T0360405

QUANTUM METHODS IN SOCIAL SCIENCE

A First Course

QUANTUM METHODS IN SOCIAL SCIENCE
A First Course

Emmanuel Haven
University of Leicester, UK

Andrei Khrennikov
Linnaeus University, Sweden

Terry Robinson
University of Leicester, UK

 World Scientific

NEW JERSEY · LONDON · SINGAPORE · BEIJING · SHANGHAI · HONG KONG · TAIPEI · CHENNAI · TOKYO

Published by

World Scientific Publishing Europe Ltd.

57 Shelton Street, Covent Garden, London WC2H 9HE

Head office: 5 Toh Tuck Link, Singapore 596224

USA office: 27 Warren Street, Suite 401-402, Hackensack, NJ 07601

Library of Congress Cataloging-in-Publication Data
Names: Haven, Emmanuel, 1965–　author. | Khrennikov, A. ĪU.
　　(Andreĭ ĪUr'evich), 1958–　author. | Robinson, Terry, (Physicist) author.
Title: Quantum methods in social science : a first course / by Emmanuel Haven
　　(University of Leicester, UK), Andrei Khrennikov (Linnaeus University, Sweden),
　　Terry Robinson (University of Leicester, UK).
Description: New Jersey : World Scientific, [2017]
Identifiers: LCCN 2016050500| ISBN 9781786342768 (hc : alk. paper) |
　　ISBN 9781786342775 (pbk : alk. paper)
Subjects: LCSH: Social sciences--Mathematical models. | Quantum theory.
Classification: LCC H61.25 .H37 2017 | DDC 300.1/53012--dc23
LC record available at https://lccn.loc.gov/2016050500

British Library Cataloguing-in-Publication Data
A catalogue record for this book is available from the British Library.

Desk Editors: Ram Mohan K/Mary Simpson

Typeset by Stallion Press
Email: enquiries@stallionpress.com

Printed in Singapore

To our Wives — Sophie, Irina, and Angelina
To our Children — Nath, Sam, Anton, Adam, and Rachel

Contents

Preface

This book is the result of a concerted effort by three academics, one physicist (Terry Robinson), one mathematician (Andrei Khrennikov), and a financial economist (Emmanuel Haven), to produce a textbook that makes accessible to advanced undergraduates an exciting new area of interdisciplinary research, namely, the application of quantum mechanical methods to topics in social science, which include economics, ecology, and psychology.

We strongly believe that new areas of scientific endeavor are ultimately more likely to find broad appeal across the scientific community if they are introduced in a pedagogical context, specifically in university courses. The authors are also united by a firm belief in interdisciplinary work, where cross-fertilization between different intellectual pursuits can shed new light on difficult problem areas. The new applications of quantum methods that are outlined in this book are a case in point. However, even though the three authors are united in their common goal, there have been inevitable differences in the ways of treating the topics that have been chosen as exemplars of the new work, as a result of these differing backgrounds. This has led to a book whose format reflects both its common overarching purpose, as well as the differing interests and methodologies of the authors. As a consequence, the book is divided into three parts, with one part from each author, which differ quite a bit in style.

The first part of the book (Terry Robinson) deals with the application of quantum operator methods to financial transactions and population dynamics. These methods are traditionally used by physicists in dealing with many-body quantum physics, such as is encountered in the quantum field theory of electromagnetic waves and in the theory of superconductors. Surprising as it may seem, this part of the book does not require any knowledge of physics at all.

Physical concepts such as energy and momentum are introduced in Part II (Emmanuel Haven). There, working from the classical physical concepts of Lagrangian and Hamiltonian mechanics, a quantum mechanical description of financial systems is developed, leading to an introduction of quantum information and its application to decision making.

The final part (Andrei Khrennikov) treats classical and quantum probability theory in some detail and deals, at a more advanced level, with the impact of quantum probabilities on shared knowledge and shared beliefs between agents in systems.

Anyone coming for the first time in contact with the methods treated in this book may well think that using techniques from quantum mechanics to elucidate thorny problems in social science seems very impractical or even far-fetched. However, appearances can be sometimes deceptive. As an example, modeling human decision making is very difficult and the use of a more generalized version of the law of total probability and a (non-Bayesian) probability update machinery (which is sourced from quantum mechanics and concretely from Born's rule determining quantum probabilities), can aid in better modeling some of the most well-known decision making paradoxes in economics and psychology, e.g., Allais, Ellsberg, and Machina paradoxes. We can go further and in fact claim that one of the main drivers of introducing the "quantum-like" framework may be traced back to a branch of quantum mechanics which has become very popular over the last few years: quantum information. In some sense, the quantum-like activity can be treated as one of the fruits from the rich pickings generated from the quantum information revolution (which is also known as the second quantum revolution).

It turns out that the quantum machine deals very well with the modeling of information. But what are "quantum-like" models?

In essence, "quantum-like" models in domains outside of quantum mechanics, do refer to models which employ techniques and formalisms from quantum mechanics, especially quantum information and probability, with the very explicit caveat that the applications to which the models pertain to, are essentially not quantum physical.

The material for this book originates in a number of different courses given by the authors in several different university departments to students with a variety of academic backgrounds. These include a course in quantum finance and social science given to final year undergraduates in the Department of Physics and Astronomy at the University of Leicester (UK), a course in quantum information given to mathematics modeling students at Linnaeus University (Sweden) and a course in quantum bio-information at Tokyo University of Science (Japan), and Moscow State University (Russia).

We should thank those students who have attended those courses. At least, with the publication of this textbook, we hope there is now available, a "one-stop" resource to get acquainted with this new subject. We have provided about 60 exercises which may aid in applying some of the concepts. We hope the textbook can entice you to read further. We hope you will peruse more advanced work in the area and even start reading some of the more specialized journals where some of this work has already been published. We hope you enjoy the trip!

Emmanuel Haven (Leicester, UK)
Andrei Khrennikov (Växjö, Sweden)
Terry Robinson (Leicester, UK)
2017

About the Authors

Emmanuel Haven was born in 1965 in Brugge, Belgium and spent his childhood in Belgium. He graduated with a BA and MA in Economics from McGill University (Canada) and he then pursued a joint PhD in Business Administration (Finance) from the John Molson School of Business, Concordia University (Canada). He started his academic career in 2000 at the Essex Business School, University of Essex and then joined the University of Leicester School of Business, where he now holds a personal chair.

Andrei Khrennikov was born in 1958 in Volgograd and spent his childhood in town Bratsk, in Siberia, north of the lake Baikal. In the period 1975–1980, he studied at Moscow State University, Department of Mechanics and Mathematics and then in 1983, he gained a PhD in mathematical physics (quantum field theory) from the same department. He started his career abroad at Bochum University and has been a Professor of Applied Mathematics at Linnaeus University, Sweden, since 1997. Since 2002, he has also held the position of director of the International Center for Mathematical Modeling in Physics, Engineering, Economics, and Cognitive Science. Research interests of Professor Khrennikov are also characterized by multiple disciples, e.g., foundations of quantum physics and quantum information, foundations of probability and mathematical modeling of cognition. He is the author of about 450 papers and 18 monographs.

Terry Robinson graduated from Birmingham University in 1968 and obtained a post-graduate Certificate in Education from Oxford in 1969. He then taught until 1976 in schools in the UK and Tanzania, returning to an academic career in 1977 after obtaining a MSc. in Experimental Space Physics from Leicester University. After working as a Lecturer in the Physics Department in the University of Dar-es-Salaam, he returned to UK and completed PhD in Ionospheric Physics at Leicester University. He was appointed to a lectureship there in 1982, and to a personal chair in 1997. He is currently an Emeritus Professor, at Leicester.

Part I

Quantum Counting: The Number Operator in a Social Science Context

Chapter 1

Introduction

1.1. What's it all about?

In this part of the book, we want to introduce some quantum tools for modeling interacting systems, which can be applied to situations in social science (see [5, 7, 11, 13, 20]). We are going to borrow these tools from what is often considered to be the most fundamental physical theory, namely, quantum field theory (QFT). That QFT is seen by many people, including, it must be said, by a lot of physicists themselves, as a mind-boggling theory, far from everyday reality, understood only by a tiny handful of brilliant minds, should not daunt the reader. We do not need to know anything about the quantum theory of fields and particles such as is needed to understand experiments carried out with the Large Hadron Collider at CERN. We are only going to need the basic mathematical tools of QFT in order to explore their application to some situations in social science. However, we will say a little about the very basic elements of the physical theory in order to set the scene and to point out what it is about them that makes them applicable to non-physical systems. But, it must be emphasized that it is not being suggested here that there is anything quantum mechanical, in the sense that physicists mean, in the social science cases that we are going to look at. That is, there are no quantum processes at the atomic level going on in the systems we are going to treat.[a]

The situation is rather like the use of differential calculus. As we know, this was invented in C17 by Leibniz and Newton to address some problems in calculating the motion of material bodies. No one would now suggest that the calculus could not be applied to population growth or financial problems. Rates of change, which is what differential calculus deals with, are mathematically the same whether they are applied to planets or bank accounts. No one is arguing that the motion of the planets can affect your bank account! It is just that we are using the same mathematical tools to look at two entirely different phenomena. The same kind of argument is true for number operator algebra that was invented to do QFT, but which can also be used on bank accounts, and much more besides, as we shall see.

Finally, we remark that besides the purely mathematical elements of quantum theory, we shall explore the basics of quantum measurement theory, which is fundamentally based on *the principle of complementarity*, proposed by Niels Bohr. He argued that it is impossible to design a single measurement procedure that can provide complete information about the state of a quantum system. For example, for a quantum particle, we cannot measure both its position and momentum in the same experimental context. We can design either a measurement procedure for position or for momentum, but not for their joint measurement. It is worth pointing out that Bohr

---

[a]Of course, everything is built from fundamental particles and physical fields, including material agents in social systems. However, we are not interested in physical processes in these agents. The entities that we will investigate are information like in nature, e.g., prices of financial assets or the beliefs of decision makers. Also, the mathematical apparatus of quantum theory is applied to such information like entities, in the same way that researchers proceed in *quantum information theory*, where quantum states are used for encoding information. Here, their concrete physical origin does not play any role. Thus, our studies in quantum social physics can be considered as a natural extension of the domain of applications of quantum information. The same approach can be applied to biological systems, from cells and proteins to brains and populations of humans, animals, and insects (see [3]).

borrowed the principle of complementarity from psychology, see, e.g., [14]. Therefore, it is not surprising that this principle has to be taken into account not only in quantum physics, but also in cognitive, psychological, and social modeling. Mathematically, this principle is encoded in non-commutativity of operators representing different observables. (Later, we shall discuss this issue in more detail.) This example shows us that borrowing of "quantum mathematics" can have fundamental methodological consequences.

1.1.1. *Three versions of physics*

Physicists generally identify three versions of physical theory including QFT, the other two being quantum mechanics (QM) and classical or pre-quantum physics. QM and classical physics are regarded as progressively less fundamental. The implication here is that QM and classical physics are approximations to QFT, in that they work under a more restricted range of circumstances, classical physics being the most approximate. Actually, this situation is probably only temporary, until an even more fundamental theory than QFT is discovered. Our aim here is to explain the basic principles involved in applying the tools of QFT, and hopefully also justify their usefulness, in a social science context. To this end, we will illustrate these new ideas by having a look at a limited number of simple applications in the areas of economics and finance and also in population migration. Our intensions are to give the reader a flavor of what this entails and hopefully engender an interest in these topics and the methodology involved, beyond the material found here, and encourage the reader to pursue matters to a deeper level to be found in the recent literature on the subject.

Historically, classical physics emerged as first of the three versions of physical theory, which were developed over an extended period between the latter part of the seventeenth century to the middle of the nineteenth century by a number of scientists, with Newton, Lagrange, and Hamilton, as the key figures. A little later, Boltzmann and Maxwell developed the classical theory of many-particle systems. QM and QFT emerged almost simultaneously, in the mid to late

1920s in order to understand phenomena on the atomic scale that could not be explained by classical physics. Classical physics can be thought of as an approximation to quantum physics in the limit when the value of Planck's famous constant, h, is made equal to zero. The Planck's constant is a ubiquitous feature of equations in both QM and QFT. It is already small at 6.67×10^{-34} Js.

In comparing classical and quantum physics, we have to remember that the latter is a fundamentally probabilistic theory. Therefore, its closest "classical relatives" are statistical physics and thermodynamics. From this viewpoint, the difference between classical and quantum can be presented in a simple way. Quantum statistics (known as Bose–Einstein and Fermi–Dirac statistics) are applicable to indistinguishable systems. Classical (Boltzmann) statistics is applicable to distinguishable systems. This is one of the crucial arguments in favor of using quantum theory (quantum statistics and probability) in social science, finance, economics. Consider for example, the dollars or pounds in your bank account, rather than the coins and bills in your pocket. The former are clearly not distinguishable from one another. Hence, we have to choose quantum statistics when dealing with them, and, in fact, we have no other choice. Later, we shall discuss peculiarities of quantum counting in more detail.

Comparing QM and QFT, we point to one of the main distinguishing features of the former: it can handle only contexts involving the fixed number of systems. Of course, there are other fundamental differences. For example, the basic version of QM is not a relativistic theory. There exists a relativistic version of QM, but it has some drawbacks and, to work in the relativistic framework, it is easier to move directly to QFT, which is a genuine relativistic theory. However, as was emphasized above, we shall not appeal to "physicalities", so we shall not explore the relativistic counterpart of the mathematical apparatus of quantum theory. Thus, we repeat once again that for our purposes the main advantage of QFT is that it can handle contexts with variable (and even indefinite) number of systems. We also recall that in our considerations "systems" have a significance purely as information, e.g., prices. Thus, if we want to work with a few fixed prices, then QM is sufficient. When dealing with a variety of appearing and disappearing financial entities, we have to use QFT again as we have no other choice. So, in modeling financial systems, QFT is preferable. However, in many problems of decision making (see [7, 11, 13] and Part III of this book), it is sufficient to use the formalism of QM.

1.1.2. *Quantizing classical physics*

Despite the dictates of the above hierarchy, physicists do not usually begin with QFT, but start to formulate theory with classical ideas in mind, at least when it comes to matters of pedagogy. This approach was strongly advocated by Dirac [9]. In classical physics, the elements of the material world are usually thought of in an idealized way, in terms of massive particles, and relevant parameters are things like the position, velocity, momentum, and energy of particles. These variables are represented by scalar quantities that are generally functions of time. Even three-dimensional vector quantities are represented by an ordered triplet of scalars in calculations. However in QM, the classical theory is said to be *quantized* by replacing the scalar variables representing the key parameters by operators. These operators then operate on state functions (wave functions) and yield scalar eigenvalues that represent quantities that can be measured in experiments. This may sound tricky enough to do, but QFT goes a step further and turns the state functions into operators. This process has been termed *second quantization*, as if one quantization were not enough! Actually, the mathematical tools of second quantization methodology that are the foundation of the concepts of QFT have recently been applied in a social science context. The most relevant of the tools of QFT to non-physical systems like those we are interested in, in a social science context is the so-called *number operator*, as we shall see shortly. Although QFT has a reputation of being unintelligible to all but a handful of physicists, we will see that the number operator is understandable in terms of a simple model of counting procedure for which the term *quantum counting* has recently been coined (see [20]).

1.1.3. *Quantum numbers*

Before saying anything specific about the possible role of QFT and second quantization in a social science context, let us briefly look at the nature of quantum physics. Quantum physics gets its name from the idea of discrete quantities or *quanta*. When we talk of a quantum of energy, we imply that energy comes in packages of definite size that depend on a set of whole numbers called *quantum numbers*. This property is unique to quantum physics. However, it is not the case that in quantum physics, energy always comes in discrete quanta. There are situations in quantum physics where energy is continuous. In contrast, in classical physics, energy is always a continuous variable and thus can, in principle, have any value.

So what gives rise to the situation in which energies are discrete in QM? Energy quanta occur when systems are localized in space in some way. This situation can arise when a particle is acted on by a force which limits its ability to free itself from a location. Such a particle is said to be bound. Such a situation arises when an electron is bound to an atom, for example. Then the electron energy takes on discrete values. In contract, a free electron that is not subject to any force can have an energy of any value.

However, even when energies are discrete, it is not the case, even in simple systems, that quantum energies always come in equal steps. For example, if a quantum particle is trapped in a deep well the energies increase as n^2, where n is a positive integer, i.e., $1, 2, 3, \ldots$ So the energies would then be proportional to $1, 4, 9, \ldots$ In contrast to this, the energy levels in a simple atom like hydrogen are proportional to n^{-2}, so the energies are proportional to $1, 1/4, 1/9, \ldots$ However, there is one very special physical system where the energies do come in equal steps. This is known as the quantum harmonic oscillator. Harmonic oscillators are very common types of physical system. The best known in every day experience is probably the simple pendulum, but oscillating springs, floating objects bobbing in water, are also fairly well known. Less obvious, but probably even more important are oscillations in the electric circuits in radio and hi-fi equipment, in computers, and also in electromagnetic fields, such as those that link our mobile phones, as well as in thermal vibrations in solids. Steps in the possible energies in all of these harmonic oscillators are proportional to 0, 1, 2, 3, ..., the set of counting numbers, including zero (which we will routinely include in this part of the book). These actually were the first quantum mechanical energy steps to be discovered. They are the very ones proposed by Max Planck to explain the energy spectrum of *black-body radiation* that started quantum theory off at the beginning of C20. In this case, the constant of proportionality for the energy steps is the famous Planck's constant, h, times the frequency of the oscillator.

1.1.4. *Quantum field theory*

Now this is where QFT comes in, because the fundamental conceptual element in QFT is the idea of quantized oscillating fields that are represented by a pair of operators called creation and annihilation operators. In QM, the harmonic oscillator is a single particle that has the same energy as a classical harmonic oscillator except that, as usual in QM, the energy forms a ladder of possible levels with steps corresponding to 0, 1, 2, 3, ..., as stated above. These energy steps are again seen in basic QFT with the major difference in interpretation. Instead of the single quantum mechanical particle climbing the ladder of energy, in QFT the 0, 1, 2, 3, ..., refer to a number of particles. The particles all have the same energy and the total energy can be 0, 1, 2, 3, ..., units, simply by having 0, 1, 2, 3, ..., particles. For example, in QM, a single particle could have three units of energy. This situation in QFT would be interpreted as three identical particles, each with one unit of energy. Thus, in the latter case, the three counts the number of particles. So, adding a unit of energy in the QM interpretation means the particle climbing one step of the ladder, whereas in the QFT interpretation it means adding a particle to the system. The increase in energy is the same in each case, but the interpretation is very different. One very important application of QFT in quantum physics is the study of what is called the *many-body problem*. The bodies in this case are usually sets of identical fundamental particles, such as electrons or photons. QFT is a much more efficient way of looking at interactions between groups of fundamental particles than QM. In particular, QFT can easily deal with variable numbers of particles, in contrast to QM.

The creation and annihilation operators play a key role here, as we shall see. As their names imply, if we start out in a state with n particles, then applying the creation operator to this state adds a particle so we get $n + 1$. By applying the annihilation operator to the state with n particles, we end up with $n - 1$. We are going to associate the role of these operators with counting identical items, and these items do not have to be fundamental particles. We will see that repeated application of creation and annihilation operators can be associated, respectively, with counting up and counting down. Another important operator emerges naturally from the mathematics behind creation and annihilation operators and that is the number operator itself. This keeps count of the number of items in the system. The mathematical structure of QFT thus lends itself to systems where whole numbers of countable objects that are more or less identical, can be added to or subtracted from. The systems that can be treated by the methods of second quantization and QFT can be characterized as a coupled system where numbers of countable items can be exchanged between different parts of the system. Examples of such identical objects could be dollars, or bags of sugar, etc. Most importantly, the tools of QFT allow us to look at the dynamical behavior of interacting systems of countable objects. Systems in social science that lend themselves to this treatment are, for example, transactions in economics and finance and migration of populations between neighboring regions. We will see that the toing and froing in such systems can be well captured by models based on QFT.

We should emphasize that using the mathematical tools of QFT in social science is in its early stages of development and the contents of this part of the book are intended only as an introduction. For a much more detailed treatment, the reader is advised to consult more advanced material such as might be found in the recent book by Bagarello [5], who has pioneered the use of second quantization methods in social science. Also, some of the treatments of the dynamics of countable objects in what follows is based on a more detailed mathematical treatment in a recent paper by Robinson and Haven [20].

1.2. Counting in culture, society, and science

1.2.1. *As simple as 1, 2, 3*

Everyone is familiar with the idea of counting. It is one of the first intellectual activities that we engage as children. We learn the names of numbers in their natural sequence: 1, 2, 3, ..., before we have any idea of what they mean, although, very quickly, children do learn to associate the counting chant (one, two, three, ...; ein, zwei, drei, ...; moja, mbili, tatu, ...) with objects to be counted and come to see that the number they stop at can tell them how many items they have in total. This sequencing process is a vital part of counting, and as we shall see in a later chapter devoted to a quantum model of the mechanics of counting, second quantization methods can mathematically reproduce this sequencing and totaling in a rather natural way. There are several complicating issues that arise in learning to count, one of which is how to classify what we mean by the things to be counted and this can throw up some interesting categorization issues. For example, there are particularly interesting issues that arise when we count fruit rather than simply counting, say apples (see [1]). Semantics and mathematics get rather intertwined here, but it was ever thus.

Counting has tremendous cultural and economic, as well as intellectual, value. How many sweets in this packet? How many potatoes on my plate? How many grains of rice in this bag? How many sheep in my flock? How many pounds in my pocket? How fast is the population of the UK changing? How fast is the number of pounds in my bank account changing? Not only does counting tell you how many things you have, it enables intelligent beings to plan for the future. Counting also plays an important role in our understanding of the natural environment, especially our appreciation of the changes in weather and climate over a year. If we know how many day–night transitions happen in a year, we can plan ahead and counter the difficulties that the changing seasons impose on our survival here on Earth; knowing the phases of the moon allows us to predict the height of sea tides, and so on. This skill has probably played a major role in man's early development, survival, and ultimate domination of the planet.

From the early 1940s, the great Swiss developmental psychologist [18], studied the ways in which children learn how to count and learn about the meaning of numbers, and his theories were extremely influential in approaches to teaching numeracy skills in early years education in the second half of C20. Interestingly, since we will be dealing with the connection between physics and counting in this part of the book, Piaget drew parallels between the way counting works and physical laws. In particular, Piaget believed conservation rules had a key role to play. This connection is particularly relevant to the quantum theory of counting that will be introduced shortly. Piaget also believed that the development of an understanding of number in children went hand in hand with the development of logical thinking, so clearly counting and intellectual development appear to be strongly connected. The subject of the acquisition of counting skills remains a topic of considerable interest in cognitive research (see [6, 22]) and is also still the subject of some controversy (see [16, 19]).

Of course, physics has an obvious and natural connection with numbers, since physics is very much a quantitative discipline. Physicists make measurements to enable them to assign numerical values to the parameters they are interested in, in order to investigate the connection between these parameters, especially when they vary in some way. This is one important way of discovering the laws, like Ohm's law of electrical resistance, Newton's law of universal gravitation and Snell's laws of optical refraction, that govern physical behavior of different aspects of the universe around us. Making measurements is also an important way of checking the laws quantitatively, via computation. Indeed, counting could be regarded as the basis of all computation (see [8]).

1.2.2. *And then there were none*

Note that, unlike the counting numbers we learn as children, Planck's quantum counting numbers include zero as well as one, two, three, etc. The zero is a bit like the joker in a pack of cards. Ace (one), two, three, etc. are all treated as regular cards, but not every card player agrees that the joker should really be treated as part of the pack and there are only a few games of cards that use a joker. Indeed, it was only as recently as the seventh century CE that zero was accepted by mathematicians as a number at all. Although the idea of zero, or more strictly, the idea of *nothingness* was known earlier, it was only after this date that zero was seen as one of the whole numbers with the same status as $1, 2, 3, \ldots$. The Indian mathematician Brahmagupta is credited with having introduced zero into the number system. Later, the Italian mathematician Fibonacci made the case for zero among mathematicians in early modern Europe, in C13.

Zero is a fundamental element in QFT where it is associated with what particle physicists refer to as the *vacuum state*. The vacuum state is not quite the same thing as the vacuum in classical physics, where it does literally mean a place with no material particles in it. In QFT, where particles are associated with excitations of a field, it means something akin to a situation in which no excitations (particles) are manifest. It can be thought of as analogous to something like a violin string. Then, the vacuum is the undisturbed string and the excited state in which particles are observed is when the string is plucked and we hear a note. These things are very hard to describe in words. At best they are essentially fairy stories; at their worst, they are simply misleading. It is probably best not to try at all, so we have to make do with second best and some slightly fuzzy analogies. That's physics. At some point, we have to accept that the only accurate description of such things is a mathematical one. Anyway, hopefully, the mathematical version of the vacuum, or a state with nothing in it, will make things somewhat clearer when we tackle the mathematical description of counting numbers that will appear a little later.

1.3. Classical or quantum representation?

In many areas of science, it is possible to identify two complementary elements that are commonly referred to as theory and experiment. This is certainly the tradition in physics, for example. However, in order to make things a little more applicable to other sciences, like economics, psychology, and ecology, and so on, it is probably better to talk about representation instead of theory, on the one hand, and the acquisition of data and information rather than experiment, on the other. Of course, this is really the purpose of theory and experiment anyway. Let us talk about data and information first.

1.3.1. *Data and information*

In many situations, though not all, data takes the form of numbers, i.e., scalars. This data is the basic information we have about a system we are interested in. It is what we feed into our computers to check our theories (rules) and make predictions about the behavior of our system. However, it should be clear, right from the start, that the information we have about our system of interest may not be complete. Being aware that our knowledge is usually only partial is important. It affects not only our ability to predict future behavior, but also affects our interpretation about what is actually happening. To a large extent, how we treat the scalar information or data is what distinguishes the classical from the quantum mechanical representation of actual systems.

1.3.2. *Representation I: The classical way*

Broadly speaking, what we shall mean by classical representation is that the key variables that describe any system of interest will be ordinary scalar functions to which numerical values can be directly attached. Thus, the representation is made up of the same kind of mathematical entities as the data. For example, in physics, we can represent current and voltage in an electric circuit by continuous variables whose values are tracked through time. In finance, we could treat income, share price or number of assets in a similar way. Note that these functions change with time in a continuous way, so the numbers are members of a set whose values are continuous, i.e., have no gaps in between. This means, we can only represent populations approximately (see Chapter 2). For example, 2.4 children, or 7.53 double-decker buses, are definite possibilities in classical representations. Numbers and the algebra of numbers are used to represent parameters in all sorts of situations, not just in physics.

The functional representation of physical variables matches well with classical probability theory (Kolmogorov measure-theoretic axiomatics, 1933), where random variables (corresponding to random measurements) are given by a special class of functions on the space of elementary events (measurable functions). The probabilistic aspects of the classical and quantum models of information will be discussed in more detail in Part III (see also [3, 13]).

1.3.3. *Representation II: The quantum way*

In contrast to the classical representation of a system, the quantum representation consists of using mathematical operator algebra to represent the variables of interest. What we mean by this will be dealt with in more detail shortly, but the key idea of an operator is that it does not immediately represent a single number value. Rather, it represents simultaneously a set, possibly an infinite set of number values, called eigenvalues. In order to extract information in the form of numerical values about the system in question, we need to operate on a state of the system. A measurement will give one of the possible set of eigenvalues. There are two main ways of mathematically representing operators in QM. One is to use differential operators. In physics, for example, momentum is associated with the differential with respect to position in space and angular momentum is associated with differentiation with respect to a rotation angle. Differential operators then operate on complex functions, called *wave functions* that represent the possible states of a system. The other common representation of operators is by square matrices, then the states on which these operators operate are column vectors. In the usual interpretation of QM, the wave function is a *probability amplitude* and the product of the wave function and its complex conjugate is a probability density. So, if we have a wave function, Ψ, then the product, $\Psi^*\Psi$, where Ψ^* is the complex conjugate of Ψ, is equal to a probability density, P (see Part III for Hilbert space representation of these basic quantum issues). In the quantum representation, we deal with equations for Ψ and work out the probability. In the classical representation, there is no probability amplitude Ψ involved at all, rather we deal directly with a probability and a probability density.

From the probabilistic viewpoint, the main difference between classical and quantum physics is that the classical Kolmogorov model of probability (based on the representation of events by set-algebra and probabilities by positive measures normalized to one) is inapplicable to incompatible observables. It is impossible (at least straight-forwardly) to describe statistical outputs of such observations by using a single Kolmogorov probability space. Thus, quantum physics showed that the domain of applications of the classical Kolmogorov axiomatics of probability theory (as any mathematical axiomatic theory) is restricted. This model can be applied to classical statistical physics and thermodynamics, but not to quantum physics. A new probability calculus based on complex probability amplitudes has to be applied, see Part III (also see [11, 13]) for concrete applications of quantum probability and the analysis of the impossibility to use classical probability.

1.3.4. *Second quantization and how to count things*

Now, as mentioned earlier, in QFT, the wave functions themselves are turned into operators, so $\psi \to \hat{a}$, and $\psi^* \to \hat{a}^+$, where $\hat{a}^+$ is the adjoint of $\hat{a}$. The meaning of these operators and in particular the adjoint will be dealt with later, but for now it can be thought of as equivalent to the conjugate, like ψ^*. Now instead of the probability density $P = \psi^*\psi$, an operator, $\hat{n} = \hat{a}^+\hat{a}$ is defined. So, there is an analogy between P and $\hat{n}$, but rather than a probability, the operator $\hat{n}$ represents a number operator, whose eigenvalues are natural numbers, 0, 1, 2, ... One thing that P and $\hat{n}$, do have in common is that they are both associated with non-negative quantities, which turns out to be a really crucial property in understanding how the number operator works.

The operator $\hat{a}$ and its adjoint can then be regarded as number operator amplitudes. The full details of these number and number amplitude operators will be treated in more detail later, in the context of quantum counting, but for now, we point out that in QFT, $\hat{n}$ represents the number of identical particles in a particular quantum state. In a notation due to Dirac, this state is given the symbol $|n\rangle$. Then operating on this state with $\hat{n}$ gives $|n\rangle = n|n\rangle$, where n is a scalar number that represents the number of particles that one would get by counting the number of particles in the state $|n\rangle$. This in itself is not particularly remarkable. What is remarkable is that if we operate on the state $|n\rangle$ with $\hat{a}$, we get a state $|n-1\rangle$, i.e., a state with one less particle. Thus $\hat{a}$ is referred to as a destruction or annihilation operator in QFT. Furthermore, if $\hat{a}^+$ operates on $|n\rangle$, we get a state $|n+1\rangle$, and so $\hat{a}^+$ is referred to as a creation operator in QFT. These operator properties were first discovered in the early years of the development of quantum theory by physicists studying the properties of atomic particles trapped by elastic forces undergoing what physicists refer to classically as simple harmonic motion. The discovery of these results lead to QFT. We will explain later how these operator properties arise in the context of the mechanics of counting, although, at this stage, it might seem strange that the physics of trapped atomic particles and fundamental quantum fields can have anything to do with counting sheep or stocks and shares, but, remarkably, it does! The common thread is the process of counting itself, and the universality of its nature, which we hope to demonstrate shortly. Once we have learned to count using these quantum methods, we can apply the same formalism to more interesting situations in which populations of things and of people are changing dynamically, i.e., with time. We will use these techniques to model changes in the assets of traders and the migration of populations between different regions. However, before that, we will look at something rather different first, namely how population changes may be dealt with classically.

Chapter 2

Classical Interlude: Modeling Population Dynamics

Before we get on to exploiting the tools of quantum physics in modeling the way populations of idealized identical items interact, in this chapter, we will look briefly at a very well-known classical model of interacting populations, which is based on the Lotka–Volterra equations (see [17]). We will do this in order to have something with which to compare the outcomes of the quantum models that we will introduce later. It will also help to see the limitations of classical models and help justify our consideration of alternative quantum models later. We will consider populations of idealized countable individuals that can change with time due to various processes such as birth, death, and inter-species competition. We wish to model these populations so that we can predict how may individuals there will be at any given time. To do this, we need a mathematical specification of the population and a mathematical rule that tells us how the population will change. In a classical formulation of the problem, we use ordinary algebra in which the variable of the system, in this case the number of individuals in the population simply represent numbers whose values can, in principle, be known exactly at any instant. We begin with a single species of (effectively) identical individuals. We next outline a simple mathematical model that specifies how this population changes with time due to birth and death. It is a very well-known example from ecology.

2.1. Population growth and decay: Just rabbits

Let us suppose we have a population of rabbits. The instantaneous population of rabbits at time t may be represented in this classical model by the function, $x(t)$, which represents an ordinary number. Suppose the rabbits are living on fertile grassland so there is an abundance of food for them. A fairly natural assumption is that the rate at which the rabbit population will grow at a time t, due to the birth of young rabbits will be proportional to $x(t)$. So if 100 individuals give birth to 20 young in a year, then we expect 200 individuals to give birth to 40 young and so on. Let the constant of proportionality be b, so the differential equation that tells us how the population changes with time is just

$$\frac{\mathrm{d}x(t)}{\mathrm{d}t} = bx(t). \tag{2.1}$$

b is essentially the birth rate per individual of the population. Equation (2.1) is easily integrated to yield $x(t) = x(0)\exp(bt)$, where $x(0)$ is just the starting population when t is zero. This solution is an example of exponential growth in the population, which is depicted in Fig. 2.1.

Now we can also presume that, over time, some proportion of the rabbit population will die of old age. The rate at which the population will change due to this effect will again be proportional to the size of the rabbit population. If the death rate per individual is c, then we

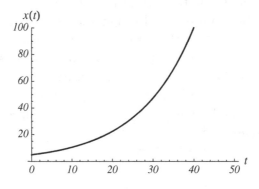

FIGURE 2.1.   Exponential growth of the rabbit population.

can modify (2.1) to

$$\frac{dx(t)}{dt} = bx(t) - cx(t), \tag{2.2}$$

where the negative sign in front of c in (2.2) reflects the fact that the death rate causes the population to fall. The solution to (2.2) is $x(t) = x(0)\exp((b-c)t)$. Now as long as $b > c$, i.e., the birth rate exceeds the death rate, then the population will still grow exponentially, but at a net growth rate of $b - c$, which is of course a lower rate than if $c = 0$. If on the other hand, the death rate were to exceed the birth rate, then the population would decline exponentially at a rate of $c - b$.

2.2. Introducing a second species: Enter the foxes

Suppose we had introduced a population of foxes onto our grassland, instead of the rabbits. Foxes cannot survive on grass alone, so we would expect their death rate to be high due to starvation as well as old age. In the foxes' case, we would then expect their death rate to exceed their birth rate and the fox population would thus decay exponentially. Now, suppose we introduce the foxes again, but this time assume there is also a rabbit population in this region of grassland. We naturally expect some interaction between the two populations, via a classical predator–prey process. The growth rate of the fox population will now be proportional to the instantaneous fox population as before, but it will also be expected to be proportional to the rabbit population too, since the more rabbits there are, the more food will be available for the foxes. So we can expect the equation that models the rate of change of the fox population to have the form

$$\frac{dy(t)}{dt} = -fy(t) + gx(t)y(t), \tag{2.3}$$

where f and g are constants of proportionality and $y(t)$ is the instantaneous fox population at time t. Note that, in the absence of the rabbits ($x(t) = 0$), the fox population would decay exponentially at a rate f, as expected.

Now, we need to model the effect of the fox population on the rabbit population. Clearly, we expect the death rate of the rabbits to be increased by the presence of the predatory foxes. We assume that this additional death rate is again proportional to the number of rabbits, but also to the number of foxes, so we get

$$\frac{\mathrm{d}x(t)}{\mathrm{d}t} = hx(t) - kx(t)y(t), \tag{2.4}$$

where h and k are constants. In the absence of the foxes $(y(t) = 0)$, we would expect the rabbit population to grow exponentially at a rate h. Indeed, h is just the same as the rate $b - c$, from Section 2.1.

Equations (2.3) and (2.4) constitute a pair of coupled differential equations that cannot be solved separately, but rather need to be solved together. The solutions for the fox and rabbit populations are now no longer exponential in form. We actually get an entirely different type of solution. Solutions to the pair of Equations, (2.3) and (2.4), which are the Lotka–Volterra equations (see [17]), have been studied extensively. The form of the solutions depends strongly on the values of the constants, $f, g, h,$ and k. An example of the kind of solution we can expect is shown in Fig. 2.2.

These solutions have been obtained numerically with the aid of Mathematica software. As can be seen from the figure, the rabbit population begins to grow because there is always plenty of food and

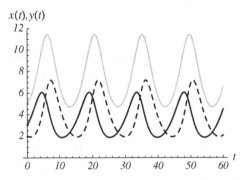

FIGURE 2.2.   Variation of the rabbit (solid curve) and fox (dashed curve) populations. The sum of the two populations is indicated by the grey curve.

initially few foxes. Initially, the fox population falls for a short time due to the small rabbit population, but, as the rabbit population increases beyond a certain level, the fox population starts to grow. Eventually, this grows to a sufficient level to reduce the rabbit population growth rate and eventually the rabbit numbers start to fall. However, then the fox population starts to decline too, due to the decline in their food supply. When the fox population is low enough, the rabbit population starts to recover and so the cycle begins all over again.

2.3. Some observations on the Lotka–Volterra model

2.3.1. *Fluctuating population numbers*

Probably the most remarkable feature of the solutions to the Lotka–Volterra equations is that the two populations repeat exactly after a certain period of time. The period is the same for both populations, although they are not generally in phase, i.e., they do not peak at the same time. Also, it is clear that although the population numbers are exactly periodic, they are not exactly sinusoidal; the peaks are sharper and the troughs broader than is the case for sinusoids. Further, it is clear that unlike sinusoids, the shapes are not mirror symmetries about either the peaks or the troughs. Sinusoids are the typical shapes one immediately thinks of for repeated cyclic processes like waves, for example. There is nothing obvious in the Lotka–Volterra equations to suggest that the solutions will be periodic. Indeed, periodic solutions do not exist for all values of the constants in the equations. In our example, we have been careful to choose values that yield the periodicity. However, it is important to see that such outcomes are possible among competing populations, when it may seem common sense to think that the foxes will always eat all of the rabbits. That this does not always happen is enlightening. The two populations, in spite of obvious one-sidedness of the competition, appear to be symbiotic in an important way. Such symbiotic fluctuating populations are seen in nature. We will see that such fluctuations, although different in origin, are also a feature of our quantum interactions models.

The oscillating nature of the solution is actually hidden within the initial equations. To see this, we can carry out a perturbation analysis on them. To do this, we assume that each population is made up of a small time-dependent part plus a much larger mean value. Thus, we assume that $x(t) = \bar{x} + \delta x(t)$ and $y(t) = \bar{y} + \delta y(t)$, where $\delta x(t)$ is assumed to always be smaller than $\bar{x}$ etc. We now substitute these back into the original equations and separate them into the time-dependent parts and also the time-independent parts that contain only mean values. In the time-dependent parts, we also neglect any terms which contain products of small values like $\delta x(t)\delta y(t)$. Now the mean values from the time-independent parts, satisfy $\bar{x} = f/g$ and $\bar{y} = h/k$. Then the time-dependent parts simplify to $\frac{\mathrm{d}\delta x(t)}{\mathrm{d}t} = -\frac{fk}{g}\delta y(t)$ and $\frac{\mathrm{d}\delta y(t)}{\mathrm{d}t} = \frac{gh}{k}\delta x(t)$, which lead to

$$\frac{\mathrm{d}^2\delta x(t)}{\mathrm{d}t^2} + fh\delta x(t) = \frac{\mathrm{d}^2\delta y(t)}{\mathrm{d}t^2} + fh\delta y(t) = 0. \qquad (2.5)$$

These two equations are those of sinusoidal oscillations of the same frequency, $\omega = \sqrt{fh}$. We can take the solutions of the form

$$x(t) = \bar{x} + (x(0) - \bar{x})\cos(\omega t) - (y(0) - \bar{y})\frac{fk}{g\omega}\sin(\omega t),$$

$$y(t) = \bar{y} + (y(0) - \bar{y})\cos(\omega t) + (x(0) - \bar{x})\frac{gh}{k\omega}\sin(\omega t), \qquad (2.6)$$

where we have used the boundary conditions, $x(0) = \bar{x} + \delta x(0)$ and $\frac{\mathrm{d}\delta x}{\mathrm{d}t}|_{t=0} = \omega\delta x(0) = -\frac{fk}{g}\delta y(0)$, etc. The approximate perturbation solution for the example in Fig. 2.2 is shown in Fig. 2.3.

As can be seen by comparing the two figures, the approximate perturbation solution gives a remarkably good estimate of the frequency and also the phase difference between the two species, in this case. The amplitude estimates are also rather good, given the crudity of the approximation involved. This is actually a little surprising since what we neglected, $\delta x(t)\delta y(t)$, is really not that small. However, it does show us that there is an intrinsic periodicity in the equations even though it is not obviously manifest at first.

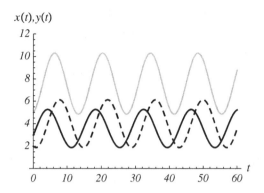

FIGURE 2.3.   The perturbation solution for the example in Fig. 2.2.

Another point to note about the population numbers in this classical case is that they cannot be represented by counting numbers. The variables of our model can be any real number and the changes occur continuously, whereas counting numbers can only change by integer steps. This does not matter much, at the computational level at least, as long as the population numbers are large. Then the change in population caused by the birth or death of an individual is only a tiny fraction of the total population. On a graph, these unit changes would look quite smooth if the population was measured in thousands. However, if we only had a few members in a population, 10 or 12, say, then the changes would look more grainy in reality, than the smooth changes that we would find in our classical model. This is one reason for at least considering a quantum model, where, as we shall see we can model changes at the individual level using operators.

2.3.2. *Eliminating one of the variables*

It is possible to eliminate one of our population variables from (2.3) and (2.4) and reduce the system to a single equation. In this case, we get

$$\frac{\mathrm{d}^2x}{\mathrm{d}t^2} - \frac{1}{x}\left(\frac{\mathrm{d}x}{\mathrm{d}t}\right)^2 - (gx - f)\frac{\mathrm{d}x}{\mathrm{d}t} + hx(gx - f) = 0. \qquad (2.7)$$

This is a remarkably complicated looking equation for such a deceptively simple system. To a certain extent, it reflects the *ad hoc* nature of the way we came up with the initial equations, which gives rise to such a non-linear result. The quantum approach turns out to produce a much simpler equation with which to model interacting systems, which reflects a much simpler set of rules for what interaction actually means at a fundamental level. We will see that the quantum approach also makes clear the role of conservation rules in constraining the solutions to the equations of motion. It is worth just examining what is conserved and hence constrained in the Lotka–Volterra model (LVM). This entails finding the so-called *integrals of the motion*, which we will look at briefly next.

2.3.3. *Integral of the motion and conserved quantities*

It is a straightforward matter, given the pair of Equations (2.3) and (2.4), to find the integrals of the motion. These are constants for the system. Suppose $K(x, y)$ is such a constant such that as $x(t)$ and $y(t)$ change their values with time then $\frac{dK}{dt} = 0$. For the LVM,

$$K = gx - ky - f \ln x + h \ln y$$

is a conserved quantity. Again there is nothing particularly remarkable about K. It is not, for example, the sum of the rabbit and fox populations. The result again reflects the *ad hoc* nature of our original equations.

It is perfectly legitimate to ask if there is a solution in which, say, the sum of the rabbit and fox populations is conserved. Indeed, one does exist for certain values of the constant coefficients, but it is not periodic. Then the values of the two populations tend asymptotically to constant values. Also, the conserved quantity, K, above also indicates that if one of the populations starts off very close to zero, then K tends to either negative or positive infinity. This leads to non-periodic and rather unrealistic behavior. As we will see, the quantum model we will explore later has very different characteristics from these.

2.3.4. *Range of applications*

The LVM has been used in a number of different areas of research. One of the earliest applications was in the study of the evolution of epidemics. A classic example of this is the study by Kermack and McKendrick [12]. The model has also been applied to economic problems, a good example being a model of the recent economic crisis of 2008 (see [15]).

Chapter 3

A Quantum Description of Systems

In this chapter, we give a short overview of the basic mathematical elements of the quantum mechanical representation of a system. By *system*, we do not necessarily mean anything physical and it certainly does not have to be thought of as a particle located in space and time. Rather it is simply something that can be characterized in a mathematical way. The basic mathematical elements that we need require no more than what is to be found in almost any modern textbook on quantum mechanics (QM) (see [4]) in which the development of the basic equations is based on symmetry arguments rather than on any analogies with classical mechanics).

3.1. Operators, states, and eigenvalues

3.1.1. *The Schrödinger equation*

The state of a system in QM is associated with a wavefunction, Ψ. We wish to study the dynamics of such a system, which means that we want to know how it changes or evolves with time. It is natural therefore to try to calculate the rate of change of Ψ, i.e., $\frac{d\Psi}{dt}$. This is where the Schrödinger equation (SE) comes in. The SE can be written in the form

$$i\frac{d\Psi}{dt} = (\hat{H}/\hbar)\Psi = \hat{\Omega}\Psi, \qquad (3.1)$$

where Ψ is a complex wavefunction, $\hat{H}$ is the Hamiltonian operator, which in physics is associated with energy, and $\hbar$ is the reduced

Planck constant ($\hbar = h/2\pi$). Actually, the physical meaning of the SE only becomes clear when $\hat{H}$ is specified for the system involved, usually in terms of its position and momentum, each of which is treated as an operator. Since we are not interested in energy here, but, as we will see, with rates of change of numbers of things, we can dispense with energy and focus on the frequency operator $\hat{\Omega}$, which has units of per unit of time, and so tells us the rate of change of, in this case, Ψ. Recall that Ψ tells us what state the system of interest is in. Once the Hamiltonian of a system is specified, then we essentially know a great deal about its behavior, so setting up the Hamiltonian is one way of predicting how a system will evolve and will be an important first step in exploring the behavior of systems of interest in the following sections. Note also that $\hat{\Omega}$ is just the Hamiltonian scaled by the reduced Planck's constant, but in what follows, we shall refer to it as just *the Hamiltonian* of the system.

3.1.2. *Linear operators*

$\hat{\Omega}$ is an example of a linear operator. Most of the operators we will be dealing with are of this type. Their basic properties are as follows: suppose that $\hat{Q}$ is some linear operator, if we operate on the sum of two state functions, $\Psi_1 + \Psi_2$, then

$$\hat{Q}(\Psi_1 + \Psi_2) = \hat{Q}\Psi_1 + \hat{Q}\Psi_2. \tag{3.2}$$

Further, if $\hat{Q}_1$ and $\hat{Q}_2$ are a pair of linear operators, then

$$(\hat{Q}_1 + \hat{Q}_2)\Psi = \hat{Q}_1\Psi + \hat{Q}_2\Psi. \tag{3.3}$$

The order of the addition above does not matter, i.e., $\hat{Q}_1 + \hat{Q}_2 = \hat{Q}_2 + \hat{Q}_1$. Also, we can apply $\hat{Q}_1$ to Ψ and then apply $\hat{Q}_2$ to the result to get $\hat{Q}_2\hat{Q}_1\Psi$. However, in general, this does not give the same result as applying $\hat{Q}_2$ first and then $\hat{Q}_1$, i.e., $\hat{Q}_2\hat{Q}_1\Psi \neq \hat{Q}_1\hat{Q}_2\Psi$. In QM, we say that $\hat{Q}_2$ does not commute with $\hat{Q}_1$, when this is the case. Then

$$(\hat{Q}_1\hat{Q}_2 - \hat{Q}_2\hat{Q}_1)\Psi = [\hat{Q}_1, \hat{Q}_2]\Psi \neq 0, \tag{3.4}$$

where $[\hat{Q}_1, \hat{Q}_2] = \hat{Q}_1\hat{Q}_2 - \hat{Q}_2\hat{Q}_1$ is called the commutation bracket. We will say more about commutation and non-commutation of operators shortly. Operators do always commute with constant scalars, so if λ is a scalar constant, then

$$\hat{Q}\lambda\Psi = \lambda\hat{Q}\Psi. \tag{3.5}$$

3.1.3. *Eigenvalue equations*

In order to determine the state Ψ of our system, we need to solve an eigenvalue equation of the form

$$\hat{\Omega}\Psi = \omega\Psi, \tag{3.6}$$

where ω is the scalar eigenvalue. In principle, (3.6) can only be solved if $\hat{\Omega}$ is a known function of some known operators that correspond to variables that describe the system, as we shall see shortly. Then there are usually a number (possibly infinite) of solutions to (3.6) called eigenfunctions or eigenstates of the system, each with a corresponding eigenvalue. If Ψ_n is such an eigenstate solution to (3.6) with eigenvalue ω_n, then

$$\hat{\Omega}\Psi_n = \omega_n\Psi_n. \tag{3.7}$$

The rules of QM say that if the system is in a state described by Ψ_n and if the frequency of the system is measured, then the result will be ω_n. In general, the system can be in a state which is a superposition of these eigenstates, such that

$$\Psi = \sum_n \alpha_n\Psi_n, \tag{3.8}$$

where α_n are numerical coefficients, which may be complex numbers. In this case, if we make a measurement on the system we do not know exactly what result we will get, but we do know it will be one of the possible eigenvalues. We do know the probability with which a particular eigenvalue will be produced, which is given by $\alpha_n^*\alpha_n$. In what follows, we consider only linear operators with a discrete spectrum. Then in the state space of such an operator, there exists a basis consisting of eigenstates.

3.1.4. *Expectation values, normalization, and orthogonality*

If $\hat{Q}$ is an operator representing some variable of interest of the system, then the expectation value associated with $\hat{Q}$ for a state Ψ is defined by

$$\langle \hat{Q} \rangle = \int \Psi^* \hat{Q} \Psi \mathrm{d}\xi, \qquad (3.9)$$

where ξ is a continuous variable that corresponds to some parameterization of the system. In physics, this is typically the position of a particle. Then the wave function is a known function $\Psi(\xi)$ of this variable and the integral can be evaluated. The expectation value is effectively an average value. In QM, this means the result of carrying out identical measurements on identical systems with identical initial conditions. In writing (3.9), it is assumed that

$$\int \Psi^* \Psi \mathrm{d}\xi = 1, \qquad (3.10)$$

then Ψ is said to be *normalized*. Each of the individual eigenfunctions of $\hat{\Omega}$ is also normalized and in addition, pairs of the eigenfunctions are orthogonal to one another, so

$$\int \Psi_n^* \Psi_m \mathrm{d}\xi = \delta_{nm}, \qquad (3.11)$$

where δ_{nm} is the Kronecker delta symbol, which has a value of 1 if $n = m$ and is zero otherwise. The main reason for wanting normalization of wave functions is that $\Psi^* \Psi$ is regarded as a probability density whose integral must amount to 1. There are a number of other important properties of operators, eigenfunctions, and eigenvalues that we are going to need, but before we look at these, we will introduce Dirac notation, which allows the expressions involved to be written in a rather succinct way.

3.2. Dirac notation

Dirac introduced a kind of shorthand way of writing integrals like those in (3.9) and (3.11), which also turns out to be a powerful way of representing quantum mechanical relations. It involves the brackets "⟨" and "⟩". Instead of explicitly writing the integral, which, let's face it, is itself a kind of shorthand, Dirac translated this into

$$\langle \hat{Q} \rangle = \langle \Psi | \hat{Q} | \Psi \rangle \tag{3.12}$$

and (3.10) becomes

$$\langle \Psi | \Psi \rangle = 1. \tag{3.13}$$

Dirac called $|\Psi\rangle$ a *ket* vector and $\langle \Psi|$ a *bra* vector. The combination in (3.12) is then a bra-ket (i.e., a bracket). The implication is also that $\langle \Psi|$ is the complex conjugate of $|\Psi\rangle$ and vice versa, i.e., $\langle \Psi| = (|\Psi\rangle)^*$ and $((\langle \Psi|)^* = |\Psi\rangle$. So, (3.13) means that

$$\||\Psi\rangle\|^2 = 1, \tag{3.14}$$

which can be interpreted to mean that the vector, $|\Psi\rangle$, has unit length. From the definition of the complex conjugate of a state vector, then if we have a second state vector, $|\Phi\rangle$, it is straightforward to show that

$$(\langle \Phi | \Psi \rangle)^* = \langle \Psi | \Phi \rangle. \tag{3.15}$$

Also, the orthonormality property can now be expressed mathematically as

$$\langle \Psi_n | \Psi_m \rangle = \delta_{nm}. \tag{3.16}$$

Also, the eigenvalue equation for $\hat{\Omega}$ can be expressed as

$$\hat{\Omega} | \Psi_n \rangle = \omega_n | \Psi_n \rangle, \tag{3.17}$$

and we should now write the SE in the form

$$i \frac{d|\Psi\rangle}{dt} = (\hat{H}/\hbar)|\Psi\rangle = \hat{\Omega}|\Psi\rangle. \tag{3.18}$$

3.3. Some special operator properties

3.3.1. *Adjoint operators*

We can construct a matrix element as follows:

$$\langle \Psi_m | \hat{Q} | \Psi_n \rangle = q_{nm}. \tag{3.19}$$

q_{nm} is an element of a matrix, in which the subscripts represent the row and column numbers (it does not really matter which way round as long as we stick to our choice throughout). Note that the diagonal elements of this matrix,

$$q_{nn} = \langle \Psi_n | \hat{Q} | \Psi_n \rangle, \tag{3.20}$$

are then the set of expectation values of the operator $\hat{Q}$ with respect to the set of eigenstates $|\Psi_n\rangle$. One can define an adjoint operator $\hat{Q}^+$ from the complex conjugate

$$\langle \Psi_m | \hat{Q} | \Psi_n \rangle^* = \langle \Psi_n | \hat{Q}^+ | \Psi_m \rangle. \tag{3.21}$$

Note then that

$$\langle \Psi_m | \hat{Q} | \Psi_n \rangle^* = \langle \Psi_n | \hat{Q}^+ | \Psi_m \rangle = q_{mn}^*, \tag{3.22}$$

where q_{mn}^* is the transpose of the matrix q_{nm}. When $m = n$, we get an expectation value

$$\langle \Psi_n | \hat{Q} | \Psi_n \rangle^* = \langle \Psi_n | \hat{Q}^+ | \Psi_n \rangle = q_{nn}^*. \tag{3.23}$$

This implies that the expectation value of $\hat{Q}^+$ is equal to the complex conjugate of the expectation value of $\hat{Q}$ for the same state of the system.

The idea of an operator adjoint plays an important role in quantum counting, so here we will outline a few of the most useful results for operators and their adjoints. First, we note that the adjoint of an operator takes us back to the original operator, rather in the way the complex conjugate of a complex number takes us back to the original number. To verify that this is the case, we note that

$$(\langle \Psi_n | \hat{Q} | \Psi_n \rangle^*)^* = \langle \Psi_n | \hat{Q}^+ | \Psi_n \rangle^* = \langle \Psi_n | \hat{Q}^{++} | \Psi_n \rangle. \tag{3.24}$$

Now, the left-hand side of the above is just $\langle \Psi_n | \hat{Q} | \Psi_n \rangle$, so, $\hat{Q}^{++} = \hat{Q}$.

Suppose in addition to operator $\hat{Q}$ and its adjoint $\hat{Q}^+$, we have another operator $\hat{R}$ and its adjoint $\hat{R}^+$. Then, as with $\hat{Q}$ and $\hat{Q}^+$, we have

$$\langle \Psi_n | \hat{R} | \Psi_n \rangle^* = \langle \Psi_n | \hat{R}^+ | \Psi_n \rangle. \tag{3.25}$$

Suppose also that we operate with $\hat{R}$ on $\hat{Q} | \Psi \rangle$ and take the complex conjugate of the result, we then have

$$(\langle \Psi_n | \hat{R}\hat{Q} | \Psi_n \rangle)^* = \langle \Psi_n | (\hat{R}\hat{Q})^+ | \Psi_n \rangle. \tag{3.26}$$

The question now is: what does $(\hat{R}\hat{Q})^+$ represent? We might guess at $\hat{R}^+\hat{Q}^+$, but we would be wrong in general. To see what it really is we note that, by splitting up $\langle \Psi_n | \hat{R}\hat{Q} | \Psi_n \rangle$ into separate parts, i.e., by writing it as $(\langle \Psi_n | \hat{R})(\hat{Q} | \Psi_n \rangle)$, then taking the complex conjugate and exploiting the definition in Equation (3.22), we get

$$((\langle \Psi_n | \hat{R})(\hat{Q} | \Psi_n \rangle))^* = (\langle \Psi_n | \hat{Q})^+)(\hat{R}^+ | \Psi_n \rangle) = \langle \Psi_n | \hat{Q}^+ \hat{R}^+ | \Psi_n \rangle. \tag{3.27}$$

Comparison of these last two equations shows us that we must have $(\hat{R}\hat{Q})^+ = \hat{Q}^+\hat{R}^+$. Note that the order is reversed by taking the adjoint. The order here is important because, unless $\hat{Q}^+$ and $\hat{R}^+$ commute, then $\hat{Q}^+\hat{R}^+ \neq \hat{R}^+\hat{Q}^+$. It is also straightforward to show that $(\hat{S}\hat{R}\hat{Q})^+ = \hat{Q}^+\hat{R}^+\hat{S}^+$, and so on. Note also that the adjoint is also linear in the sense that $(\hat{R} + \hat{Q})^+ = \hat{R}^+ + \hat{Q}^+$.

3.3.2. Hermitian operators

Here, we briefly consider what are referred to as Hermitian operators. These are an important set of operators in quantum theory that have real eigenvalues. This is an important property in QM since observables are associated with real numbers and are thus represented by Hermitian operators. The normal Hamiltonian is Hermitian. For physicists, real eigenvalues are particularly important since eigenvalues correspond to measurements made on a system and physicists like their measurements to have real values. Another important reason for the Hamiltonian being real is that it leads to the Heisenberg equation of motion, which we will encounter shortly, having a simple form (see Section 3.4). We can find a clue as to what kind of operators necessarily have real eigenvalues by looking at the results in the last section. Equation (3.23) shows that the expectation value of the adjoint of an operator is the complex conjugate of the expectation value of the operator itself. So, if the adjoint was identical with the operator, then the expectation values would have to be real. Suppose $\hat{Q}$ has a set of eigenvectors $|\Phi_n\rangle$ and corresponding eigenvalues q_n, such that

$$\hat{Q}|\Phi_n\rangle = q_n|\Phi_n\rangle. \tag{3.28}$$

From this, we can infer that

$$\langle\Phi_n|\hat{Q}|\Phi_n\rangle = q_n \tag{3.29}$$

and

$$\langle\Phi_n|\hat{Q}^+|\Phi_n\rangle = q_n^*. \tag{3.30}$$

Thus, if $\hat{Q}^+ = \hat{Q}$, then $q_n^* = q_n$. Hence, q_n must be real. Operators that are equal to their own adjoints are termed *self-adjoint*. So, Hermitian operators are essentially self-adjoint operators.

There are some useful corollaries to the above results. Suppose $\hat{R}$ is not a Hermitian (self-adjoint) operator. However, it is easy to show that the sum $\hat{R}+\hat{R}^+$ is Hermitian, since $(\hat{R}+\hat{R}^+)^+ = \hat{R}^+ + \hat{R}$, which is the same as $\hat{R}+\hat{R}^+$.

Finally, we note that since $(\hat{Q}\hat{R})^+ = \hat{R}^+\hat{Q}^+$, then it follows that $(\hat{Q}^+\hat{Q})^+ = \hat{Q}^+\hat{Q}$. Thus, $\hat{Q}^+\hat{Q}$ is automatically Hermitian and necessarily has real eigenvalues. This turns out to be a crucial result that we will exploit shortly in the section on positive operators and then later in the theory of quantum counting.

3.3.3. *Operator functions*

We are familiar with the idea of a function of scalar variables like x and y. So, the function x^2 takes the set of numbers represented by x and maps them into a new set of numbers obtained by calculating x^2. We want to be able to do something similar for operators. For example, although the Hamiltonian, $\hat{\Omega}$, is an operator, we still want to be able to integrate (3.18) as if $\hat{\Omega}$ were an ordinary number and find

$$|\Psi(t)\rangle = \exp(-i\hat{\Omega}t)|\Psi(0)\rangle. \tag{3.31}$$

The question is: how do we define or even justify such a step? Well here's how. We begin with an eigenvalue equation for an operator, say $\hat{Q}$, thus

$$\hat{Q}|\Phi\rangle = q|\Phi\rangle, \tag{3.32}$$

where $|\Phi\rangle$ and q are the eigenstates and eigenvalues, respectively. Suppose we operate again with $\hat{Q}$ and recall that operators commute with scalars, so $\hat{Q}$ commute with q, then

$$\hat{Q}^2|\Phi\rangle = q\hat{Q}|\Phi\rangle = q^2|\Phi\rangle, \tag{3.33}$$

where $\hat{Q}^2$ is a shorthand for $\hat{Q}\hat{Q}$. Clearly, we could repeat this process to any order and get

$$\hat{Q}^n|\Phi\rangle = q^n|\Phi\rangle. \tag{3.34}$$

From the above result, we can write the following series:

$$\left(1 + \frac{\hat{Q}}{1!} + \frac{\hat{Q}^2}{2!} + \frac{\hat{Q}^3}{3!} + \cdots\right)|\Phi\rangle = \left(1 + \frac{q}{1!} + \frac{q^2}{2!} + \frac{q^3}{3!} + \cdots\right)|\Phi\rangle. \tag{3.35}$$

For the terms in the bracket on the right-hand side, summed to infinity, we would have no hesitation in writing $\exp q$. By the same token, we write the terms in the bracket on the left-hand side as $\exp \hat{Q}$. By this way of working, we can define any analytic function of $\hat{Q}$, $f(\hat{Q})$ by

$$f(\hat{Q})|\Phi\rangle = f(q)|\Phi\rangle. \tag{3.36}$$

So, going back to Equation (3.31), we can now understand $\exp(-i\hat{\Omega}t)$ as

$$\exp(-i\hat{\Omega}t) = 1 + \frac{-it\hat{\Omega}}{1!} + \frac{(-it\hat{\Omega})^2}{2!} + \frac{(-it\hat{\Omega})^3}{3!} + \cdots. \tag{3.37}$$

By differentiating this expression term by term, one can check that the SE is formally satisfied by $|\Psi(t)\rangle = \exp(-i\hat{\Omega}t)|\Psi(0)\rangle$.

One final point about functions of operators in the context of commutation relations. Given the way the function of an operator is defined, then

$$[\hat{Q}, f(\hat{Q})] = 0. \tag{3.38}$$

It is obvious that $[\hat{Q}, \hat{Q}] = \hat{Q}\hat{Q} - \hat{Q}\hat{Q} = 0$, but also $[\hat{Q}, \hat{Q}^2] = \hat{Q}\hat{Q}\hat{Q} - \hat{Q}\hat{Q}\hat{Q} = 0$, and so on. So, $[\hat{Q}, \hat{Q}^n] = 0$ for any n. Hence, any analytic function of $\hat{Q}$, $f(\hat{Q})$, commutes with $\hat{Q}$ itself.

3.3.4. *When do operators commute?*

It is not necessarily true that an eigenstate of the Hamiltonian operator $\hat{\Omega}$ is also an eigenstate of some other operator, say $\hat{Q}$. Then we expect

$$\hat{Q}|\Psi_n\rangle = \sum_m q_{nm}|\Psi_m\rangle. \tag{3.39}$$

Then we generally find that $\hat{Q}\hat{\Omega} \neq \hat{\Omega}\hat{Q}$. This is an example of the non-commutation of operators we introduced earlier, i.e., $[\hat{Q}, \hat{\Omega}] \neq 0$. The non-commutation comes from the fact that $\hat{Q}$ does not share the same set of eigenstates as $\hat{\Omega}$. Then

$$(\hat{Q}\hat{\Omega} - \hat{\Omega}\hat{Q})|\Psi_n\rangle = \sum_m q_{nm}(\omega_n - \omega_m)|\Psi_m\rangle \neq 0, \tag{3.40}$$

as long as $\omega_n \neq \omega_m$, whenever $n \neq m$, which we will assume to be the case here. It is straightforward to show that if two operators do share the same set of eigenvectors, then they will commute as follows:

Suppose

$$\hat{Q}|\Phi\rangle = q|\Phi\rangle \tag{3.41}$$

and

$$\hat{R}|\Phi\rangle = r|\Phi\rangle, \tag{3.42}$$

where q and r are respective eigenvalues. Then

$$\hat{R}\hat{Q}|\Phi\rangle = q\hat{R}|\Phi\rangle = qr|\Phi\rangle \tag{3.43}$$

and

$$\hat{Q}\hat{R}|\Phi\rangle = r\hat{Q}|\Phi\rangle = rq|\Phi\rangle. \tag{3.44}$$

Since $rq = qr$, then subtracting gives

$$[\hat{Q}, \hat{R}]|\Phi\rangle = 0 \tag{3.45}$$

and so $\hat{Q}$ and $\hat{R}$ commute.

3.3.5. *Expansion of commutation brackets*

Situations will arise where the commutation bracket will contain products of operators and we will need to know how to simplify them. It is straightforward to show, by explicitly writing out the brackets that, for any three operators, $\hat{Q}$, $\hat{R}$, and $\hat{S}$, then

$$[\hat{Q}, \hat{R} + \hat{S}] = [\hat{Q}, \hat{R}] + [\hat{Q}, \hat{S}]. \tag{3.46}$$

A little more tricky is the result:

$$[\hat{Q}, \hat{R}\hat{S}] = \hat{R}[\hat{Q}, \hat{S}] + [\hat{Q}, \hat{R}]\hat{S}. \tag{3.47}$$

Similarly,

$$[\hat{Q}\hat{R}, \hat{S}] = \hat{Q}[\hat{R}, \hat{S}] + [\hat{Q}, \hat{S}]\hat{R}. \tag{3.48}$$

Looking at this last relation, the trick is to write $\hat{Q}\hat{R}\hat{S} - \hat{S}\hat{Q}\hat{R}$ as

$$\hat{Q}\hat{R}\hat{S} - \hat{Q}\hat{S}\hat{R} + \hat{Q}\hat{S}\hat{R} - \hat{S}\hat{Q}\hat{R}.$$

Note that we have added and subtracted the same terms in the middle of the sequence above. The first two terms are just $\hat{Q}[\hat{R}, \hat{S}]$ and the second two are $[\hat{Q}, \hat{S}]\hat{R}$.

3.3.6. *Positive operators*

We have seen that Hermitian operators are a special set of operators in QM that have real eigenvalues. They may be represented by self-adjoint operators, i.e., an operator, say $\hat{Q}$, such that $\hat{Q}^+ = \hat{Q}$. Now, we want to go further and see what kind of operator has non-negative eigenvalues. Clearly, such an operator would also have to be Hermitian (self-adjoint) because non-negative numbers are also real numbers. If $\hat{Q}$ can be expressed as $\hat{Q} = \hat{A}^+ \hat{A}$, where $\hat{A}$ is some operator that has an adjoint, $\hat{A}^+$, then we can show that the eigenvalues of $\hat{Q}$, assuming that it has any, must be non-negative. Let

$$\hat{Q}|\Psi\rangle = q|\Psi\rangle. \qquad (3.49)$$

Thus,

$$\langle\Psi|\hat{Q}|\Psi\rangle = \langle\Psi|\hat{A}^+\hat{A}|\Psi\rangle = \||\hat{A}|\Psi\rangle\|^2 = q. \qquad (3.50)$$

Since $\||\hat{A}|\Psi\rangle\|^2 \geq 0$, then q must be non-negative. So, we can conclude that if an operator can be expressed as the product of an operator and its adjoint, then it will have non-negative eigenvalues. Operators with non-negative eigenvalues are sometimes called *positive* or *positive definite* operators, although more accurately, if ≥ 0 applies, rather than just $>$, then they should strictly be called *positive semi-definite*. We will need an operator of this type later when we explore the properties of the number operator whose eigenvalue spectrum is the set of natural or counting numbers.

3.4. Heisenberg operators

Up to now, (3.1) and (3.18) imply that the wave function Ψ and the corresponding state vector $|\Psi\rangle$ that satisfy the time-dependent SE are time-dependent. Then, the operators like $\hat{\Omega}$ and $\hat{Q}$ are treated as independent of time. Heisenberg developed an approach to QM in which the states were independent of time, but the operators were considered as functions of time. Suppose an operator $\hat{Q}$, which is itself not a function of time, t, operates on a state, $|\Psi(t)\rangle$ that is an explicit function of time. Then the expectation value of $\hat{Q}$ is $\langle\Psi(t)|\hat{Q}|\Psi(t)\rangle$. Now, we assume that $|\Psi(t)\rangle$ is a solution of the time-dependent SE and so can be expressed as $|\Psi(t)\rangle = \exp(-i\hat{\Omega}t)|\Psi(0)\rangle$. Similarly, its conjugate can be written $\langle\Psi(t)| = \langle\Psi(0)|\exp(i\hat{\Omega}t)$, where we have used $(\exp(-i\hat{\Omega}t))^+ = \exp(i\hat{\Omega}t)$ and that $(\hat{\Omega})^+ = \hat{\Omega}$. Thus, we can write

$$\langle\Psi(t)|\hat{Q}|\Psi(t)\rangle = \langle\Psi(0)|\exp(i\hat{\Omega}t)\hat{Q}\exp(-i\hat{\Omega}t)|\Psi(0)\rangle. \qquad (3.51)$$

We can thus define a new operator $\hat{Q}(t)$, which is now an explicit function of t, such that

$$\hat{Q}(t) = \exp(i\hat{\Omega}t)\hat{Q}(0)\exp(-i\hat{\Omega}t). \tag{3.52}$$

Note that $\hat{Q}(t)$ only reduces to $\hat{Q}(0)$ if $\hat{Q}(0)$ commutes with $\hat{\Omega}$, which it generally is not assumed to do. Formal differentiation of $\hat{Q}(t)$ then yields

$$i\frac{\mathrm{d}\hat{Q}(t)}{\mathrm{d}t} = \hat{Q}(t)\hat{\Omega} - \hat{\Omega}\hat{Q}(t) = [\hat{Q}(t), \hat{\Omega}]. \tag{3.53}$$

The above equation is called the Heisenberg equation of motion (HEM). It is complementary to the SE as a method of putting the dynamical behavior of a system in mathematical form. As with the SE, the key starting point for setting up such an equation is to determine the form of the Hamiltonian, Ω, which determines the behavior of the system. Once the Hamiltonian is known the dynamics follow. One important consequence of the HEM that is immediately obvious from its form is that if any operator commutes with the Hamiltonian, Ω, then the time derivative of that operator is zero. Such an operator is termed *an integral of the motion*. The implication is that the operator and its expectation values are invariant, i.e., independent of time. Such quantities are invaluable guides on how systems treated by Hamiltonian methods behave. In the following sections, we will make use of both the Schrödinger and Heisenberg equations.

The rule (3.53) has a number of interesting properties that are worth noting. First, if $\hat{Q}^+(t)$ is the adjoint of $\hat{Q}(t)$, then, from the definition of adjoint, $\hat{Q}^+(t) = \exp(i\hat{\Omega}t)\hat{Q}^+(0)\exp(-i\hat{\Omega}(t))$, which has exactly the same form as (3.52) and so, the differential of the adjoint obeys (3.53) too.

In what follows, we will be interested in the way systems vary in time. As we have seen in the Heisenberg representation, it is the operators that vary in time and the state vectors or functions are constant in time. From a practical predictive point of view, we will be interested in how the expectation values of the operators, which are just numbers that correspond to what is measured, vary with time. We will formally write the expectation values as functions of time. For example, for operator $\hat{Q}(t)$,

$$Q(t) = \langle \hat{Q}(t) \rangle = \langle \Psi(0)|\hat{Q}(t)|\Psi(0)\rangle. \tag{3.54}$$

Now, since the state vectors and their conjugates are invariant, then, when we come to differentiate the expectation value of $\hat{Q}(t)$, we get

$$\frac{\mathrm{d}\langle \hat{Q}(t) \rangle}{\mathrm{d}t} = \frac{\mathrm{d}\langle \Psi(0)|\hat{Q}(t)|\Psi(0)\rangle}{\mathrm{d}t} = \langle \Psi(0)|\frac{\mathrm{d}\hat{Q}(t)}{\mathrm{d}t}|\Psi(0)\rangle. \tag{3.55}$$

This means that the rate of change of the expectation value of a Heisenberg-type operator is equal to the expectation value of the rate of change of the operator, i.e.,

$$\frac{\mathrm{d}\langle \hat{Q}(t) \rangle}{\mathrm{d}t} = \left\langle \frac{\mathrm{d}\hat{Q}(t)}{\mathrm{d}t} \right\rangle. \tag{3.56}$$

This is an important result that will be used with operator differential equations in the following chapters. Clearly, since the derivative of a derivative is also a derivative, the same rule applies to higher derivatives too. Heisenberg operators and the Heisenberg equation of motion play a crucial role in the quantum mechanical models of population changes and trading that are treated later. These operators underpin the idea of quantum counting that is introduced in the next chapter.

3.5. Exercises

Exercise 1. Check that

$$|\Psi(t)\rangle = \exp(-i\hat{\Omega}t)|\Psi(0)\rangle$$

formally satisfies the Schrödinger equation.

Exercise 2. Given three linear operators, $\hat{A}$, $\hat{B}$, and $\hat{C}$, show the validity of the following expressions involving commutation brackets:

(i) $[\hat{A}, \hat{B} + \hat{C}] = [\hat{A}, \hat{B}] + [\hat{A}, \hat{C}]$
(ii) $[\hat{A}, \hat{B}\hat{C}] = \hat{B}[\hat{A}, \hat{C}] + [\hat{A}, \hat{B}]\hat{C}$

Exercise 3. Given $[\hat{A}, \hat{B}] = 1$, use the above relations to show that $[\hat{A}, \hat{B}^2] = 2\hat{B}$.

Exercise 4. In a way similar to the above result, also simplify:

  (i) $[\hat{A}, \hat{B}^3]$,
  (ii) $[\hat{A}, \hat{B}^n]$, where n is a natural number.
(iii) $[\hat{A}^2, \hat{B}^2]$.

Chapter 4

Quantum Counting

4.1. The mechanics of counting

In Chapter 2, we had a brief look at population modeling using classical methods. No counting was involved since the population numbers were treated as scalar variables which were functions of time. The numbers involved were not intrinsically counting numbers. They could be any real number on a continuous number line. What controlled the time dependence of the populations was the algebraic rules in the form of differential equations that we imposed. These were concocted in a rather *ad hoc* manner, based on a notion of what might cause the growth and decay of the populations and how we might quantify these processes in relation to the population numbers and some arbitrary constants.

Quantum counting is an attempt to model the operation of counting in a mathematical way that reflects the fact that we are dealing with counting numbers, which do not form a continuum on the number line. In counting, the sequence of numbers is as important as the total. We go from 0 to 1, to 2, to 3 and so on in a very systematic way. The aim is to give us the total when we stop counting. This is just how counting works. Research has been carried out to see if humans can ascertain the number of individual items in a group of identical items without going through this systematic counting out procedure (see [10]). It turns out that the maximum number that can be correctly estimated without explicit counting is just four!

As we know, there are jumps between counting numbers such that neighboring ones, on the number line, differ in value by one. We could imagine counting up as climbing the rungs of a ladder, and, by the same token, interpret descending the ladder as counting down. However, counting is more than repeatedly adding (or subtracting) one. We do not count up by repeating "and one, and one, and one, ... etc.", or repeating "less one, less one, less one, ... etc", when counting down. We would not know where we were on the ladder if this is all we did. The point of counting is to know where one is on this number ladder. So counting involves both *repetition* and *remembering*. The mathematical approach to counting must have a memory store that labels what rung we are on, on the ladder, as well as being able to increase or decrease that position by one. In spoken counting, we have a different name for each number. In mathematics and computation, we use a unique symbol from a set of (usually arabic) numerals to label each number. What we need to do then, is to devise a mathematical operation that captures both the memory aspect, as well as the process of adding or subtracting one. This is where quantum counting comes in. The term *quantum counting* has recently been introduced by Robinson and Haven [20] in relation to the foundational aspects of physics, starting with quantum field theory (second quantization) as the fundamental theory and deriving quantum theory and classical physics as approximations to it.

4.1.1. *Repetition, cyclic processes, and clocks*

One way of characterizing counting is as repetition. In counting up, we keep adding one to the previous number. This is what specifies the order of counting numbers. This repeated action of adding one is essentially a cyclic process and this cyclic aspect is one clue as to how to represent counting mathematically. A good way of visualizing this repetition or cyclic process is by representing it as a clock face. We are used to the idea of a clock as something which counts the hours. In some languages, the word for hour is the same as the word for clock (e.g., German: Uhr; Swahili: saa). Fig. 4.1 shows a very simple clock face with a single pointer (hand).

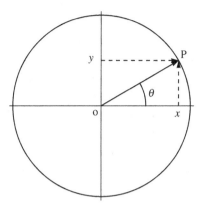

FIGURE 4.1.   A cyclic process represented by a pointer rotating steadily around a clock face.

The orientation of the pointer, OP, can be specified by a clock angle. For normal clocks, the clock angle would be taken from the 12 o'clock position and measured clockwise, of course. However, here we follow mathematical convention and utilize a pair of Cartesian coordinates x, and y, whose origin coincides with the center of the clock face. The angle, θ is then measured counter-clockwise from the positive x axis. The position of the tip of the pointer, P can be specified in terms of the coordinates, (x, y). If OP is a distance r, then $x = r\cos\theta$ and $y = r\sin\theta$.

Let us assume that the pointer moves at a constant rate around the clock face, then the angle θ is defined by an angular frequency (sometimes called angular velocity), ω_0, such that $\theta = \omega_0 t$, and t is just time. ω_0 is related to the period, T, i.e., the time taken for one complete revolution, by $\omega_0 = 2\pi/T$. Note that after a whole number, n, revolutions of the pointer, t changes by nT and θ changes by $2\pi n$. So, the pointer is in exactly the same position again after a time nT. This means that just by looking at the position of the pointer at a given instant, we cannot know the time to within a whole number of periods. This ambiguity is called aliasing. Before developing quantum counting using operator algebra, it is useful to point out a powerful mathematical simplification to specifying the position of the pointer on the clock face.

4.1.2. *Phasors: The complex plane as a clock counter*

Instead of using a pair of real time-dependent coordinates $(x(t), y(t))$, where $x(t) = r\cos(\omega_0 t)$ and $y(t) = r\sin(\omega_0 t)$, to specify the position of the pointer, these two functions can be combined into a single complex amplitude, $a(t) = x(t) - iy(t) = r(\cos(\omega_0 t) - i\sin(\omega_0 t)) = r\exp(-i\omega_0 t)$. So, $a(t) = r\exp(-i\omega_0 t)$ is a complex amplitude that rotates clockwise on the clock face, which is now regarded as a complex plane. Similarly, the complex conjugate, $a^*(t) = r\exp(i\omega_0 t)$ rotates counter-clockwise in the complex plane. $a(t)$, expressed in this complex number form is called a *phasor*. Such quantities are extensively used in physics to represent oscillations and waves. The quantum operator versions of $a(t)$ and $a^*(t)$ play a crucial role in quantum counting.

In the complex plane, the angle θ is mathematically more properly called a phase angle rather than a clock angle. The complex plane representation of the clock face is also called an Argand diagram. The Argand diagram does not have to represent an actual plane in space, rather it should be thought of as representing a cyclic system in which the pointer indicated the phase of the cycle being represented. In the Argand diagram, the x-axis is called the real axis and the y-axis is called the imaginary axis. Then a complex number $x + iy$ is represented by the vector (x, y), where x is the real part and y the imaginary part of the complex number.

With this representation, it is straightforward to understand the aliasing idea, as follows. If $(x(t), y(t))$ represents the system at time t, then $(x(t+nT), -y(t+nT))$ represents the system at a time which is just n periods later, where n is a whole number (counting number or integer). Now, if $\omega_0 t = \theta$, then $\omega_0(t + T) = \theta + 2\pi n$. So, $x(t + nT) = r\cos(\theta + 2\pi n)$ and $y(t + nT) = -r\sin(\theta + 2\pi n)$. However, as is well known, $\cos(\theta + 2\pi n) = \cos\theta$ and $\sin(\theta + 2\pi n) = \sin\theta$. Thus, $x(t + nT) = x(t)$ and $y(t + nT) = y(t)$, and hence $a(t + nT) = a(t)$. Consequently, the system repeats its position after any whole number of cycles.

4.2. Generating a spectrum of integers with the integer operator

We are going to apply the Schrödinger equation (SE) to the clock face counter in a particular way. If we divide both sides of the SE by ω_0, we get

$$i\frac{d|\Psi\rangle}{\omega_0 dt} = \frac{\hat{\Omega}}{\omega_0}|\Psi\rangle. \tag{4.1}$$

Recall that ω_0 is a constant rotation rate, and $\theta = \omega_0 t$, so, differentiation with respect to θ is the same as differentiation with respect to $\omega_0 t$. Then, we can write (4.1) as

$$i\frac{d|\Psi\rangle}{\omega_0 dt} = i\frac{d|\Psi\rangle}{d\theta} = \hat{Z}|\Psi\rangle, \tag{4.2}$$

where the operator $\hat{Z} = \hat{\Omega}/\omega_0$. Given that the eigenvalues of $\hat{\Omega}$ are frequencies (see (3.7)), then clearly the operator $\hat{Z}$ will have eigenvalues that are the ratio of two frequencies, which are just dimensionless numbers. To see exactly what these numbers are for our clock face counter, we need to solve the eigenvalue equation

$$i\frac{d|\Psi(\theta)\rangle}{d\theta} = \lambda|\Psi(\theta)\rangle, \tag{4.3}$$

where λ is an, as yet, unknown set of eigenvalues and $|\Psi(\theta)\rangle$ is a set of eigenfunctions that will represent the possible eigenstates of the system that correspond to the eigenvalues.

Now (4.3) is easily integrated to give $|\Psi(\theta)\rangle = \exp(-i\lambda\theta)|\Psi(0)\rangle$. However, recall that the clock face counter is in the same state after one complete cycle, i.e., when $\theta \to \theta + 2\pi$. This means that $|\Psi(\theta)\rangle = |\Psi(\theta + 2\pi)\rangle$, but then we must have $\exp(-i\lambda\theta)|\Psi(0)\rangle = \exp(-i\lambda(\theta + 2\pi))|\Psi(0)\rangle$. This necessarily implies that $\exp(-i2\lambda\pi) = 1$ and hence $\lambda = n$, where n is an integer. So, the operator $\hat{Z} = id/d\theta$ has a set of eigenfunctions $|\Psi_n(\theta)\rangle = \exp(-in\theta)|\Psi_n(0)\rangle$, with corresponding integer eigenvalues, n. It is a simple matter to check that

$$\hat{Z}|\Psi_n(\theta)\rangle = i\frac{\mathrm{d}|\Psi_n(\theta)\rangle}{\mathrm{d}\theta} = n|\Psi_n(\theta)\rangle, \qquad (4.4)$$

by explicit differentiation of $|\Psi_n(\theta)\rangle = \exp(-in\theta)|\Psi_n(0)\rangle$ with respect to θ. Since the operator $\hat{Z}$ generates a spectrum of integers, $\ldots -3, -2, -1, 0, 1, 2, 3, \ldots$, then we can call the operator $\hat{Z}$ the integer operator. However, what we really want is an operator that generates a spectrum of counting numbers (including zero), i.e., $0, 1, 2, 3, \ldots$. We will see how to do that next, by noting that natural numbers, unlike integers, are all non-negative.

4.3. Generating a spectrum of natural numbers with the number operator

The Nobel Prize-winning physicist, Julian Schwinger, made a clever and important observation concerning the integer operator $\hat{Z}$, when he was studying the angular momentum of atomic systems (see [21]). It turns out that $\hat{Z}$ multiplied by the reduced Planck constant, $\hbar$, is the operator for a component of angular momentum of a quantum particle. This is not too surprising, since our clock counter is rotating, at least in the complex plane of the Argand diagram. Schwinger pointed out that an integer is always the difference between two natural numbers. This is a really significant idea in the context of integer and number operators.

Here, we will apply Schwinger's idea in a way that is a little different from how he applied it. We note that the set of integers comprises a set of natural numbers, including zero, $0, 1, 2, 3, \ldots$, together with the set of their additive inverses, $0, -1, -2, -3, \ldots$. Zero is a common element of these two sets, but that causes no particular problem. If we apply operator $\hat{Z}$ to a subset of its eigenfunctions, $|\Psi_n(\theta)\rangle$, where the values of n are non-negative, i.e., $n = 0, 1, 2, 3, \ldots$, then we will get only non-negative eigenvalues. We can let $\hat{Z} = \hat{n}$ where $\hat{n}$ is a natural number operator that only has non-negative eigenvalues, but is only allowed to act on the eigenfunctions with subscripts $n \geq 0$. We could do the same thing for the non-positive eigenvalues, but with a little thought, we would have to use a different natural number operator. We could let $\hat{Z} = -\hat{n}_-$, when it operates on $|\Psi_n(\theta)\rangle$, with $n \leq 0$. In what follows, we only need one set of natural numbers so we will use $\hat{n}$ and the eigenfunctions with non-negative eigenvalues always take $n \geq 0$.

Now that we have an operator $\hat{n}$ that we know has only non-negative eigenvalues we can factorize it into the product of a pair of factors, one an operator amplitude $\hat{a}$ and the other its adjoint, $\hat{a}^+$, as pointed out in Section 3.3.6. So let us write $\hat{n} = \hat{a}^+ \hat{a}$, where the properties of the factors $\hat{a}$ and its adjoint are yet to be determined. $\hat{a}$ is what Robinson and Haven [20] refer to as a number amplitude operator, because the relationship between $\hat{n}$ and $\hat{a}$ is analogous to the relationship between a probability density and the wave function in quantum mechanics, which is regarded as a probability density amplitude. Our next task is to deduce what these properties are. Now we know that

$$\langle \Psi_n | \hat{n} | \Psi_n \rangle = n = \langle \Psi_n | \hat{a}^+ \hat{a} | \Psi_n \rangle = \| \hat{a} \Psi_n \rangle \|^2. \tag{4.5}$$

The last term shows clearly that $n \geq 0$. Next we need a phase symmetry procedure introduced in Robinson and Haven [20]. This involves noticing that $\hat{n} = \hat{a}^+ \hat{a}$ is invariant to a phase change in $\hat{a}$. To see what this means, let us write the form of $\hat{a}$ that does not depend on a phase angle θ as $\hat{a}(0)$, and then introduce a phase shift of θ in $\hat{a}(0)$ by $\hat{a}(\theta) = \hat{a}(0) \exp(-i\theta)$. Then of course, the adjoint of $\hat{a}(\theta)$ is $\hat{a}^+(\theta) = \hat{a}^+(0) \exp(i\theta)$. So, we have

$$\hat{n} = \hat{a}^+(0)\hat{a}(0) = \hat{a}^+(\theta)\hat{a}(\theta), \tag{4.6}$$

since $\hat{a}^+(\theta)\hat{a}(\theta) = \hat{a}^+(0) \exp(i\theta) \exp(-i\theta))\hat{a}(0) = \hat{a}^+(0)\hat{a}(0)$. However, note that now we have not only introduced phase dependence into the operators $\hat{a}(\theta)$ and $\hat{a}^+(\theta)$, but time dependence too, since we can take the phase as the clock angle, $\theta = \omega_0 t$.

Now, if $\hat{a}(\theta)$ is a function of phase and time, it must have the form of a Heisenberg operator and must obey the Heisenberg equation of motion (HEM). If we divide the Heisenberg equation by ω_0 and treat the differentiation with respect to phase again, we get, in general

$$i\frac{d\hat{a}(\theta)}{d\theta} = \hat{a}(\theta)\hat{Z} - \hat{Z}\hat{a}(\theta) = [\hat{a}(\theta), \hat{Z}]. \tag{4.7}$$

However, if we restrict the operators to operating on eigenstates with non-negative eigenvalues, as before, then we can replace $\hat{Z}$ by $\hat{n}$ once again so

$$i\frac{d\hat{a}(\theta)}{d\theta} = [\hat{a}(\theta), \hat{n}] = [\hat{a}(\theta), \hat{a}^+(\theta)\hat{a}(\theta)]. \tag{4.8}$$

Since we know that $\hat{a}(\theta) = \hat{a}(0)\exp(-i\theta)$, the we know that $i\frac{d\hat{a}(\theta)}{d\theta} = \hat{a}(\theta)$, so

$$\hat{a} = [\hat{a}, \hat{n}] = \hat{a}\hat{n} - \hat{n}\hat{a}. \tag{4.9}$$

We do not need to explicitly indicate the argument of $\hat{a}$ in (4.9), because $\exp(-i\theta)$ is a common factor and can be canceled. So $\hat{a}$ can stand for $\hat{a}(0)$ or $\hat{a}(\theta)$. $\hat{n}$, of course, does not depend on θ.

It turns out that we can use Equation (4.9) to work out what the properties of $\hat{a}$ and its adjoint are. These are not at all obvious. We certainly cannot assume what their eigenstates are, or even whether they have any. We certainly cannot assume that their eigenstates are the set $|\Psi_n\rangle$. Recall that if we operate with the natural number operator $\hat{n}$ on a state $|\Psi_n\rangle$ with $n \geq 0$, then $\hat{n}|\Psi_n\rangle = n|\Psi_n\rangle$. Now, let us operate on $|\Psi_n\rangle$ with the terms in (4.9). Then we get, after a little rearranging

$$n(\hat{a}|\Psi_n\rangle) = (n-1)(\hat{a}|\Psi_n\rangle). \tag{4.10}$$

This equation shows that the state obtained by operating with $\hat{a}$ on $|\Psi_n\rangle$, i.e., $\hat{a}|\Psi_n\rangle$, is also an eigenstate of $\hat{n}$. Indeed, we can see that this new state must have an eigenvalue of $n-1$. Thus, we can deduce that it must be proportional to $|\Psi_{n-1}\rangle$. So, let us put $\hat{a}|\Psi_n\rangle = \beta|\Psi_{n-1}\rangle$, where β is a scaler that can depend on n, but that we can assume, without loss of generality, is real. However, we know that $(\|\hat{a}|\Psi_n\rangle\|)^2 = n$, and so $(\|\beta|\Psi_{n-1}\rangle\|)^2 = n$. But, we also have, $(\|\beta|\Psi_{n-1}\rangle\|)^2 = \beta^2\langle\Psi_{n-1}|\Psi_{n-1}\rangle = \beta^2$. So, $\beta = \sqrt{n}$. So, we have shown that

$$\hat{a}|\Psi_n\rangle = \sqrt{n}|\Psi_{n-1}\rangle. \tag{4.11}$$

In a similar fashion, but starting with $i\frac{\mathrm{d}\hat{a}^+(\theta)}{\mathrm{d}\theta} = -\hat{a}^+(\theta)$, it can be shown that

$$\hat{a}^+|\Psi_n\rangle = \sqrt{n+1}|\Psi_{n+1}\rangle. \tag{4.12}$$

Now (4.12) implies that $\hat{a}^+|\Psi_{n-1}\rangle = \sqrt{n}|\Psi_n\rangle$. So, if we operate on (4.11) with $\hat{a}^+$ we get

$$\hat{a}^+\hat{a}|\Psi_n\rangle = \sqrt{n}\hat{a}^+|\Psi_{n-1}\rangle = n|\Psi_n\rangle, \tag{4.13}$$

as expected, since $\hat{a}^+\hat{a} = \hat{n}$. But note that

$$\hat{a}\hat{a}^+|\Psi_n\rangle = (n+1)|\Psi_n\rangle, \tag{4.14}$$

so, we can conclude that $\hat{a}\hat{a}^+ \neq \hat{a}^+\hat{a}$, i.e., $[\hat{a}, \hat{a}^+] \neq 0$. Indeed, if we subtract (4.13) from (4.14), we get

$$[\hat{a}, \hat{a}^+] = 1, \tag{4.15}$$

which confirms that $\hat{a}^+$ does not commute with $\hat{a}$.

4.4. Occupation number notation and properties of $\hat{a}$ and $\hat{a}^+$

4.4.1. *Occupation number notation*

Recall that the operators $\hat{n}$, $\hat{a}$, and its adjoint $\hat{a}^+$ all operate on the state $|\Psi_n\rangle$. The only thing important about this state, as far as we are concerned, is the subscript n, which essentially completely specifies $|\Psi_n\rangle$. So, from now on we will just specify $|\Psi_n\rangle$ with $|n\rangle$. Then we get

$$\hat{a}|n\rangle = \sqrt{n}|n-1\rangle,$$
$$\hat{a}^+|n\rangle = \sqrt{n+1}|n+1\rangle,$$
$$\hat{n}|n\rangle = n|n\rangle. \tag{4.16}$$

The notation $|n\rangle$ for the state is indicative of the fact that we will interpret this state as one with n *things* in it. For this reason, the notation is called an *occupation number representation*. As we will see, this notation proves particularly useful for representing more complicated situations in which several different populations are involved.

4.4.2. *Everything stops at zero*

If we apply $\hat{a}$ to the state $|n\rangle$, with n things in it, we get a state with $n-1$ things in it, i.e., $\sqrt{n}|n-1\rangle$ to be precise. Now what happens if we apply $\hat{a}$ once more, to the result, i.e., if we apply $\hat{a}^2$ to $|n\rangle$. Well, we just get

$$\hat{a}^2|n\rangle = \sqrt{n}\hat{a}|n-1\rangle = \sqrt{n(n-1)}|n-2\rangle, \qquad (4.17)$$

which means we now have $n-2$ things in the state. Now suppose we applied $\hat{a}$, n times to $|n\rangle$, i.e., what is $\hat{a}^n|n\rangle$? All we have to do is continue with rule Equation (4.16) and then we wind up with

$$\hat{a}^n|n\rangle = \sqrt{n!}|0\rangle. \qquad (4.18)$$

The state $|0\rangle$ is a perfectly acceptable state. It is just one with nothing in it! We will just call this the empty state. It does not itself mean the same as zero. It is not nothing. It is a state, albeit one with nothing in it. Do not forget that an empty box is still a box; an empty hand is still a hand, etc. Note that the coefficient of this empty state above is the square root of factorial n. Now suppose we operate once more with $\hat{a}$, i.e., we operate $n+1$ times on $|n\rangle$ with $\hat{a}$. We then get

$$\hat{a}^{n+1}|n\rangle = \sqrt{n!}\hat{a}|0\rangle = \sqrt{n! \times 0}|-1\rangle. \qquad (4.19)$$

This looks like we get to the state $|-1\rangle$, which would be very awkward. How would we interpret having a state with -1 things in it? However, if we look at the result more carefully we see that the coefficient of the state is zero, since the square root of factorial n times zero is zero. So, we do not get to $|-1\rangle$ after all, since $\hat{a}^{n+1}|n\rangle = 0$, which means we get no state at all. What if we try again with another $\hat{a}$? We get

$$\hat{a}^{n+2}|n\rangle = \sqrt{n! \times 0 \times -1}|-2\rangle = 0. \qquad (4.20)$$

The result is the same as before because once the factor zero appears in the coefficient, it stays there when further factors of $\hat{a}$ are applied. It is not difficult to see that

$$\hat{a}^m|n\rangle = 0, \tag{4.21}$$

whenever $m > n$. Thus the state $|0\rangle$ is an impenetrable barrier, which cannot be crossed from above. Once the state is empty, it cannot be emptied further. Actually this should not be totally surprising, since the preceding analysis was premised on the assumption that $\hat{n}$ could only have non-negative (integer) eigenvalues. We have shown that this assumption is consistent with the resulting properties of $\hat{a}$.

4.4.3. *Building the state $|n\rangle$ from scratch*

Above, we showed that counting down from $|n\rangle$ stops at $|0\rangle$, whatever the value of n (it is always positive or zero of course). It is sometimes useful to use the opposite technique and build the state $|n\rangle$ from scratch, starting with an empty state. So, starting with $\hat{a}^+|0\rangle = \sqrt{1}|1\rangle = |1\rangle$, and then $\hat{a}^+\sqrt{1}|1\rangle = \sqrt{2 \times 1}|2\rangle = \sqrt{2}|2\rangle$ and so on, we eventually end up with

$$\hat{a}^{+n}|0\rangle = \sqrt{n!}|n\rangle, \tag{4.22}$$

after n applications of the operator $\hat{a}^+$. Then we can write

$$|n\rangle = \frac{\hat{a}^{+n}}{\sqrt{n!}}|0\rangle. \tag{4.23}$$

4.4.4. *Commutation brackets with functions of $\hat{a}$ and $\hat{a}^+$*

A useful extension to the commutation relation $[\hat{a}, \hat{a}^+] = 1$ is worth noting for use later. Using the expansion rule for commutation brackets, we get the following:

$$[\hat{a}, \hat{a}^{+2}] = 2\hat{a}^+,$$
$$[\hat{a}, \hat{a}^{+3}] = 3\hat{a}^{+2},$$

and so on. So, in general, $[\hat{a}, \hat{a}^{+M}] = M\hat{a}^{+(M-1)}$. One can go further by assuming that in general, any analytic function of $\hat{a}^+$ can be written as an infinite polynomial in $\hat{a}^+$, in which case,

$$[\hat{a}, f(\hat{a}^+)] = \frac{\mathrm{d}f(\hat{a}^+)}{\mathrm{d}\hat{a}^+}. \tag{4.24}$$

Similarly, one can show that

$$[f(\hat{a}), \hat{a}^+] = \frac{\mathrm{d}f(\hat{a})}{\mathrm{d}\hat{a}}. \tag{4.25}$$

Chapter 5

Quantum Transactions

5.1. The quantum trader

The number operator algebra that we have just developed is designed
to add to and subtract from totals of countable objects. This is the
essential basis for a mathematical model of trading in which traders
add to and subtract from numbers of goods and amounts of money
by exchanging them (see [5]). However, we are going to begin with a
non-trading trader. This may seem a pointless exercise, but it is only
by knowing how to set up the equations of motion for an isolated
non-interacting case that we can start to explore more complicated
and hence more interesting situations. This is equivalent to a physicist starting with an isolated system. The reason for doing this is
that usually such systems are the simplest to deal with, since they
do not, by definition, interact with anything else. For example, for a
single particle in Newtonian classical physics that does not interact
with anything means that no forces act on it. Such a particle obeys
Newton's first law of motion and continues in a state of rest or uniform motion in a straight line. This means that nothing happens to
a truly isolated system in mechanics. We will see what the equivalent
to Newton's first law of motion is for an isolated trader.

Let us assume that a trader, called A, has a number, n of tradable
assets. We can associate a quantum number amplitude operator, $\hat{a}$
and its adjoint $\hat{a}^+$ with A, such that the number operator associated
with A is $\hat{n} = \hat{a}^+\hat{a}$. Now, as mentioned previously, what we need
to know about a system in order to be able to predict its behavior
is its Hamiltonian. The good news about the single trader problem

is that we know very well what behavior to expect, so specifying the Hamiltonian will allow us to check the self-consistency of the problem.

The starting point is (4.8), i.e.,

$$i\frac{d\hat{a}}{d\theta} = [\hat{a}, \hat{n}],$$

where we know that $\hat{a}(\theta) = \hat{a}(0)\exp(-i\theta)$. Recalling that θ is associated with a clock-like angle in the complex plane and that $\theta = \omega_0 t$, then substituting this latter relation into the equation above gives

$$i\frac{d\hat{a}}{dt} = [\hat{a}, \hat{\Omega}], \tag{5.1}$$

where $\hat{\Omega} = \omega_0\hat{n}$. So, $\hat{\Omega} = \omega_0\hat{n}$ is the Hamiltonian operator for our lone trader. We can recognize (5.1) is the Heisenberg equation of motion (HEM) for the operator $\hat{a}(t)$. It is a simple matter to check that

$$i\frac{d\hat{a}}{dt} = \omega_0[\hat{a}, \hat{a}^+\hat{a}] = \omega_0\hat{a}, \tag{5.2}$$

where we have used $[\hat{a}, \hat{a}^+\hat{a}] = [\hat{a}, \hat{a}^+]\hat{a} = \hat{a}$. Clearly, $\hat{a}(t) = \hat{a}(0)\exp(-i\omega_0 t)$ satisfies the HEM. We also can see that the HEM for $\hat{n}$ gives us the rate of change of the number. We get

$$i\frac{d\hat{n}}{dt} = \omega_0[\hat{n}, \hat{n}] = 0, \tag{5.3}$$

which means that the rate of change of the number is identically zero. This is no surprise, since our trader is not trading with anyone and we should expect the number to stay fixed. The mathematical reason for this result is that $\hat{n}$ commutes with the Hamiltonian, so $[\hat{n}, \hat{\Omega}] = 0$, hence $\frac{d\hat{n}}{dt} = 0$. This should be pretty obvious, for this trivially straightforward case.

5.2. Several non-trading traders

Let us suppose we now have two traders, A and B, but do not allow them to trade. We represent the first in a similar manner to the lone trader in the previous section, with number amplitude operator, $\hat{a}$ and its adjoint $\hat{a}^+$, associated with A, such that the number operator associated with A is $\hat{n} = \hat{a}^+\hat{a}$. Then we expect $\hat{a}(t)$ to have the form $\hat{a}(t) = \hat{a}(0)\exp(-i\omega_a t)$, where now the phase angle of A's number amplitude operator is $\omega_a t$. We would also now expect the Hamiltonian operator for A to be $\hat{\Omega}_a$ to be $\hat{\Omega}_a = \omega_a \hat{n}$. We should expect something very similar for B, since the two traders do not interact. So let B be represented by a number amplitude operator $\hat{b}$ and its adjoint $\hat{b}^+$, such that the number operator associated with B is $\hat{m} = \hat{b}^+\hat{b}$. We would expect $\hat{b}(t)$ to have the form $\hat{b}(t) = \hat{b}(0)\exp(-i\omega_b t)$ and the Hamiltonian representing B to be $\hat{\Omega}_b$ with $\hat{\Omega}_b = \omega_b \hat{m}$. Now what about a Hamiltonian for the whole system, A and B combined? First, we expect the individual number operators each to remain fixed since A and B are each really lone traders in their own enclosed system, so the total $\hat{n} + \hat{m}$ must be fixed too. In a similar way, we can argue that the Hamiltonian of the whole system of A and B combined so

$$\hat{\Omega} = \hat{\Omega}_a + \hat{\Omega}_b = \omega_a \hat{n} + \omega_b \hat{m}. \tag{5.4}$$

The state vector of the system can be written in occupation number form with two entries, $|n, m\rangle$, where now, instead of (4.16), we write

$$\hat{a}|n, m\rangle = \sqrt{n}|n - 1, m\rangle,$$
$$\hat{a}^+|n, m\rangle = \sqrt{n + 1}|n + 1, m\rangle,$$
$$\hat{n}|n, m\rangle = n|n, m\rangle. \tag{5.5}$$

Similarly, we expect, in a self-explanatory way

$$\hat{b}|n, m\rangle = \sqrt{m}|n, m - 1\rangle,$$
$$\hat{b}^+|n, m\rangle = \sqrt{m + 1}|n, m + 1\rangle,$$
$$\hat{m}|n, m\rangle = m|n, m\rangle. \tag{5.6}$$

Since $\hat{a}$ can only affect A and not B, etc. Now we still want (5.1) to hold, so

$$i\frac{d\hat{a}}{dt} = [\hat{a}, \hat{\Omega}] = \omega_a[\hat{a}, \hat{a}^+\hat{a}] + \omega_b[\hat{a}, \hat{b}^+\hat{b}] = \omega_a\hat{a}. \tag{5.7}$$

Now the first commutation bracket gives us the correct final answer, so the second is redundant and logically must be zero. Thus, on expanding the bracket, we must have $[\hat{a}, \hat{b}^+] = 0$ and $[\hat{a}, \hat{b}] = 0$. So amplitude operators associated with different traders commute with each other. This is an important and quite general rule, which will be the case even when the traders trade (interact) with one another.

We can extend the above analysis to any number of non-interacting traders and expect the Hamiltonian of the whole system to have the form

$$\hat{\Omega} = \sum_k \omega_k \hat{a}_k^+ \hat{a}_k, \tag{5.8}$$

where $\hat{a}_k$ is the number amplitude operator associated with kth trader. The number of assets this trader possesses is then $\hat{n}_k = \hat{a}_k^+ \hat{a}_k$. The state of the system would be written as $|n_1, n_2, \ldots, n_k, \ldots\rangle$ and the commutation rules would be

$$\begin{aligned} [\hat{a}_i, \hat{a}_j] &= 0, \\ [\hat{a}_i, \hat{a}_j^+] &= \delta_{ij}, \end{aligned} \tag{5.9}$$

for all i, j. We also get $\mathrm{d}n_i/\mathrm{d}t = 0$, for all i, as a result.

Now for something a bit more useful.

5.3. Allowing the traders to trade

Next, we want to show how we can use number amplitude operators to set up a simple trading model in which the traders interact with one another. Consider again the pair of traders A and B above, in a state represented once more by $|n, m\rangle$. Let us operate on this state with $\hat{a}^+ \hat{b}$. It is easy to see that we get $\hat{a}^+ \hat{b}|n, m\rangle = \sqrt{(n+1)m}|n+1, m-1\rangle$. So the operator $\hat{a}^+ \hat{b}$ turns the state, $|n, m\rangle$ into the state, $|n+1, m-1\rangle$. Now one can think of this process in two ways. Either we just have one extra appearing in the assets of trader A and one item disappearing from the items trader B possesses, or we can think of trader A receiving an item from trader B, i.e., we can think of $\hat{a}^+ \hat{b}$ as an *exchange operator*. The operator $\hat{b}^+ \hat{a}$ by the same token has the reverse effect, i.e., $\hat{b}^+ \hat{a}|n, m\rangle = \sqrt{n(m+1)}|n-1, m+1\rangle$.

We can construct a simple interaction Hamiltonian, $\hat{\Omega}_I$, that is Hermitian, as is required by quantum theory, of the form [5]

$$\hat{\Omega}_I = V(\hat{a}^+\hat{b} + \hat{b}^+\hat{a}), \tag{5.10}$$

where we take V as a real constant. We can check that $\hat{\Omega}_I$ is Hermitian by noting that $(\hat{a}^+\hat{b})^+ = \hat{b}^+\hat{a}$, etc. so, $(\hat{\Omega}_I)^+ = \hat{\Omega}_I$.

If we operate with $\hat{\Omega}_I$ on $|n, m\rangle$, we get $V(\sqrt{(n+1)m}|n+1, m-1\rangle + \sqrt{n(m+1)}|n-1, m+1\rangle)$, so clearly $|n, m\rangle$ is not an eigenstate of $\hat{\Omega}_I$. Indeed, neither $\hat{n}$ nor $\hat{m}$ commute with $\hat{\Omega}_I$. This is hugely significant for such a system, because it means that $\hat{n}$ and $\hat{m}$ are not constants of the motion. They are both going to vary with time. We will look at a simple example of this type next. This will display the basic properties of a trading system.

5.4. A simple transaction model: Two traders

5.4.1. *Setting up the Hamiltonian*

We now want to bring interaction or trading between our traders A and B. If we consider the Hamiltonian in (5.4) as our basic non-trading situation, which we will call $\hat{\Omega}_0 = U\hat{a}^+\hat{a} + W\hat{b}^+\hat{b}$, then, if we add trading to the situation, we get a complete trading Hamiltonian of the form

$$\hat{\Omega} = \hat{\Omega}_0 + \hat{\Omega}_I = U\hat{a}^+\hat{a} + W\hat{b}^+\hat{b} + V(\hat{a}^+\hat{b} + \hat{b}^+\hat{a}). \tag{5.11}$$

Now let us see what happens to the numbers of assets of each trader by applying the HEM to the pair of trading traders.

5.4.2. *Applying the HEM to the population numbers*

Recall that $[\hat{a}, \hat{a}^+] = 1$, $[\hat{b}, \hat{b}^+] = 1$, $[\hat{a}, \hat{b}] = 0$, $[\hat{a}, \hat{b}^+] = 0$, etc. Then

$$i\frac{d\hat{n}}{dt} = [\hat{a}^+\hat{a}, \hat{\Omega}] = V(\hat{a}^+\hat{b} - \hat{b}^+\hat{a}) \tag{5.12}$$

and

$$i\frac{d\hat{m}}{dt} = [\hat{b}^+\hat{b}, \hat{\Omega}] = -V(\hat{a}^+\hat{b} - \hat{b}^+\hat{a}). \tag{5.13}$$

Thus, adding together the above equations gives

$$\frac{d(\hat{n} + \hat{m})}{dt} = 0, \tag{5.14}$$

which implies that the sum $\hat{n} + \hat{m}$, is independent of time. This result is both useful in the calculations to come and also an important indicator of the nature of the trading interaction. Conservation rules like this put constraints on what the outcome can be.

5.4.3. *A direct method of solution*

Differentiating (5.12) once more w.r.t time gives

$$-\frac{d^2\hat{n}}{dt^2} = \left[i\frac{d\hat{n}}{dt}, \hat{\Omega} \right] = -V[\hat{a}^+\hat{b} - \hat{b}^+\hat{a}, \hat{\Omega}], \tag{5.15}$$

which results in

$$\frac{d^2\hat{n}}{dt^2} + (W - U)V(\hat{a}^+\hat{b} + \hat{b}^+\hat{a}) + 2V^2(\hat{n} - \hat{m}) = 0. \tag{5.16}$$

We can eliminate the awkward second term in this equation by noting that

$$V(\hat{a}^+\hat{b} + \hat{b}^+\hat{a}) = \hat{\Omega} - U\hat{n} - W\hat{m}. \tag{5.17}$$

So, (5.16) now becomes

$$\frac{d^2\hat{n}}{dt^2} + (W - U)(\hat{\Omega} - U\hat{n} - W\hat{m}) + 2V^2(\hat{n} - \hat{m}) = 0. \tag{5.18}$$

Note that in evaluating the time derivatives above, we used the following relations that are a consequence of the basic commutation relations involving $\hat{a}$ and $\hat{b}$ and their corresponding adjoints: $[\hat{a}^+\hat{a}, \hat{a}^+\hat{b}] = \hat{a}^+\hat{b}$, $[\hat{a}^+\hat{a}, \hat{b}^+\hat{a}] = -\hat{b}^+\hat{a}$, $[\hat{b}^+\hat{b}, \hat{a}^+\hat{b}] = -\hat{a}^+\hat{b}$, $[\hat{b}^+\hat{b}, \hat{a}^+\hat{b}] = -\hat{a}^+\hat{b}$, $[\hat{b}^+\hat{b}, \hat{b}^+\hat{a}] = \hat{b}^+\hat{a}$, and $[\hat{a}^+\hat{b}, \hat{b}^+\hat{a}] = \hat{a}^+\hat{a} - \hat{b}^+\hat{b} = n - m$.

We should now turn the operator equation into a scalar equation and solve for the numbers as a function of time. These scalar numbers will be expectation values, which, it must be remembered, are a kind of average value. This is straightforward. At time $t = 0$, let us write the number of the items that A has to be $n(0)$ and for B, $m(0)$. So, the initial state of the system is the state $|n(0), m(0)\rangle$. All this means is that $\langle n(0), m(0)|\hat{n}(0)|n(0), m(0)\rangle = n(0)$, etc. However, since in the Heisenberg representation, the states are independent of time, then $|n(0), m(0)\rangle$ represents the state vector *for all time*. This does not mean the expectation values are constant in time, since the operators are generally time-dependent. We formally define the time-dependent expectation value of A's number of items as $n(t) = \langle n(0), m(0)|\hat{n}(t)|n(0), m(0)\rangle$ [5].

In turning the differential equation of the operator $\hat{n}(t)$ into a scalar equation, we also need to evaluate, $\langle \hat{\Omega} \rangle$, the expectation value of the Hamiltonian that contains the awkward term $\hat{a}^+\hat{b} + \hat{b}^+\hat{a}$. However, at $t = 0$, the expectation value of terms like $\hat{a}^+\hat{b}$ are automatically zero, since $\langle n(0), m(0)|\hat{a}^+(0)\hat{b}(0)|n(0), m(0)\rangle = 0$. This is because $\hat{a}^+(0)\hat{b}(0)|n(0), m(0)\rangle = \sqrt{n(0)m(0)}|n(0) + 1, m(0) - 1\rangle$. On the other hand, it is equally important to realize that when $t \neq 0$, then $\langle n(0), m(0)|\hat{a}^+(t)\hat{b}(t)|n(0), m(0)\rangle \neq 0$, in general, since we do not know the relationships between $\hat{a}(t)$ and $\hat{b}(t)$ and $|n(0), m(0)\rangle$.

Now $[\hat{\Omega}, \hat{\Omega}] = 0$ means that $\hat{\Omega}$ is independent of time and so $\langle \hat{\Omega} \rangle$ must be constant. Then we have

$$\langle \hat{\Omega} \rangle = \langle n(0), m(0)|\hat{\Omega}|n(0), m(0)\rangle = Un(0) + Wm(0). \qquad (5.19)$$

Recall also that $\frac{\mathrm{d}\langle \hat{n} \rangle}{\mathrm{d}t} = \langle \frac{\mathrm{d}\hat{n}}{\mathrm{d}t} \rangle$ etc, hence

$$\frac{\mathrm{d}^2 n(t)}{\mathrm{d}t^2} + n(t)((W - U)^2 + 4V^2) = (W - U)^2 n(0) + 2V^2(n(0) + m(0)). \qquad (5.20)$$

This equation is more simply written as

$$\frac{\mathrm{d}^2 n(t)}{\mathrm{d}t^2} + n(t)\omega^2 = K, \qquad (5.21)$$

where ω is a frequency given by

$$\omega^2 = (W - U)^2 + 4V^2 \qquad (5.22)$$

and K is a constant. The solution then takes the general form

$$n(t) = n_0 + n_1 \cos(\omega t) + n_2 \sin(\omega t), \qquad (5.23)$$

where n_0, n_1, and n_2 are constants to be determined by the initial conditions. These are, first, substituting $t = 0$ into (5.23) gives $n(0) = n_0 + n_1$. Second, we know that the first derivative of $n(t)$ is zero at $t = 0$, since, from Equation (5.12), $i\frac{d\hat{n}}{dt} = V(\hat{a}^+\hat{b} - \hat{b}^+\hat{a})$ and we have already shown that the right-hand side gives zero contribution to the expectation value at $t = 0$. From (5.23), $\frac{dn(t)}{dt}|_{t=0} = \omega n_2 = 0$, so $n_2 = 0$. We also know the initial value of the second derivative of $n(t)$ at $t = 0$, from (5.18), is $2V^2(m(0) - n(0))$. So differentiating (5.23) twice gives $2V^2(m(0) - n(0)) = -\omega^2 n_1$.

With these three initial conditions, we find the full solution for $n(t)$ is

$$n(t) = \frac{((W - U)^2 + 2V^2)n(0) + 2V^2 m(0) + 2V^2(n(0) - m(0))\cos(\omega t)}{(W - U)^2 + 4V^2}.$$

(5.24)

We can now easily find the solution for $m(t)$. We showed that the sum of the two number operators was independent of time, which means that $n(t) + m(t) = n(0) + m(0)$. So from $m(t) = n(0) + m(0) - n(t)$, one finds that

$$m(t) = \frac{((W-U)^2 + 2V^2)m(0) + 2V^2 n(0) + 2V^2(m(0) - n(0))\cos(\omega t)}{(W - U)^2 + 4V^2}.$$

(5.25)

Note the symmetry in these two solutions. Essentially, the solution for $m(t)$ is the same as the for $n(t)$ but with $n(0)$ and $m(0)$ interchanged. An example of what this solution looks like is shown in Fig. 5.1.

We will discuss the results in detail in the next section, but it is important to point out one aspect straightaway, and that is that the values of the populations in the graphs in Fig. 5.1. vary sinusoidally and hence continuously. So we do not see just whole numbers in the results. The reason for this is that we have plotted the time-dependent expectation values. These are not the same as eigenvalues, but rather represent averages of many repeated experiments. So we get real numbers and not just whole numbers, as a result. It is rather like finding the average of the number of children in families. We know that individual families have 0, 1, 2, 3, etc., children, but, if we

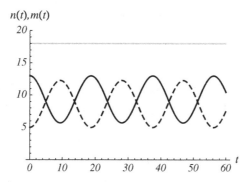

FIGURE 5.1. Variations of assets (solid and dashed curves) in two-trader transactions. The grey line indicates the total assets.

averaged these out over the whole country, the average value would certainly not be a whole number.

This simple two-trader model is an important indicator of how quantum interaction models work in general. We will see this model can be applied to other situations with the same kind of results. For example, we will see this behavior again when we come to population migration. The two-trader model also helps to understand what happens when more traders are involved. So in the next section, we summarizes the key characteristics of the two-trader model.

5.5. Key characteristics of the simple quantum two-trader model

The quantum two-trader model above is an example of the way interacting populations can be modeled. There are similarities as well as significant differences between the quantum model of interacting populations as indicated by the two-trader model above and the classical Lotka–Volterra model (LVM), discussed earlier. First, there are oscillations in the populations as functions of time, which lead to exact repetitions of the state of the systems in both the classical and quantum cases. However, in the quantum case, the oscillations are exactly sinusoidal, which is not the case in the classical system. Also, the variations in the quantum model are always exactly out of phase, i.e., there is a $180°$ (π) phase difference, whereas in the LVM, there is a phase difference between the two populations but it is less than $180°$.

However, the most important difference between the quantum and classical cases is that the quantum case is subject to a very simple conservation rule, i.e., both $n(t)$ and $m(t)$ oscillate, while their sum remains constant. There is no such simple conservation rule in the classical case. The frequency of oscillation, ω, is also easy to ascertain in the quantum case; it just depends on the interaction rate V, and also on the constants U and W, but then only on the difference between them. Note also that the amplitude of the oscillation is proportional to $n(0) - m(0)$, so that if the two traders start out with the same number of assets, then their assets do not change on an individual basis. Thus, there has to be a difference in the number of assets held by the traders at the start for their asset numbers to fluctuate with time. This is an interesting characteristic that is not shared by the fluctuating populations in the LVM, where neither the frequency of oscillation nor the amplitudes are easily obtained from the contents in the original equations. There, even if the two populations start out equal, then both, in general, vary with time. Another contrast with the behavior of the LVM is the behavior when one of the traders has no assets to begin with. For example if $m(0) = 0$, i.e., trader B starts with no assets, we get the result in Fig. 5.2, for our quantum model. The model shows that trader B immediately begins to acquire assets from trader A, only to lose and then regain them again. Trader B initially loses assets to A and so on.

One final important point about the quantum model, which helps us simplify more complicated situations later, if $W = U$, then both U and W have no effect on the result, which reduces to

$$n(t) = \frac{m(0) + n(0) + (n(0) - m(0))\cos(2Vt)}{2},$$

$$m(t) = \frac{m(0) + n(0) + (m(0) - n(0))\cos(2Vt)}{2}. \qquad (5.26)$$

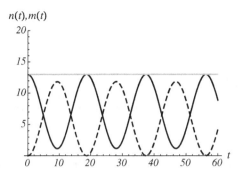

FIGURE 5.2. Variations of assets (solid and dashed curves) in two-trader transactions for the case when trader B starts with no assets. The grey line indicates
the total assets.

The results are identical to what one would get if $U = W = 0$, so we
could model this situation with the Hamiltonian

$$\hat{\Omega} = \hat{\Omega}_I = V(\hat{a}^+\hat{b} + \hat{b}^+\hat{a}). \tag{5.27}$$

This greatly simplifies the operator analysis when applying the HEM
and we end up with a result that, although slightly simpler than the
$W \neq U$ case, still retains the basic oscillatory characteristics of the
more general situation. We will use this simplification of just utilizing
the interaction part of the Hamiltonian in more complicated multi-
trader cases later.

5.6. Eigenfrequency approach

Thus far, we have tackled the two-trader problem using what we have
called a direct approach in which the HEM is used to determine differential equations for the number operators. These operator equations
are then turned into differential equations for the expectation values
of the number operators which are then solved as coupled linear
equations, similar to those found in classical cases. This approach
works well when only a few traders are involved and we will follow
this type of solution later when we have a look at the case of a few
traders. It is simple to understand and rather direct in the way it
gets to the numbers as functions of time. However, it becomes rather
unwieldy when many more interacting agents are involved. There is

an alternative, rather more standard, method called the *eigenvalue method* that can be applied systematically, however many traders are involved. In this section, we will illustrate the method for the case of two traders. The eigenvalue method involves finding the time derivatives of the number amplitude operators, rather than the number operators themselves. This leads to a set of coupled equations that can be treated systematically by matrix methods. The systematization of the solutions is greatly aided by the existence of software routines that can find the eigenvalues and eigenvectors of matrices to very large order. For further details, see [5].

So, applying the HEM to $\hat{a}$ and $\hat{b}$ with the aid of the Hamiltonian,

$$\hat{\Omega} = U\hat{a}^+\hat{a} + W\hat{b}^+\hat{b} + V(\hat{a}^+\hat{b} + \hat{b}^+\hat{a}),$$

leads to

$$i\frac{\mathrm{d}\hat{a}}{\mathrm{d}t} = [\hat{a}, \hat{\Omega}] = U\hat{a} + V\hat{b},$$

$$i\frac{\mathrm{d}\hat{b}}{\mathrm{d}t} = [\hat{b}, \hat{\Omega}] = W\hat{b} + V\hat{a}. \tag{5.28}$$

Clearly, the above equations form a coupled pair. They are solved as an eigenvalue problem by assuming that $\hat{a}$ and $\hat{b}$ are both proportional to $\exp(-i\omega t)$. Substituting these relations into the above differentials then gives, in matrix form

$$\begin{pmatrix} \omega - U & -V \\ -V & \omega - W \end{pmatrix} \begin{pmatrix} \hat{a} \\ \hat{b} \end{pmatrix} = 0. \tag{5.29}$$

The solutions for the eigenfrequency, ω, are found by setting the determinant of the "two by two" matrix equal to zero. This results in a quadratic equation for ω, of the form

$$\omega^2 - (U + W)\omega + UW - V^2 = 0, \tag{5.30}$$

which thus has two solutions. These are

$$\omega_1 = \frac{U + W + \sqrt{(U - W)^2 + 4V^2}}{2},$$

$$\omega_2 = \frac{U + W - \sqrt{(U - W)^2 + 4V^2}}{2}. \tag{5.31}$$

The eigenvectors of this system comprise a pair of two-component unit column vectors. Because, they each have two components whose squares sum to unity, they can be written in the form

$$\begin{pmatrix} \cos\alpha \\ \sin\alpha \end{pmatrix},$$

where α is an as yet unknown angle. The first eigenvector will satisfy

$$\begin{pmatrix} \omega_1 - U & -V \\ -V & \omega_1 - W \end{pmatrix} \begin{pmatrix} \cos\alpha \\ \sin\alpha \end{pmatrix} = 0. \tag{5.32}$$

This gives us two equations for $\tan\alpha$, but they both yield the same result, which is

$$\tan\alpha = \frac{W - U + \sqrt{(W-U)^2 + 4V^2}}{2V}, \tag{5.33}$$

from which $\cos\alpha$ and $\sin\alpha$ can be deduced. The second eigenvector can be found in a similar way with ω_2 instead of ω_1 substituted in the eigenvalue equation. The resulting second eigenvector turns out to be

$$\begin{pmatrix} -\sin\alpha \\ \cos\alpha, \end{pmatrix},$$

which is orthogonal to the first eigenvector, as it should be.

We can now write the time-dependent solutions for $\hat{a}$ and $\hat{b}$ in the form

$$\hat{a}(t) = \hat{c}(0)\exp(-i\omega_1 t)\cos\alpha + \hat{d}(0)\exp(-i\omega_2 t)\sin\alpha,$$

$$\hat{b}(t) = -\hat{c}(0)\exp(-i\omega_1 t)\sin\alpha + \hat{d}(0)\exp(-i\omega_2 t)\cos\alpha. \tag{5.34}$$

The meaning of $\hat{c}$ and $\hat{d}$ here becomes clear if we substitute the above results for $\hat{a}$ and $\hat{b}$ back into the Hamiltonian. Then we get, after some tedious algebra

$$\hat{\Omega} = \omega_1\hat{c}^+\hat{c} + \omega_2\hat{d}^+\hat{d}. \tag{5.35}$$

So, $\hat{c}$ and $\hat{d}$ are independent operators and act like a pair of non-trading traders, C and D. This means that, if we construct number operators for $\hat{c}$ and $\hat{d}$, such that $\hat{p} = \hat{c}^{+}\hat{c}$ and $\hat{q} = \hat{d}^{+}\hat{d}$, then, $\frac{d\hat{p}}{dt} = 0$ and $\frac{d\hat{q}}{dt} = 0$.

We can also show, by direct substitution that

$$\hat{a}^{+}\hat{a} + \hat{b}^{+}\hat{b} = \hat{c}^{+}\hat{c} + \hat{d}^{+}\hat{d}. \tag{5.36}$$

The left-hand side of (5.36) is just the total number $\hat{n} + \hat{m}$ in the original description of the system, and the right-hand side is just the total number $\hat{p} + \hat{q}$ in the second description in terms of the eigen-operators. So the total are the same in both cases.

Finally, the time-dependent forms of the expectation values $n(t)$ and $m(t)$ may be found using the the expressions for $\hat{a}(t)$ and $\hat{b}(t)$ above. This is done by setting $t = 0$ in (5.34) and writing

$$\hat{a}(0) = \hat{c}(0) \cos \alpha + \hat{d}(0) \sin \alpha,$$
$$\hat{b}(0) = -\hat{c}(0) \sin \alpha + \hat{d}(0) \cos \alpha. \tag{5.37}$$

These expressions are then treated as a pair of simultaneous equations for $\hat{c}(0)$ and $\hat{d}(0)$. One obtains

$$\hat{c}(0) = \hat{a}(0) \cos \alpha - \hat{b}(0) \sin \alpha,$$
$$\hat{d}(0) = \hat{a}(0) \sin \alpha + \hat{b}(0) \cos \alpha. \tag{5.38}$$

Having found $\hat{c}(0)$ and $\hat{d}(0)$ in terms of $\hat{a}(0)$ and $\hat{b}(0)$, the results are substituted back into (5.34). Thus, for $\hat{a}(t)$, one obtains

$$\hat{a}(t) = (\hat{a}(0) \cos^2 \alpha - \hat{b}(0) \cos \alpha \sin \alpha) \exp(-i\omega_1 t)$$
$$+ (\hat{a}(0) \sin^2 \alpha + \hat{b}(0) \cos \alpha \sin \alpha) \exp(-i\omega_2 t). \tag{5.39}$$

Then, one evaluates $n(t) = \langle n_0, m_0 | \hat{a}^{+}(t)\hat{a}(t) | n_0, m_0 \rangle$ and obtains

$$n(t) = \hat{n}(0)(\cos^4 \alpha + \sin^4 \alpha) + 2\hat{m}(0) \cos^2 \alpha \sin^2 \alpha$$
$$+ 2(n(0) - m(0)) \cos^2 \alpha \sin^2 \alpha \cos((\omega_1 - \omega_2)t). \tag{5.40}$$

Substituting for $\cos \alpha$ and $\sin \alpha$ in terms of U, W, and V, one obtains exactly the same expression for $n(t)$ as was obtained by the direct method that was used in Section 5.4.3. $m(t) = \langle n_0, m_0 | \hat{b}^+(t) \hat{b}(t) | n_0, m_0 \rangle$ is found simply from the the total number conservation rule once more, so that $m(t) = n(0) + m(0) - n(t)$.

A further point of interest here is that the time-dependence of $n(t)$ and $m(t)$ is contained in a term $\cos((\omega_2 - \omega_1)t)$, and $\omega_2 - \omega_1$ is just the same as $\omega = \sqrt{(W - U)^2 + 4V^2}$ as in (5.24) and (5.25). Even though there are two different frequencies, ω_1 and ω_2 involved in the operator amplitudes, both number operators, $\hat{n}(t)$ and $\hat{m}(t)$ oscillate with the same frequency, $\omega_2 - \omega_1$, as was found with the direct method above.

5.7. Stable trading partnerships

We can invert (5.34) and write the time-dependent operators $\hat{c}(t) = \hat{c}(0) \exp(-i\omega_1 t)$ and $\hat{d}(t) = \hat{d}(0) \exp(-i\omega_2 t)$ in terms of $\hat{a}(t)$ and $\hat{b}(t)$, thus

$$\hat{c}(t) = \hat{a}(t) \cos \alpha - \hat{b}(t) \sin \alpha,$$
$$\hat{d}(t) = \hat{a}(t) \sin \alpha + \hat{b}(t) \cos \alpha. \tag{5.41}$$

Although we initially thought of this system as a pair of interacting traders, A and B, whose assets fluctuate with time, as in Fig. 5.1, we have found that this is equivalent to a pair of traders, C and D, who do not trade and whose assets do not vary in time. What are we to make of this? The first thing to say is that within the quantum physics world, this kind of thing happens. For instance, in the QFT description of a pair of interacting particles, electrons say, as the pair enter the interaction, then they can be considered as forming some kind of compound system, where the individual electrons are not distinguishable. Such a situation arises, for example in the Bardeen–Cooper–Schrieffer (BCS) theory of superconductors (see [2]), where a pair of electrons forms a single compound *quasi-particle* called a *Cooper pair*. Here, (5.41) can be interpreted as a pair of compound traders, each having a contribution from the traders A and B. So A and B cannot be thought of as separate identities. Their trading makes them interdependent, but, if we take some part of each (the proportions are fixed by the size of $\cos \alpha$, which, in turn, depend on U, W, and V), then we can have a pair of stable subsystems, C and D, with time-independent assets. The interaction that emerges from our simple quantum transaction model has a somewhat collaborative nature that conserves assets overall. Contrast this result with the classical LVM, whose character is much more competitive.

5.8. Several trading traders

Any arbitrary number of trading traders may be modeled by a Hamiltonian of the form

$$\hat{\Omega} = \sum_n U_n \hat{a}_n^+ \hat{a}_n + \sum_{i,j} V_{ij} \hat{a}_i^+ \hat{a}_j. \tag{5.42}$$

The first sum represents the situation if there was no interaction (trading) between the traders, in which case after applying the HEM, one finds that $\frac{d\hat{n}_i(t)}{dt} = 0$ for all of the traders. If the second term is included, then $\frac{d\hat{n}_i(t)}{dt} \neq 0$. However, using the rules of the commutators we can show that

$$\sum_i \frac{d\hat{n}_i(t)}{dt} = 0, \tag{5.43}$$

i.e., the sum of all of the rates of changes in the numbers of assets is zero, which implies the total number of assets is fixed. Let's look at an example of three interacting traders next.

5.8.1. *A three-trader example*

Consider a specific Hamiltonian for three traders, A, B, and C, of the form

$$\hat{\Omega} = V_1(\hat{a}^+ \hat{b} + \hat{b}^+ \hat{a}) + V_2(\hat{b}^+ \hat{c} + \hat{c}^+ \hat{b}), \tag{5.44}$$

which means that A trades with B, while B trades with A and C, which constitutes a simple trading chain. Note that we have neglected the non-interacting part of the Hamiltonian. As we saw in the two-trader case, this still reproduces the intrinsic variability of the system, but greatly simplifies the operator manipulation in the application of the HEM. Let's now use the HEM for the above Hamiltonian to obtain the rates of change of assets of the traders. We let $\hat{n} = \hat{a}^+\hat{a}$, $\hat{m} = \hat{b}^+\hat{b}$ and $\hat{p} = \hat{c}^+\hat{c}$ be the number operators for the assets of A, B and C, respectively and get

$$i\frac{d\hat{n}}{dt} = [\hat{a}^+\hat{a}, \hat{\Omega}] = V_1(\hat{a}^+\hat{b} - \hat{b}^+\hat{a}),$$

$$i\frac{d\hat{m}}{dt} = [\hat{b}^+\hat{b}, \hat{\Omega}] = V_1(\hat{b}^+\hat{a} - \hat{a}^+\hat{b}) + V_2(\hat{b}^+\hat{c} - \hat{c}^+\hat{b}),$$

$$i\frac{d\hat{p}}{dt} = [\hat{c}^+\hat{c}, \hat{\Omega}] = V_2(\hat{c}^+\hat{b} - \hat{b}^+\hat{c}). \tag{5.45}$$

If we add together the derivatives in the above array of differential equations, it is easy to see that pairs of terms cancel and we are left with $\frac{d(\hat{n}+\hat{m}+\hat{p})}{dt} = 0$, so that, again the total number of assets is conserved. This is a useful relation since it means we can eliminate one of the variables from the system, as we shall see below. The next step is to substitute the derivatives of each of the number operators back into the HEM to obtain a set of second derivatives, just as we did in the two trader case. This yields a set of coupled linear differential equations of the form

$$\frac{d^2\hat{n}}{dt^2} + 2V_1^2(\hat{n} - \hat{m}) + V_1V_2(\hat{a}^+\hat{c} + \hat{c}^+\hat{a}) = 0,$$

$$\frac{d^2\hat{p}}{dt^2} + 2V_2^2(\hat{p} - \hat{m}) + V_1V_2(\hat{a}^+\hat{c} + \hat{c}^+\hat{a}) = 0. \tag{5.46}$$

We have to go to still higher order to get rid of unwanted terms, so

$$\frac{d^3\hat{n}}{dt^3} + 2V_1^2\left(\frac{d\hat{n}}{dt} - \frac{d\hat{m}}{dt}\right) + V_1^2V_2(\hat{b}^+\hat{c} - \hat{c}^+\hat{b}) + V_1V_2^2(\hat{b}^+\hat{a} - \hat{a}^+\hat{b}) = 0. \tag{5.47}$$

Eliminating the awkward terms by using the expression for the lower order derivatives gives

$$\frac{d^3\hat{n}}{dt^3} + (4V_1^2 + V_2^2)\frac{d\hat{n}}{dt} + 3V_1^2\frac{d\hat{p}}{dt} = 0,$$

$$\frac{d^3\hat{p}}{dt^3} + (4V_2^2 + V_1^2)\frac{d\hat{p}}{dt} + 3V_2^2\frac{d\hat{n}}{dt} = 0. \tag{5.48}$$

We can then eliminate $\hat{p}$ to give

$$\frac{d^5\hat{n}}{dt^5} + 5(V_1^2 + V_2^2)\frac{d^3\hat{n}}{dt^3} + 4(V_1^2 + V_2^2)^2\frac{d\hat{n}}{dt} = 0. \qquad (5.49)$$

We can turn this into a scalar equation for $n(t)$ by replacing $\hat{n}$ by $n(t)$ using the expectation value method we used earlier. The resulting scalar equation for $n(t)$ has exactly the same form as (5.49) and this has a solution of the form

$$n(t) = n_0 + n_1\cos(\omega t) + n_2\cos(2\omega t), \qquad (5.50)$$

where $\omega = \sqrt{V_1^2 + V_2^2}$ and n_0, n_1 and n_2 are constants, which can be evaluated from the boundary conditions, $n(0) = n_0 + n_1 + n_2$, $\frac{d^2\hat{n}}{dt^2}|_{t=0} = -\omega^2(n_1 + 4n_2)$ and $\frac{d^4\hat{n}}{dt^4}|_{t=0} = \omega^4(n_1 + 16n_2)$. Then one finds

$$n_2 = \frac{V_1^2(V_1^2(n(0) - m(0)) + V_2^2(p(0) - m(0)))}{2\omega^4} \qquad (5.51)$$

and

$$n_1 = \frac{2V_1^2}{\omega^2}(n(0) - m(0)) - 4n_2, \qquad (5.52)$$

together with $n_0 = n(0) - n_1 - n_2$. Following a similar procedure as before, we can obtain a solution for $p(t)$ and then by knowing that the sum of the assets is fixed, we can obtain an expression for $m(t)$. Figure 5.3 shows the solution for $n(t)$, $m(t)$, and $p(t)$ obtained in this way.

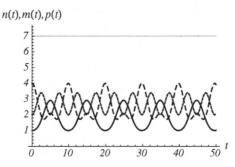

FIGURE 5.3.   The assets (solid, short, and long dashes) in a trading chain of three traders. The grey line indicates the total assets.

Periodic fluctuations can be seen again in this case although they are more complicated than the two trader case, due to the mixing of more frequencies associated with the increased number of eigenfrequencies. As more traders are added to the system, the number of eigenfrequencies increases and the more complicated become the fluctuations.

5.9. Independent subsystems: Worlds within worlds

Consider a system of N traders, labeled, A_n, where n is $1, 2, 3, \ldots, N$, who all trade with each other, coexisting with another pair of traders, B and C, who only trade with each other and not at all with any of A_n. The interaction Hamiltonian of the whole trading system then has the form

$$\hat{\Omega} = \sum_{i,j} V_{ij} \hat{a}_i^+ \hat{a}_j + V(\hat{b}^+ \hat{c} + \hat{c}^+ \hat{b}). \tag{5.53}$$

The terms inside the summation sign represent the contributions of the A_n and the last two terms of B and C. It is a straightforward matter to apply the HEM to this system and obtain the rates of change of the assets of B and C, which are

$$i\frac{d\hat{m}}{dt} = [\hat{b}^+ \hat{b}, \hat{\Omega}] = V(\hat{b}^+ \hat{c} - \hat{c}^+ \hat{b}),$$

$$i\frac{d\hat{p}}{dt} = [\hat{c}^+ \hat{c}, \hat{\Omega}] = V(\hat{c}^+ \hat{b} - \hat{b}^+ \hat{c}). \tag{5.54}$$

Thus, the variation in the numbers of assets of B and C are not affected at all by any of the traders A_n. Thus the trading pair of B and C form an independent subsystem in which their total assets $m + p$ together remain fixed. The total assets of the A_n is likewise fixed, independent of B and C. It is sometimes useful to be able to identify independent subsystems within more complex systems in order to simplify calculations. However, as we saw earlier, if we allow one of the members of the independent subsystem to trade with one the member of the rest of the traders, by adding a term like

$$V_{kb}(\hat{b}^+ \hat{a}_k + \hat{a}_k^+ \hat{b}),$$

then not only does the number of assets of B become indirectly dependent on *all* of the A_n, and not just directly dependent on A_k, but the assets of trader C, in spite of having no direct contribution to the interaction Hamiltonian, all become dependent on the A_n.

5.10. Asymmetrical trading

5.10.1. *Different exchange rates*

Thus far, we have a pair-trading model in which the rate at which trader A gains or loses items is the same as the rate trader B loses or gains items, through the conservation rule

$$\frac{d(\hat{n} + \hat{m})}{dt} = 0.$$

Note that the above expression implies that if one of the rates is positive the other must be negative, at any instant, so that one of the traders must be losing assets when the other is gaining, unless both rates are zero. This is a rather inflexible situation, but second quantization methods can be made to accommodate a less symmetrical trading scheme in which

$$\frac{d\hat{n}}{dt} \neq -\frac{d\hat{m}}{dt}.$$

To do this, we begin again by describing a state of this trading pair in occupation number formalism as $|n(0), m(0)\rangle$, with A starting out with $n(0)$ assets and B with $m(0)$ as before. But now consider a trading Hamiltonian of the form [5]

$$\hat{\Omega}_I = V(\hat{a}^{+3}\hat{b}^2 + \hat{b}^{+2}\hat{a}^3). \tag{5.55}$$

This kind of Hamiltonian is still Hermitian, as it needs to be, but it is also non-linear in the sense that the number amplitude operators appear in it to powers greater than 1. We can check that $\hat{a}^{+3}\hat{b}^2|n(0), m(0)\rangle$ produces a state, $|n(0) + 3, m(0) - 2\rangle$ and $\hat{b}^{+2}\hat{a}^3|n(0), m(0)\rangle$ produces a state, $|n(0) - 3, m(0) + 2\rangle$, so that A's assets can go up or down by three while B's go up or down by 2. As we will see this leads to a new conservation rule, different from the total number of assets $n(t) + m(t) = n(0) + m(0)$ that we got in the linear case treated previously.

5.10.2. *A new integrals of the motion*

Consider a more general Hamiltonian of the form

$$\hat{\Omega} = U\hat{a}^+\hat{a} + W\hat{b}^+\hat{b} + V(\hat{a}^{+P}\hat{b}^Q + \hat{b}^{+Q}\hat{a}^P), \tag{5.56}$$

where P and Q are positive integers. We again use the HEM to evaluate $dn(t)/dt$ by evaluating $[a^+a, \Omega]$. As in the equal trading case, the first two terms in Ω commute with $n(t)$ and so do not contribute. The final term is a bit more tricky to evaluate. We will need the result that, if $[a, a^+] = 1$, then $[a, a^{+P}] = Pa^{+(P-1)}$ and $[a^P, a^+] = Pa^{(P-1)}$. These results come from repeated application of the commutation expansion described in Section 4.4.4. Thus $[a^P, a^+] = a[a^{P-1}, a^+] + [a, a^+]a^{P-1}$, etc. The second term in this expansion is just a^{P-1} and the first term is expanded again. Then one finds that

$$i\frac{d\hat{n}}{dt} = PV(\hat{a}^{+P}\hat{b}^Q - \hat{b}^{+Q}\hat{a}^P). \tag{5.57}$$

In a similar way, we can obtain $dm(t)/dt$ and find that

$$i\frac{d\hat{m}}{dt} = -QV(\hat{a}^{+P}\hat{b}^Q - \hat{b}^{+Q}\hat{a}^P). \tag{5.58}$$

Thus, we can observe a new constant of the system by noting that

$$\frac{1}{P}\frac{d\hat{n}}{dt} + \frac{1}{Q}\frac{d\hat{m}}{dt} = 0. \tag{5.59}$$

So, unless $P = Q$, the rates at which the assets of A and B change are no longer equal and opposite. Also, unless $P = Q$, the total number of assets, $n(t) + m(t)$, is no longer conserved and we get a new integral of the motion. It is easy to show that

$$\frac{n(t)}{P} + \frac{m(t)}{Q} = \frac{n(0)}{P} + \frac{m(0)}{Q} = I_0, \qquad (5.60)$$

where I_0 is the constant of the motion. Note that when $P = 1$ and $Q = 1$, the system constant is $n_0 + m_0$, the total number of items, so we recover the linear result. However, note that when either P or Q (or both) are not equal to unity, then the total number is not conserved. It is possible though to interpret this rule in straightforward way, if we rewrite (5.59) as

$$\frac{\mathrm{d}\hat{n}}{\mathrm{d}t} = -\frac{P}{Q}\frac{\mathrm{d}\hat{m}}{\mathrm{d}t}. \qquad (5.61)$$

This means that the rate at which A loses or gains assets is P/Q times the rate that B loses or gains assets, so that the rates of trading are asymmetrical. In the example above where $P = 3$ and $Q = 2$, then A trades $3/2$ times faster than B. It is interesting to note that although P and Q themselves have to be whole numbers, any ratio of rates that is a rational number can be modeled, in principle. Let us look at a simple worked example to illustrate the dynamics of the asymmetrical trading case.

5.10.3. *A worked example, $P = 1$, $Q = 2$*

In general, the time-dependence of $n(t)$ and $m(t)$ is difficult to work out when P and Q differ from unity. To illustrate this, we will take the simplest non-linear case with $P = 1$ and $Q = 2$. Then the Hamiltonian is

$$\hat{\Omega} = U\hat{a}^+\hat{a} + W\hat{b}^+\hat{b} + V(\hat{a}^+\hat{b}^2 + \hat{b}^{+2}\hat{a}). \qquad (5.62)$$

Consequently,

$$i\frac{\mathrm{d}\hat{n}}{\mathrm{d}t} = V(\hat{a}^+\hat{b}^2 - \hat{b}^{+2}\hat{a}). \qquad (5.63)$$

Similarly,

$$i\frac{\mathrm{d}\hat{m}}{\mathrm{d}t} = -2V(\hat{a}^+\hat{b}^2 - \hat{b}^{+2}\hat{a}). \qquad (5.64)$$

Thus, as expected, $n(t) + m(t)/2 = I_0$, a constant.

Substituting the result for $\frac{d\hat{n}}{dt}$ into the HEM once more, we get

$$\frac{d^2\hat{n}}{dt^2} + (2W - U)V(\hat{a}^+\hat{b}^2 + \hat{b}^{+2}\hat{a}) + V^2(4\hat{n} + 2\hat{m} + 8\hat{n}\hat{m} - 2\hat{m}^2) = 0.$$

$$(5.65)$$

We can eliminate $\hat{m}$ using the constant I_0, i.e., $\hat{m} = 2(I_0 - \hat{n})$ and the awkward second term by using the Hamiltonian, i.e., $\hat{\Omega} - U\hat{a}^+\hat{a} - W\hat{b}^+\hat{b} = V(\hat{a}^+\hat{b}^2 + \hat{b}^{+2}\hat{a})$. Thus

$$\frac{d^2\hat{n}}{dt^2} + ((2W - U)^2 + 32V^2 I_0)\hat{n}$$

$$= 24V^2\hat{n}^2 - (2W - U)(\hat{\Omega} - 2W I_0) + 4V^2(2I_0^2 - I_0). \quad (5.66)$$

At this point, we need to turn the time-dependent operator equation into a time-dependent expectation value equation as we did in the linear case. However, because of the term involving $\hat{n}^2$, we have an extra difficulty. We can use $\langle \hat{n} \rangle = n(t)$ and $\langle \frac{d\hat{n}}{dt} \rangle = \frac{dn(t)}{dt}$ as before, but because in general $\langle n^2 \rangle \neq \langle n \rangle^2$, then $\langle n^2 \rangle$ acts as another time-dependent variable. The reason for this is similar to why, in statistics, if one has a set of data values that represent some measurable variable x, then one can find the mean $\langle x \rangle$ by adding all of the x values and dividing by the number of data points. Similarly, the mean $\langle x^2 \rangle$ can be found by adding all of the values x^2 and dividing by the number of data points. Then we would not expect $\langle x^2 \rangle$ to be equal to $\langle x \rangle^2$, unless, that is, all of the data points had the same value. In this case, there is no spreading of the data points, which can be interpreted as a lack of noise in the data. This is the basis of an approximation that we will look at next.

5.10.4. *An approximate solution*

We can use a technique, borrowed from quantum optics, to get an approximate solution to our non-linear problem. It is a technique that turns the non-linear equation that contains operators into one that only contains scalar functions. To carry out this switch, we make the assumption that the operator $\hat{n}$ can be replaced by its expectation

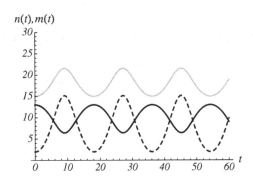

FIGURE 5.4.   Variations of assets (solid and dashed curves) in two-trader transactions with asymmetrical trading. The grey curve indicates the total assets, which is no longer fixed.

value, which is just a time dependent scalar function. This relies on the assumption that we can neglect the difference between the expectation value of the square and the square of the expectation value for the number operator. In quantum optics this is associated with neglecting so-called *quantum noise*. An example of the kind of solution to these equations can be found in Fig. 5.4. Note, that in this case, the total number of assets is no longer a fixed quantity.

Because we have a non-linear equation, the result, though periodic, is not quite sinusoidal, unlike the equal trading case that we looked at earlier. Also, in the non-linear case the frequency of the oscillations depends on the amplitudes, as is usual in non-linear problems.

5.11. Exercises

Exercise 5. (i) A Hamiltonian that characterizes a two-trader system may be written as

$$\Omega = \alpha \hat{a}_1^+ \hat{a}_1 + \beta \hat{a}_2^+ \hat{a}_2 + \gamma(\hat{a}_2^+ \hat{a}_1 + \hat{a}_1^+ \hat{a}_2)$$

where $\hat{a}_1$ and $\hat{a}_2$ are annihilation operators and α, β, and γ, are constants, such that the number operators associated with the annihilation operators and their respective adjoints represent the assets of each trader at each instant. Explain qualitatively what the effect of the term in the brackets is.

(ii) Using the Hamiltonian above, and the HEM, show that the number operators are individually time-dependent when γ is non-zero, but that their sum is invariant.

(iii) Use the HEM to find the time derivatives of $\hat{a}_1$ and $\hat{a}_2$ and hence find the eigenfrequencies, ω_1 and ω_2 of the system.

(iv) For the case when $\alpha = \beta$, $\hat{a}_1(t)$ has the form

$$\hat{a}_1(t) = \frac{1}{2}((\hat{a}_1(0) + \hat{a}_2(0))\exp(-i\omega_1 t) + (\hat{a}_1(0) - \hat{a}_2(0))\exp(-i\omega_2 t)).$$

Use this result to show that

$$n_1(t) = \frac{1}{2}((n_1(0) + n_2(0)) + (n_1(0) - n_2(0))\cos(2\gamma t)).$$

where $n_1(t) = \langle n_1(0), n_2(0)|\hat{n}_1(t)|n_1(0), n_2(0)\rangle$.

(v) Also deduce $n_2(t)$ and sketch the variations of $n_1(t)$ and $n_2(t)$ as functions of time, given that $n_1(0) = 10$ and $n_2(0) = 16$.

Exercise 6. Describe the meaning of the following interaction term in the Hamiltonian for a two-trader system:

$$\Omega = \lambda(\hat{a}^+\hat{b}^3 + \hat{b}^{+3}\hat{a}),$$

where λ is a constant and $\hat{a}$ and $\hat{b}$ are annihilation operators. Using the HEM, determine the rates of changes of the assets held by each trader and deduce the conserved quantity.

Chapter 6

Quantum Migration

So far, we have examined systems that, although they have a dynamical aspect, in that the number of countable items involved, e.g., the assets of traders, has varied in time, there has been no indication of spatial movement. In this chapter, we will briefly examine how the quantum Hamiltonian methods we have developed so far can be applied to situations in which populations, they could be people, or non-human animals for example, move about within a spatial region. The good news is that we do not really need to learn any new mathematics. With a little adjustment to the conceptual elements involved, we can apply what we have learned directly to the population migration situation. To do this, we can think of an array of identical cells that are in contact, into which, or out of which, members of a population can move. It makes sense to allow the population to move only between neighboring cells. This process is often called *nearest neighbor hopping*. The simplest system in which we can apply our methods consists of a one-dimensional line of identical adjacent cells.

6.1. Nearest neighbor hopping in one dimension

Consider the chain of cells arranged as in Fig. 6.1. With each cell we can associate a number amplitude operator, its adjoint and the corresponding number operator, so that the set of these operators for the ith cell in the sequence is $\hat{a}_i$, $\hat{a}_i^+$, and $\hat{n}_i$, where $\hat{n}_i = \hat{a}_i^+ \hat{a}_i$. The state of the system is represented in occupation number formalism as $|n_1, n_2, \ldots, n_i, \ldots, n_N\rangle$, where N is the total number of cells in the row.

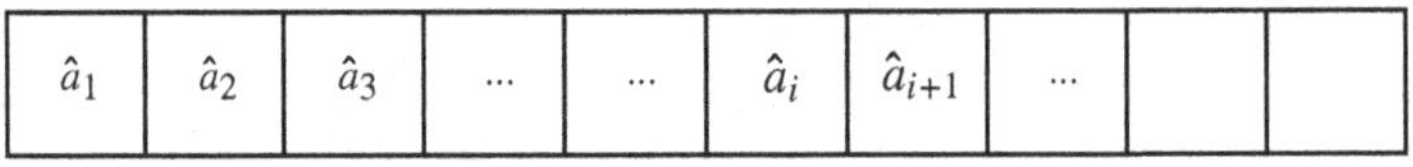

| $\hat{a}_1$ | $\hat{a}_2$ | $\hat{a}_3$ | ... | ... | $\hat{a}_i$ | $\hat{a}_{i+1}$ | ... | | |

FIGURE 6.1.   A row of cells along which a population can migrate by moving between neighboring cells.

The general the interaction Hamiltonian that describes hopping between *neighboring cells* has the form

$$\hat{\Omega} = \sum_i V_i(\hat{a}_i^+ \hat{a}_{i+1} + \hat{a}_{i+1}^+ \hat{a}_i). \tag{6.1}$$

The first term inside the summation takes a unit of population out of the $(i+1)$th cell and puts it in the ith, while the second does the opposite. It might be thought that there are other possibilities, such as a term like $\hat{a}_i^+ \hat{a}_{i-1}$, but a little thought and maybe writing out the terms explicitly will show that such terms are included in the sum already. The coefficients V_i control the rate at which the members of the population hop between cells, and are as usual considered to be real numbers.

Now, let us do a simple example, involving only three neighboring cells. Consider a simple specific Hamiltonian of the form

$$\hat{\Omega} = V(\hat{a}_1^+ \hat{a}_2 + \hat{a}_2^+ \hat{a}_1 + \hat{a}_2^+ \hat{a}_3 + \hat{a}_3^+ \hat{a}_2), \tag{6.2}$$

which involves only the first three neighboring cells. The members of the population can pass from cell 1 to cell 2 and vice versa, and from cell 2 to cell 3 and vice versa. The rate of movement between the cells, V is the same along the whole chain. This, of course, means that the population hopping rate is the same everywhere. This is a model of what is termed a *homogeneous* medium.

The point of doing this particular problem is not only that it nicely illustrates the way population migrations can be modeled using second quantization methods, but we have actually solved this problem before in Section 5.8.1. Compare the Hamiltonian above with that in (5.44) and it will be seen that the Hamiltonians are essentially identical if we set the coefficients in (5.44) all equal to V. Then we can immediately write the solutions for the time-dependent population numbers of each cell from equations $n(t), m(t)$, and $p(t)$.

$n_1(t), n_2(t), n_3(t)$

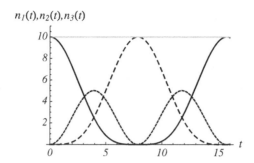

FIGURE 6.2. Population migration from cell to neighboring cell. The continuous curve illustrates cell 1; the short dashes, cell 2, and the longer dashes, cell 3. The grey line indicates the total population.

We all know that as before the population summed over all the cells does not change, but that the population is just being continually redistributed. This clearly is a nice property for the system to have, if we are modeling a fixed total number of migrating individuals.

Now in order to illustrate the behavior of our system, we will look at a specific initial situation, which is a kind of test bed for what is predicted. We are going to assume that initially the whole population is in the first cell, so that at the start there are no individuals in cells two and three. The results for the first few time steps are illustrated in Fig. 6.2.

What we can see in Fig. 6.2 is that after a short time interval, the population (10) of cell 1 starts to decline while that of cell 2 starts to increase. A little later, the population of cell 3 also starts to increase due to migration from cell 2. This is clearly consistent with movement along the row of cells. After about three units of time, the population in cell 1 has fallen to the level to which that in cell 2 has risen, and there is also a substantial population in cell 3. After four units of time, the population in cell 2 peaks and subsequently also starts to fall and we can see a majority of the population has entered cell 3. After about seven units of time, cells 1 and 2 are both empty and the whole population is in cell 3. Subsequently, the population begins to move back towards cell 1 and after about 15 units of time, the population is all back in cell 1. Subsequently, the whole process repeats itself and the population continues to bounce backwards and forwards along the row, as indicated. It is worth pointing out that this behavior, although quite understandable, is different from what would be expected from classical diffusion theory, where eventually the population would settle down with equal numbers in each cell. In the quantum case, the oscillatory behavior would continue for ever.

6.2. Exercises

Exercise 7. (i) A population of identical individuals is distributed among a number of identical cells arranged in a matrix of rows and columns in a two-dimensional grid. Using creation and annihilation operators, where the annihilation operator $\hat{a}_{ij}$ corresponds to the cell in the ith row and jth column, construct an Hermitian interaction Hamiltonian that describes the movement of individuals between adjacent cells, either along rows or along columns, but not both, in which the population of the whole grid remains fixed during the population movement.

(ii) How would you indicate the following situations, (a) all cells are equally accessible in all directions from any starting point, (b) it is easier to move along rows than along columns, and (c) certain regions of the grid are out of bounds?

Chapter 7

More Elaborate Systems

7.1. Buying and selling models

In our simple two-trader model, we have only used the exchange of single types of items. A transaction in this scheme involves an item passing from a trader A_1 to a trader A_2 and a second transaction involves the reverse process. Consider now a situation in which traders exchange goods for cash. In other words, we want to model transactions that involve both buying and selling and not just simple exchange as before. As an example, consider the situation in which each transaction consists of an exchange of an item of goods for a portion of cash, say. Let the number of items of goods belonging to A_1 be represented by $\hat{n}_1 = \hat{a}_1^+ \hat{a}_1$ and those of A_2 be $\hat{n}_2 = \hat{a}_2^+ \hat{a}_2$, but now let the two traders each have numbers of portions of cash, $\hat{k}_1 = \hat{c}_1^+ \hat{c}_1$ and $\hat{k}_2 = \hat{c}_2^+ \hat{c}_2$, to exchange for the goods. We can take the state vector of the system in occupation number notation to be $|n_1(0), n_2(0), k_1(0), k_2(0)\rangle$.

Bagarello [5] has introduced the idea of *selling* and *buying* operators, which, for a two-trader system, may be defined in the following way. For our trader A_1, the selling operator would be $\hat{x}_1 = \hat{c}_1^+ \hat{a}_1$. The effect this has on the state vector $|n_1(0), n_2(0), k_1(0), k_2(0)\rangle$ is to turn it into $|n_1(0) - 1, n_2(0), k_1(0) + 1, k_2(0)\rangle$. Of course, we would also need to multiply this by $\sqrt{n_1(0)(k_1(0) + 1)}$. A_2 also has a selling operator that will be given by $\hat{x}_2 = \hat{c}_2^+ \hat{a}_2$. This will turn $|n_1(0), n_2(0), k_1(0), k_2(0)\rangle$ into $|n_1(0), n_2(0) - 1, k_1(0), k_2(0) + 1\rangle$, multiplied by $\sqrt{n_2(0)(k_2(0) + 1)}$.

Now selling can be considered as part of a transaction that is complemented by buying. A buying operator can be constructed simply by taking the adjoint of a selling operator, so, the buying operators of A_1 and A_2 are respectively, $\hat{x}_1^+ = \hat{a}_1^+ \hat{c}_1$ and $\hat{x}_2^+ = \hat{a}_2^+ \hat{c}_2$. Thus, we expect a transaction that involves A_1 selling to A_2 to be of the form $\hat{x}_2^+ \hat{x}_1$. Now bearing in mind what has gone before, we can expect the reverse transaction to take place, i.e., $\hat{x}_1^+ \hat{x}_2$, in which A_1 is the buyer and A_2 the seller. Implicit in the definitions of these buying and selling operators is that the price of each good is fixed. For the moment, let us fix it at one unit of cash. We will investigate the effects of price in more detail later.

These two transactions then contribute to an interaction Hamiltonian of the form

$$\hat{\Omega}_I = V(\hat{x}_1^+ \hat{x}_2 + \hat{x}_2^+ \hat{x}_1), \tag{7.1}$$

where V is real ensures that $\hat{\Omega}_I$ is Hermitian, as required if we wish to use the HEM in problems involving this type of interaction. Then we can model the situation in which each transaction involves an exchange of goods as well as cash by a Hamiltonian that has a non-interacting part, $\hat{\Omega}_0$ as well as the interacting part, $\hat{\Omega}_I$ that can be written explicitly as

$$\hat{\Omega} = U_1 \hat{n}_1 + U_2 \hat{n}_2 + W_1 \hat{k}_1 + W_2 \hat{k}_2 + V(\hat{a}_1^+ \hat{c}_2^+ \hat{a}_2 \hat{c}_1 + \hat{a}_2^+ \hat{c}_1^+ \hat{a}_1 \hat{c}_2). \tag{7.2}$$

Next, we look for the integrals of the motion and conserved quantities for this trading model, involving just two traders.

7.2. Integrals of the motion

First let us use the HEM, with the above Hamiltonian, to calculate the rates of change of $\hat{n}_1$, $\hat{n}_2$, $\hat{k}_1$, and $\hat{k}_2$. We get

$$i \frac{d\hat{n}_1}{dt} = V(\hat{a}_1^+ \hat{c}_2^+ \hat{a}_2 \hat{c}_1 - \hat{a}_2^+ \hat{c}_1^+ \hat{a}_1 \hat{c}_2),$$

$$i \frac{d\hat{n}_2}{dt} = -V(\hat{a}_1^+ \hat{c}_2^+ \hat{a}_2 \hat{c}_1 - \hat{a}_2^+ \hat{c}_1^+ \hat{a}_1 \hat{c}_2),$$

$$i\frac{\mathrm{d}\hat{k}_1}{\mathrm{d}t} = V(\hat{a}_1^+\hat{c}_2^+\hat{a}_2\hat{c}_1 - \hat{a}_2^+\hat{c}_1^+\hat{a}_1\hat{c}_2),$$

$$i\frac{\mathrm{d}\hat{k}_2}{\mathrm{d}t} = -V(\hat{a}_1^+\hat{c}_2^+\hat{a}_2\hat{c}_1 - \hat{a}_2^+\hat{c}_1^+\hat{a}_1\hat{c}_2). \tag{7.3}$$

It is straightforward to show that $\frac{\mathrm{d}(\hat{n}_1+\hat{n}_2)}{\mathrm{d}t} = 0$ and $\frac{\mathrm{d}(\hat{k}_1+\hat{k}_2)}{\mathrm{d}t} = 0$, so the total number of goods possessed by the traders is fixed and also the total cash. However, there are two other interesting integrals of the motion. These are $\frac{\mathrm{d}(\hat{n}_1-\hat{k}_1)}{\mathrm{d}t} = 0$ and $\frac{\mathrm{d}(\hat{n}_2-\hat{k}_2)}{\mathrm{d}t} = 0$. We can express the differential relations as conserved quantities and get $n_1(t) + n_2(t) = N$, $k_1(t) + k_2(t) = K$, $n_1(t) - k_1(t) = D$ and $n_2(t) - k_2(t) = E$. So for each trader individually, the difference between their number of goods and their cash is fixed. This is rather unexpected, but it does help in solving the equations of motion.

7.3. Solving the equations of motion

One can get to a solution of the time-dependent set of equations by finding their second derivatives. We only need one because the conservations rules will give us the other three. So let us find the second derivative of $\hat{n}_1$. We will first simplify the Hamiltonian by dropping the non-interaction terms as we have previously. So setting $U_1 = U_2 = W_1 = W_2 = 0$, then

$$\frac{\mathrm{d}^2\hat{n}_1}{\mathrm{d}t^2} = 2V^2(\hat{n}_2\hat{k}_2(\hat{n}_1 + \hat{k}_1 + 1) - \hat{n}_1\hat{k}_1(\hat{n}_2 + \hat{k}_2 + 1)). \tag{7.4}$$

We can eliminate all of the operators except $\hat{n}_1$ with the aid of the conservation rules above. Then we get

$$\frac{\mathrm{d}^2\hat{n}_1}{\mathrm{d}t^2} = 2V^2((N - \hat{n}_1)(K + D - \hat{n}_1)(2\hat{n}_1 - D + 1)$$
$$- \hat{n}_1(\hat{n}_1 - D)(N + K + D + 1 - 2\hat{n}_1)). \tag{7.5}$$

This is a non-linear equation which we will again solve approximately by using the same kind of technique we used in Section 5.10.4.

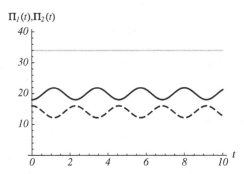

FIGURE 7.1. Portfolio values (solid and dashed curves) of a pair of traders exchanging goods and cash assuming a fixed price for the goods. The grey line indicates the total value of the two portfolios.

So we simply replace the operator in Eq. (7.5) by its scalar expectation value. The other three variables, $n_2(t)$, $k_1(t)$ and $k_2(t)$ are obtained from the conservation rules above.

Since we are now dealing with a situation in which the traders have both cash as well as goods, it is useful to use the concept of the *portfolio* (see [5]) to characterize the value of their assets. The values of the portfolios, $\Pi_1(t)$ and $\Pi_2(t)$, of the two traders are defined as the sum of the values of the goods and cash for each trader, i.e., $\Pi_1(t) = P_0 n_1(t) + k_1(t)$ and $\Pi_2(t) = P_0 n_2(t) + k_2(t)$, where P_0 is the fixed price of each good. In the present case, of course, we have $P_0 = 1$. An example of how the two portfolio values behave is shown in Fig. 7.1.

In this simple example, the values of the portfolios oscillate sinusoidally in a manner we have come to expect from the linear and linearized models. Note also that the sum of the two portfolios is conserved in this case.

7.4. Further refinements: Supply and price

A way of improving the realism of this trading model is to allow the price of the goods to vary with time. One possible way in which the price of the goods might change is through a supply control mechanism. This can be modeled by adding a term, $\hat{\Omega}_s$, to the Hamiltonian in (7.2). The idea of this addition to the Hamiltonian is that, if the supply number goes up by one unit then the price of one good goes down by one unit, and vice versa. Such a process can be modeled by (see [5])

$$\hat{\Omega}_s = \hat{P} + \hat{S} + \hat{p}^+\hat{s} + \hat{s}^+\hat{p}, \qquad (7.6)$$

where $\hat{P} = \hat{p}^+\hat{p}$ is the price operator whose expectation values measure the price at any given time and $\hat{p}$ and $\hat{p}^+$ respectively lower and raise the price by one unit. Similarly, $\hat{S} = \hat{s}^+\hat{s}$ is the supply operator whose expectation values measure the number of goods available at any given time and $\hat{s}$ and $\hat{s}^+$ respectively lower and raise the number of goods available by one unit. The form of this Hamiltonian is familiar from Section 5.4 and its meaning is straightforward to interpret. The first two terms are just the amounts associated with the price and the supply. These would not change in time if there were no further terms. The third and fourth terms are interaction terms that model the effect of supply on price and vice versa.

Now note that in this case, $\hat{\Omega}_s$ contains no operators in common with the original Hamiltonian in (7.2) (see also Section 5.9). So, the original system and the price–supply system constitute a pair of independent subsystems that may be solved separately. Thus we can retain the solutions in the previous section for $n_1(t)$, $n_2(t)$, $k_1(t)$, and $k_2(t)$, and just solve for the expectation values $P(t)$ and $S(t)$. These solution have exactly the same forms as the solution for our simple two-trader model in Section 5.4.3, with $U = W = V = 1$. The expectation values $P(t)$ and $S(t)$ then take the form

$$P(t) = \frac{1}{2}(P(0) + S(0) + (P(0) - S(0))\cos(2t))$$

and

$$S(t) = \frac{1}{2}(P(0) + S(0) + (S(0) - P(0))\cos(2t)). \qquad (7.7)$$

The above modification would also feed through to the definition of the portfolio values. An obvious new definition of the portfolio expectation values of the two traders would be $\Pi_1(t) = P(t)n_1(t) +$

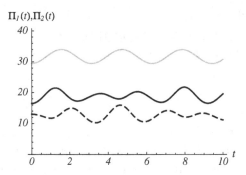

FIGURE 7.2. Portfolio values (solid and dashed curves) of a pair of traders exchanging goods and cash, allowing the price of the goods to vary with time due to the effects of supply. The grey curve indicates the total value of the two portfolios.

$k_1(t)$ and $\Pi_2(t) = P(t)n_2(t) + k_2(t)$. The effect of supply and price on the portfolios above is shown in Fig. 7.2.

We can see that introducing supply and price into the picture has a significant impact on the portfolio values of our traders. First, the sum of the values of the two portfolios is no longer constant. Second the fluctuations in their values are no longer of a simple sinusoidal nature. This is because the frequency of the price variations is not the same as the frequency of the variations in the number of goods, so the two get mixed together in the products of prices and the numbers of goods. However, such a system does not quite capture the true characteristics of the situation, since, if the price of the goods varies, then we should expect that to impact on the amount cash that A_1 and A_2 exchange. We might expect this then to modify the buying and selling operators. For example, A_1's selling operator might be now expected to look like be $\hat{x}_1 = \hat{c}_1^{+P(t)}\hat{a}_1$, which would mean that the A_1 would now receive $P(t)$ units of cash for a good. While this latter modification improves the self-consistency of the model, it greatly increases its mathematical difficulty. This is beyond the scope of the present introductory treatment (see Bagarello's book [5] for more details).

Chapter 8

Conclusions

In this part of the book, we have explored in a very elementary way the use of the number operator and its companions, the number amplitude operators, that correspond to creation and annihilation operators in QFT, to model some simple systems in which populations of people, goods, cash etc. vary in time, through being exchanged between different elements of the system as a whole. We have picked extremely simple systems with only a few agents to illustrate the principles involved. We have stressed a key property of this approach to be the existence of certain conservation rules. This is a really important aspect of the modeling and something that physicists always look for in dealing with physical systems, whether they be treated classically of by quantum methods. Whether the system involves galaxies or a few atoms, a physicist will insist that fundamental quantities like energy and momentum are conserved as the system evolves. This constraint is vital in deciding on the validity of the model. It is very easy to write lines of computer code with a perfectly correct set of equations, but which overall do not keep some conserved quantity constant. Models of isolated systems that do not constrain totals of energy and momentum to be fixed should certainly be deemed invalid. The reason is that it is possible to demonstrate mathematically that the accepted theories of physics conserve these quantities. Moreover, the conserved quantities tell physicists precisely what parameters they need to model. For example, physics tells us to measure and keep track of the product of mass times velocity (momentum) and one half times mass, times velocity squared (kinetic energy). Using mass times velocity cubed, for example, would be a waste of time, since it is not part of the great accounting process that controls motion in the universe. It is precisely these features of a physical system that tell the physicist that it is a waste of time thinking about a perpetual motion machine, or something that gives energy for nothing. In contrast, many non-physically based systems models have no all-enveloping theory that tells the modeler what parameters to choose for modeling. With the Lokta–Volterra model (LVM) for example, it seems intuitively obvious to pick the population values of rabbits and foxes and write an albeit *ad hoc* equation for their variation in time. But why not pick the population number squared? There is nothing to tell us not to. The same appears true of financial models. One picks income, or price or tax. Why not use some combination or some function of these quantities? There are no rules, apart from convention or intuition that constrains the choice of such variables. Why should this matter, well, it could lead to a prediction of something for nothing. The equivalent of a perpetual motion machine might then seem possible in finance or economics. Is continuous economic growth really possible? This may look as feasible as a perpetual motion machine did before the rules of physics were properly understood.

Whether the QFT-based models that we have looked at, albeit briefly, offer any more reliable way to predict economic or social science outcomes remains to be seen, but we can be sure what is contained in them. This at least means we can design models that conserve certain quantities and keep them in bounds. It means we are better able to build models that do things we understand. The Hamiltonian approach is particularly well suited to being able to create systems with known global properties. The details of model predictions, such as individual behavior, still need to be calculated, but at least one knows that there is some control over what can be expected from such models.

References — Part I

[1] Aerts, D.; Sozzo, S.; Veloz, T. (2015). The quantum nature of identity in human thought: Bose-Einstein statistics for conceptual indistinguishability. *International Journal of Theoretical Physics* 54, 4430–4443.

[2] Annett, J.F. (2004). *Superconductivity, Superfluids and Condensates.* Oxford University Press, Oxford.

[3] Asano, M.; Khrennikov, A.; Ohya, M.; Tanaka, Y.; Yamato, I. (2015). *Quantum Adaptivity in Biology: From Genetics to Cognition.* Springer, Heidelberg.

[4] Auletta, G.; Fortunato, M.; Paris, G. (2009). *Quantum Mechanics.* Cambridge University Press, Cambridge.

[5] Bagarello, F. (2013). *Quantum Dynamics for Classical Systems.* J. Wiley, New York.

[6] Brannon, E.M. (2002). The development of ordinal numerical knowledge in infancy. *Cognition* 83, 223–240.

[7] Busemeyer, J.R.; Bruza, P.D. (2012). *Quantum Models of Cognition and Decision.* Cambridge University Press, Cambridge.

[8] Cockshott, P.; Mackenzie, L.M.; Michaelson, G. (2015). *Computation and its Limits.* Oxford University Press, Oxford.

[9] Dirac, P.A.M. (1964). *Lectures on Quantum Mechanics.* Belfer Graduate School of Science, Yeshiva University, New York.

[10] Gross, H.J. (2012). The magical number four: A biological, historical and mythological enigma. *Communicative & Integrative Biology* 5(1), 1–2.

[11] Haven, E.; Khrennikov, A. (2013). *Quantum Social Science.* Cambridge University Press, Cambridge.

[12] Kermack, W.O.; McKendrick, A.G. (1927). A contribution to the mathematical theory of epidemics. *Proceedings of the Royal Society A* 115, 700–721.

[13] Khrennikov, A. (2010). *Ubiquitous Quantum Structure: From Psychology to Finance.* Springer, Heidelberg.

[14] Khrennikov, A. (2015). Quantum-like modeling of cognition. *Frontiers in Physics* 3, art. 77. doi.org/10.3389/fphy.2015.00077

[15] Korobeinikov, A. (2009). Financial crisis: An attempt of mathematical modelling. *Applied Mathematics Letters* 22, 1882–1886.

[16] Margolis, E.; Laurence, S. (2008). How to learn natural numbers: Inductive inference and the acquisition of number concepts. *Cognition* 106, 924–939.

[17] Murray, J.D. (1993). *Mathematical Biology*. Springer-Verlag, New York.

[18] Piaget, J. (1965). *The Child's Conception of Number*. Norton Co, New York.

[19] Rips, L.J.; Asmuth, J.; Bloomfield, A. (2006). Giving the boot to the bootstrap: How not to learn the natural numbers. *Cognition* 101, B51–B60.

[20] Robinson, T.R.; Haven, E. (2015). Quantization and quantum-like phenomena: A number amplitude approach. *International Journal of Theoretical Physics* 54, 4576–4590.

[21] Schwinger, J. (2015). *On Angular Momentum*. Dover Publications, Mineola, New York.

[22] Wynn, K. (1990). Children's understanding of counting. *Cognition* 36, 155–193.

Part II

The Quantum-Like Paradigm with Simple Applications

Chapter 9

Taking a Step Back

9.1. Introduction

The first part of the book introduced you to an approach many aspiring physicists will learn about once they take a more advanced module in quantum mechanics. First, quantization does require that position and momentum are operators and there is a commutation relation. As you have seen from Part I in the book, *second quantization* assumes that position and momentum are numbers and fields are now operators. But let us be very careful about the main message of the first part of this book: we can in effect come up with a theory which is almost physics-free so to speak! We should keep this in mind while we progress throughout the book.

In part III of the book, we will be able to say much more on how first quantization is particularly useful in the area of decision making (DM). We will be very interested in considering how we can formalize the so-called non-Boolean information processing by decision makers. The idea of "information" is central in part III and also, to an extent, in this part of the book. But again let us keep in mind the query — how "tied" we are to physics in applying those formalisms to social science?

The title of this part of the book uses the words "quantum-like". The quantum-like approach which has now been applied to a variety of areas of the social sciences such as politics, economics, and psychology, assumes that the wave function itself portrays information. From the outset, it is important we say clearly what we mean with the quantum-like approach (we also use the words "quantum-like paradigm" (see [48])). The central argument of this paradigm is that the quantum wave function is informational in nature. If that way of thinking is palatable, then the next step consists in arguing that the quantum formalism itself becomes useful to model processes which are steered by "information". It is important to stress that the quantum-like paradigm does NOT imply that macroscopic processes (or any processes) outside of the quantum physical scale exhibits quantum mechanical features. They may do so, but it is much more likely they do not. Thus, the quantum formalism is really an *operational* formalism.

This chapter wants to take a step back. Before we introduce more cases, which will highlight the use of the quantum formalism as an operational formalism in social science, it may be good to consider the historical context in which such applications may be embedded in.

As is the case with many new applications in virtually every domain of knowledge, there is the question of longevity. For how long will this new promising contribution last? Will it be just a fashion which will die out or will it rather leave a much more durable footprint? Many examples abound, which show this eternal opposition between lasting and non-lasting impressions upon the edifice of knowledge, that new domains of inquiry may bring. Fuzzy set theory is an example of a movement which made impressive contributions to areas such as applied engineering and operations research, but it was probably less successful in areas such as academic finance, for instance. It is fair to say the fuzzy set theory approach lost some of its momentum since its heyday in the 1990s. Can the same be said for the "econophysics"[a] movement? Probably not. The quest for applying to good use (in social science), formalisms from statistical mechanics has succeeded to a large extent in uncovering the existence of power laws in a lot of financial data. The heat equation and

---

[a]Maybe we can loosely define "econophysics" as an area of applications in physics which applies concepts from statistical mechanics to a variety of areas of social science and the humanities.

the so-called Kolmorogov backward partial differential equation can be shown to have made crucial contributions to the most successful theory in academic finance, i.e., option pricing theory. And more contributions can be added. Further on, in this part of the book, we will consider how the core Hamiltonian framework can actually become a model input in very basic microeconomic theory. This is an important contribution. Why? We need to make the point that once we can show that a formalism from physics, when used as an operational formalism, can actually be employed to model a phenomenon in social science, then we have achieved something. The contribution here consists in augmenting the existing modeling in the social science domain. This goes beyond explaining a phenomenon with a new formalism. Indeed, once a new formalism lies at the base of a model, then the explanation of the phenomenon can potentially be gaining bigger depth. The phenomenon can be re-produced or also predicted via the use of the said model, rather than just explained.

For the novice reader, who knows little about the sociology of imported formalisms, it is quite prudent to say that there is substantial opposition from established disciplines in the social sciences toward the import of such formalisms. One of the most famous economists of the twentieth century, Nobel Laureate Paul Samuelson did frown upon using analogies between concepts of different disciplines (see [85]). We may wonder whether Paul Samuelson was unhappy about such analogies simply because he believed physics based models, when they are applied to economics are just merely metaphors? Ferdinand Verhulst would define a model as being a function of metaphors and some "quantitative and/or qualitative bits" (see [94]). We can delve deeper into this but this book is not the place to do so.

However, to attempt to give a slightly more augmented feel of the sociological dimension of importing a foreign formalism into one's own discipline, it is important to consider the "other side of the fence". We mean: how do physicists themselves think about exporting those formalisms? Benoit Mandelbrot indicated that when social science borrows from physics, the type of randomness assumed in models is not of the type which may well occur in reality. He distinguishes "mild" from "wild" randomness (see [75]). Consider another remark from an MIT Ph.D. in engineering who said that if we were to "...assume you try to measure the temperature of water with a thermometer. Your sample size should be on the order of 10^{23} molecules......translating this sample size to financial data (say S&P[b] returns (on sec/sec basis)): it would take a lot of years of S&P second-by-second returns to collect enough data to give you a probability distribution that allows you to make the connection between finance at the 'quantum' level and finance at the 'classical physics' level." (see [35]). In the first part of the book, we alluded to energy conservation, a concept of crucial importance in physics. It is surely not obvious how we can argue for the existence of an analogous concept in economics. Gallegati *et al.* [43, p. 5] remarked that "income is not, like energy in physics, conserved by economic processes". We can continue our list. For instance, states in classical mechanics are totally reversible in time. Which processes in social science are totally reversible?

This introduction seems to enter a direction where we implicitly claim that in fact the reader should better not bother continue reading! But this is not what we try to say. In fact, the methods we will cover in this part of the book (and the same can be said for the other approaches in parts I and III of the book) are beneficial to model deviations precisely from very formal behaviors in social science! This is, on *prima facie*, seriously contradictory. On the one hand, we seem to imply that social science phenomena can not possibly behave in the same rigorous ways as physical phenomena do. Hence, why bother then using physics formalisms when they manifestly can not help us to better model the "wild behavior" of social science events. But it is nearly the opposite: the formalisms do show they can accommodate very non-formal DM for instance. We will cover this in the last chapter of this part of the book and in a much more in depth treatment in part III of the book.

---

[b]S&P is the abbreviation of "Standard and Poor's", which is a US financial services company.

But let us continue confusing ourselves a little more.... We know from the animal world that certain species can be very good at finding optimal solutions to difficult problems. In economics, we are taught that we, as consumers, will maximize the satisfaction retrieved from consuming goods for a given a certain budget constraint. We make thus the argument that it is our human model which uses mathematical concepts to explain how we function. We may well be born with an optimizer template in our head (just like, for instance, bacteria have such a template), but the formal rendering (or approximation) of this template is expressed with formal models using mathematics and they may indeed be sourced from physics.

We finish this introduction with an indication on what comes next in this part of the book. In the next section, we introduce some basic concepts from classical mechanics and then discuss how the potential function and the wider Lagrangian (Hamiltonian) framework can really have meaning within a social science environment. We also discuss financial option pricing. We consider how the Brownian motion plays a key role in this theory and how the Kolmogorov backward partial differential equation emerges as the central equation.

In the next chapter, we will discuss how information, via the formal use of the wave function can be shown to be of use in a social science context. The last chapter of this part of the book introduces you to the concept of quantum probability and DM. Part III of the book will discuss this topic in much greater depth.

9.2. Some basic ideas from classical mechanics

9.2.1. *Energy conservation*

We know from our high-school courses in physics that force is directed in such a way that it pushes a particle to a lower potential. If the potential energy is denoted by the function $V(x)$ (this could be a time-dependent function too), then it is natural to write that the force, F is such that: $F = -\frac{dV}{dx}$. Another crucial issue we learned from our high-school physics modules was that total energy, E, being the sum of potential and kinetic energy, needs to be conserved, i.e., $\frac{dE}{dt} = 0$. This is a very important condition and, from the outset, it is very difficult to think of an analog of such conservation principle within an economics setting, for instance. Note that potential energy does not need to be conserved: only total energy is conserved.

Assume that we have a time-dependent potential V, and let us write:

$$\frac{\mathrm{d}V}{\mathrm{d}t} = \frac{\mathrm{d}V}{\mathrm{d}x}\frac{\mathrm{d}x}{\mathrm{d}t} \tag{9.1}$$

and consider $\frac{\mathrm{d}x}{\mathrm{d}t} = v$, where v is velocity. Kinetic energy is given by $T = \frac{1}{2}mv^2$. The importance of total energy conservation can be underlined as follows. If we consider what is needed to impose that[c] $\frac{\mathrm{d}E}{\mathrm{d}t} = 0$, we need to write:

$$\frac{\mathrm{d}E}{\mathrm{d}t} = \frac{\mathrm{d}V}{\mathrm{d}t} + \frac{\mathrm{d}T}{\mathrm{d}t} = \frac{\mathrm{d}V}{\mathrm{d}x}v + mv\frac{\mathrm{d}v}{\mathrm{d}t} = \frac{\mathrm{d}V}{\mathrm{d}x}v + mva \tag{9.2}$$

and energy conservation, $\frac{\mathrm{d}E}{\mathrm{d}t} = 0$ requires thus that:

$$v\left(\frac{\mathrm{d}V}{\mathrm{d}x} + ma\right) = 0, \tag{9.3}$$

which is rewritten as: $v(ma - F) = 0$ and this yields Newton's second law.

9.2.2. *First analogs with social science*

Can we espouse those basic notions to an economics setting? Maybe to some degree. One could define the economics version of kinetic energy by: $\frac{1}{2}\sum_{j=1}^{n} m_j v_j^2$; where m_j is the number of shares of stock j and

$$v_j(t) = \dot{q}_j(t) = \lim_{\Delta t \to 0} \frac{q_j(t + \Delta t) - q_j(t)}{\Delta t}, \tag{9.4}$$

where t is time and q_j is the price of asset j (say the price of the share of the jth corporation).

---

[c]This is simply the time derivative towards total energy E.

We can define a price vector:

$$\overrightarrow{q(t)} = (q_1(t), q_2(t), \ldots q_n(t)), \qquad (9.5)$$

where the dimension of the vector is simply given by the number of corporations. The phase space of prices, could be seen as a product space $Q \times V$; where $V \equiv \mathbb{R}^n$ if n corporations are considered and $\overrightarrow{v} = (v_1, v_2, \ldots v_n) \in V$, and $\overrightarrow{q} = (q_1, q_2, \ldots, q_n) \in Q$.

A simple example of the above analogy could be as follows. Assume two corporations, "1" and "2" which operate in the same sector. Assume there is an identical change in price, but a higher level of share emission in corporation "1" as opposed to corporation "2", then there is higher "kinetic energy" in corporation "1" as opposed to corporation "2".

The analog of potential energy in economics can also be of interest. We can think of an interaction between firms of the same sector, where for instance it would be natural to consider price differences. As an example, $(q_1 - q_2)^2$ could indicate the squared difference of prices of comparable (or identical?) assets made from corporation "1" as opposed to corporation "2". Alternatively, we could also consider a potential function which is time-dependent of the following format: $(q_1 - q_2)^{2t}$, with t being time. When time passes, the potential function becomes narrower and narrower. If for instance, $q_1 - q_2$ were to measure the price difference between two identical goods made by two different companies, then the price difference between those goods is narrowed with the passage of time because of the increased arrival of information over time. If we imagine a probability density function to be associated with this potential, then the minimum point of the potential will be the most likely point.

9.2.3. *The Lagrangian and the action functional*

One can also define the so-called Lagrangian: $\mathcal{L} = T - V$. A more advanced course in physics may discuss the notion of stationary "action". The so-called action of a trajectory is defined as $\mathcal{A} = \int_{t_o}^{t_1} \mathcal{L}(x, \dot{x}) \mathrm{d}t$, where t is time. As the superb book of Susskind and Hrabovsky [89] shows, it is essential that the Lagrangian is the difference between kinetic and potential energy (and not the sum — see the next section). The authors report that the stationary action principle crops up in a very wide spectrum of physics, whether it be classical mechanics but also relativity theory and quantum mechanics. We will be coming back below to some social science-based uses of the action idea.

It is useful to consider some of the essential ideas behind the least action principle, especially the consequence of minimizing action is extremely beautiful. We follow Susskind and Hrabovsky [89, p. 105] and Jammer [62, p. 23]. Least action can be written as: $\delta \mathcal{A} = \int_{t_o}^{t_1} \mathcal{L}(x, \dot{x}) \mathrm{d}t = 0$, where $\dot{x} = \frac{\mathrm{d}x}{\mathrm{d}t}$. As the authors indicate, the function which one minimizes here is a function of an incredibly large amount of variables (think of the many many variables you need to construct the trajectory). The action, as a quantity, is a function of a function, and is therefore called a *functional*. The outcome of the minimization process yields the Euler–Lagrange equation:

$$\frac{\mathrm{d}}{\mathrm{d}t}\left(\frac{\partial \mathcal{L}}{\partial \dot{x}}\right) = \frac{\partial \mathcal{L}}{\partial x}, \tag{9.6}$$

from where we can recover: $F = m.a.$

9.2.4. *The birth of the Hamiltonian*

The above example of the time-dependent potential, $(q_1 - q_2)^{2t}$, would require us to write that the Lagrangian is now $\mathcal{L}(x, \dot{x}, t)$. Following Susskind and Hrabovsky [89, pp. 147–149], consider

$$\frac{\mathrm{d}\mathcal{L}}{\mathrm{d}t} = \frac{\partial \mathcal{L}}{\partial x}\frac{\partial x}{\partial t} + \frac{\partial \mathcal{L}}{\partial \dot{x}}\frac{\partial \dot{x}}{\partial t} + \frac{\partial \mathcal{L}}{\partial t} \tag{9.7}$$

and using the Euler–Lagrange relation: $\frac{\mathrm{d}}{\mathrm{d}t}(\frac{\partial \mathcal{L}}{\partial \dot{x}}) = \frac{\partial \mathcal{L}}{\partial x}$ and noting that $\frac{\partial \mathcal{L}}{\partial \dot{x}}$ is momentum,[d] p, then one can rewrite the above total derivative as

$$\frac{\mathrm{d}\mathcal{L}}{\mathrm{d}t} = \frac{\partial p}{\partial t}\frac{\partial x}{\partial t} + p\frac{\partial \dot{x}}{\partial t} + \frac{\partial \mathcal{L}}{\partial t}, \tag{9.8}$$

---

[d] A more correct name is generalized (conjugate) momentum.

which can now easily be rewritten as: $\frac{d\mathcal{L}}{dt} = \dot{p}\dot{x} + p\ddot{x} + \frac{\partial\mathcal{L}}{\partial t}$ and which can be further re-written as

$$\frac{d\mathcal{L}}{dt} = \frac{d}{dt}(p\dot{x}) + \frac{\partial\mathcal{L}}{\partial t}. \tag{9.9}$$

If one then sets: $\mathcal{H} = p\dot{x} - \mathcal{L}$, then this quantity, when the time derivative is taken, simply yields

$$\frac{d\mathcal{H}}{dt} = \frac{d}{dt}(p\dot{x}) - \frac{d\mathcal{L}}{dt} = \frac{d}{dt}(p\dot{x}) - \frac{d}{dt}(p\dot{x}) - \frac{\partial\mathcal{L}}{\partial t}. \tag{9.10}$$

This beautiful result shows that the time-dependence of the Lagrangian makes that the time derivative of the quantity $\mathcal{H}$ is non-zero.

The movement from the Lagrangian formalism: $\mathcal{L}(x, \dot{x})$ to $\mathcal{L}(x, \dot{x}, t)$ brings us into the Hamiltonian framework, and the quantity $\mathcal{H}$ is the Hamiltonian. We can say that with a time-dependent potential the so-called "Hamiltonian conservation", $\frac{d\mathcal{H}}{dt} = 0$ is not obtained. As the authors also show, using the definition of $\mathcal{L} = T - V = \frac{m}{2}\dot{x}^2 - V$ and the momentum $m\dot{x}$ and replacing those definitions into $\mathcal{H} = p\dot{x} - \mathcal{L}$, simply yields

$$m\dot{x}^2 - \frac{m}{2}\dot{x}^2 + V = T + V. \tag{9.11}$$

Note thus, that the Hamiltonian indicates the *sum* of potential and kinetic energies, while the Lagrangian denotes the *difference* between kinetic and potential energy.

9.2.5. *Momentum conservation in finance?*

Recall the above example of the potential function which considers the difference in price on similar assets sourced from different corporations. We could write the potential function as: $V(x_1 - x_2)$, where x_1 is the price of asset "1" and x_2 is the price of asset "2".

We could borrow a Lagrangian, which is described in Susskind and Hrabovsky [89, p. 126] as

$$\mathcal{L} = \frac{m}{2}\left(\dot{x}_1^2 + \dot{x}_2^2\right) - V(x_1 - x_2). \tag{9.12}$$

Let us define, in a financial context a price average and price discordance, as respectively: $x_{av} = \frac{x_1+x_2}{2}$ and $x_{disc} = \frac{x_1-x_2}{2}$. We can rewrite the above $\mathcal{L}$ in the form of time derivatives: $\dot{x}_{av}^2 = \frac{(\dot{x}_1^2+\dot{x}_2^2)^2}{4}$ and $\dot{x}_{disc}^2 = \frac{(\dot{x}_1^2-\dot{x}_2^2)^2}{4}$. We observe that $\dot{x}_{av}^2 + \dot{x}_{disc}^2 = \frac{1}{2}(\dot{x}_1^2+\dot{x}_2^2)$ so that $\dot{x}_1^2 + \dot{x}_2^2 = 2(\dot{x}_{av}^2 + \dot{x}_{disc}^2)$ and therefore we can rewrite the Lagrangian as: $\mathcal{L} = m(\dot{x}_{av}^2 + \dot{x}_{disc}^2) - V(x_1 - x_2)$. More importantly, since $x_1 - x_2 = 2x_{disc}$, we can rewrite the Lagrangian as

$$\mathcal{L} = m(\dot{x}_{av}^2 + \dot{x}_{disc}^2) - V(2x_{disc}). \tag{9.13}$$

Here are a couple of interesting issues we can raise:

(1) Note the non-symmetry in variables on the side of the kinetic term and the potential term.
(2) Note that there is both a common variable for velocity and position: x_{disc}. However, the x_{av} only exists for velocity. Following Susskind and Hrabovsky [89, p. 125], the x_{av} variable is cyclic.
(3) Another interesting issue which relates to $V(x_1 - x_2)$ is that $\dot{p}_1 = -\frac{\partial}{\partial x_1}V(x_1-x_2) = -V'(x_1-x_2)$ and $\dot{p}_2 = -\frac{\partial}{\partial x_2}V(x_1-x_2) = V'(x_1 - x_2)$. Hence

$$\dot{p}_1 + \dot{p}_2 = 0 \tag{9.14}$$

and this indicates so-called momentum conservation. A counter example to this conservation is quite easy to show. Say if $V(x_1, x_2) = V(cx_1 - dx_2)$, then: $\dot{p}_1 = -cV'(cx_1 - dx_2)$ and $\dot{p}_2 = dV'(cx_1 - dx_2)$, so to impose momentum conservation one needs to multiply $-cV'(cx_1 - dx_2)$ with d and $dV'(cx_1 - dx_2)$ with c:

$$-cdV'(cx_1 - dx_2) + dcV'(cx_1 - dx_2) = 0. \tag{9.15}$$

(4) We finally note the above example is not awkward from a finance perspective. We can well define finance equivalents of $\dot{x}_{av}^2$ and $\dot{x}_{disc}^2$ and the potential function is also rationalizable from a

finance perspective. From a finance perspective, how important is the asymmetry in the variables and the momentum conservation which obtains here? As is well known, momentum conservation is narrowly linked to Newton's third law.

9.2.6. *Conservation: How important is it?*

As we have seen from the above, energy conservation is tightly connected to Newton's second law and momentum conservation is tightly connected to Newton's third law. We mentioned at the beginning of this section that in economics, we can barely make an argument for the existence of an equivalent level of energy conservation. Accounting transactions will exhibit a semblance of conservation, via the debit/credit set up. However, how will the gains in productivity in an economy be espoused with the idea of conservation? Gallegati *et al.* [43, p. 5 said it very well]: ".....income is not, like energy in physics, conserved by economic processes. Therefore, it is a fundamental fallacy to base economic models on a principle of conservation...."

9.3. Applying basic classical mechanics to finance and economics: Some examples

In this section, we will consider several examples where we show how some of the concepts we defined above can be used in finance and economics. We consider the following examples:

- Example 1: a synergetics approach in behavioral economics,
- Example 2: an action functional and arbitrage,
- Example 3: re-modeling equilibrium pricing with a Lagrangian framework.

9.3.1. *Example 1: A synergetics approach in behavioral economics*

Thomas Lux's work provides for some of the very first applications of classical mechanics (more precisely statistical mechanics) within the setting of so-called behavioral finance. A key paper in that regard is Lux [73].

In that work, Lux follows to some extent in the footstep of Hermann Haken [46] who introduced the field of "synergetics". Lux [73, p. 5] defines synergetics as a "collection of methods....for analysis of the dynamic evolution of multi-component systems with interactions among their constituent parts."

Lux defines a population $2N$ of so-called "naive" traders and he divides them in a group of optimistic (n^+ of them) and pessimistic traders (n^- of them), so that $n^+ + n^- = 2N$. He then defines expressions for the transition probabilities for traders to move from a depressed to an optimistic group (and vice versa):

$$\pi_{+-} = v \exp(U) \tag{9.16}$$

and

$$\pi_{-+} = v \exp(-U) \tag{9.17}$$

with $U = \alpha_1 x + \alpha_2 \dot{p}/v$; where $\dot{p}$ is the time derivative of price; x is an opinion index; v determines the frequency of transitions and α_i measure the strength of each x (opinion) versus $\dot{p}/v$ (observed price change/trend). Interestingly enough, Lux provides for the use of the so-called "master equation" (in fact, he also refers to earlier work by Aoki [1] which already introduced this in the economics literature).

The master equation can be seen to lie at the base[e] of the derivation of the Fokker–Planck partial differential equation (PDE, henceforth). This PDE describes the time evolution of a probability density function over a particle's position. This PDE is also known under the name of the *forward* Kolmogorov PDE. Below, we will discuss the so-called Black–Scholes PDE, which is an example of a *backward* Kolmogorov PDE. See [93, 96].

The dynamics of the opinion and price can be captured by what Lux [73, p. 9] defines as "the probability of the system to occupy state $\{x, p\}$ at time t." This probability is denoted as $Q(x, p; t)$. If the conditional probability to move from state i to state i' per unit

---

[e]The so-called Kramers–Moyal expansion is essential here.

of time is denoted as $w_{ii'}$, then Lux writes the master equation as

$$\frac{dQ(x,p;t)}{dt} = \sum_{x'}(w_{xx'}Q(x',p;t) - w_{x'x}Q(x,p;t))$$
$$+ \sum_{p'}(w_{pp'}Q(x,p';t) - w_{p'p}Q(x,p;t)). \qquad (9.18)$$

Pinpointing the statistics which would derive from the above equation depends on some assumptions (Dirac delta assumption on state variables etc...) and Lux [73, p. 10] (Appendix A in that paper) describes those conditions in a very detailed way. The paper then continues to determine very useful expressions for the time evolution of both the mean opinion index and the mean price. Furthermore, variances of the said variables are also receiving a time-dependent expression. All of this provides for a rich framework where for instance transient dynamics resulting from a shock can be described.

We noted above the use of the master equation within a behavioral economics context. We need to mention that master equations are also widely used in quantum theory. Physicists use the Markov approximation to the quantum master equation, known as the *Gorini–Kossakowski–Sudarshan–Lindblad* (GKSL) equation. See [79]. This mathematical tool was explored to model the process of DM with quantum-like features. See, for instance, [4, 5, 68, 69].

9.3.2. *Example 2: An action functional and arbitrage*

As we have started discussing in the section above, the action concept is a functional (i.e., a function of a function). Great care needs to be exercised to apply such concepts within an economics or a finance environment. We will consider in this section a first application of this functional in finance. In the next example, we revisit the action functional but in an even more fundamental way.

Ilinski [61] provides for an interesting application of an action functional within a very basic finance context. Let us set up the example. Assume we face the following two situations:

(1) We have cash at t_i and we have as objective to buy shares at time t_{i+1}. We can write that if the interest we have on the cash, which is having value of 1 unit of currency at time t_i, is given by r_0, then the future value of this 1 unit of currency value over a period of time Δ is given by $\exp(r_0\Delta)$. We can then write that the ratio $\frac{\exp(r_0\Delta)}{S_{i+1}}$ will yield the number of shares you can buy at time t_{i+1} at price S_{i+1}.

(2) Alternatively, we can buy the shares at price, S_i and at time t_i. The return on the shares over the same period of time, Δ, we now denote with r_1. In a similar way, as in situation 1, we can write that $\frac{\exp(r_1\Delta)}{S_i}$ will yield the number of shares we now have.

In a financial market where we cannot realize any risk free profits, it should *not* be that either:

$$\frac{\exp(r_0\Delta)}{S_{i+1}} > \frac{\exp(r_1\Delta)}{S_i} \text{ or } \frac{\exp(r_1\Delta)}{S_i} > \frac{\exp(r_0\Delta)}{S_{i+1}}. \tag{9.19}$$

In the first case, $\exp(r_0\Delta)S_{i+1}^{-1}\exp(-r_1\Delta)S_i > 1$, while in the second case, $\exp(r_1\Delta)S_i^{-1}\exp(-r_0\Delta)S_{i+1} > 1$.

In a perfect world, we should thus require that

$$\exp(r_1\Delta)S_i^{-1}\exp(-r_0\Delta)S_{i+1} + \exp(r_0\Delta)S_{i+1}^{-1}\exp(-r_1\Delta)S_i - 2 = 0. \tag{9.20}$$

Ilinski [61] then formulates a so-called "non-arbitrage" condition, which essentially is a condition which prevents any opportunity to make a risk free profit. This condition is encapsulated in an action functional, $\mathcal{A}$, as follows:

$$\mathcal{A} = \sum_{i=-\infty}^{\infty} \alpha_i(\exp(r_1\Delta)S_i^{-1}\exp(-r_0\Delta)S_{i+1}$$
$$+ \exp(r_0\Delta)S_{i+1}^{-1}\exp(-r_1\Delta)S_i - 2); \tag{9.21}$$

where α_i is dependent on variance. This action is to be minimized. Note the interesting occurrence of a constant potential function in the above expression.

9.3.3. *Example 3: Re-modeling equilibrium pricing with a Lagrangian framework*

Some background for non-economists. There exists a lot of literature on using concepts from information theory and classical mechanics in economics and finance. However, a very challenging task consists in assessing whether basic models in economics and finance can be enlarged or generalized by the use of techniques from statistical mechanics. One outstanding example where a basic model, i.e., the one of equilibrium pricing in economics, is generalized by using such concepts is contained in the work of Belal Baaquie. In the development below, we follow the paper by Baaquie [8], but it is important one takes note of several other papers which apply the more general approach to real commodities (see therefore also [9, 10]).

An introductory course in microeconomics will virtually always introduce theoretical building blocks around the topic of how demand and supply in an economy can be determined. An intuitive starting point for wanting to demand a good must, almost by default, imply there must be somewhere a preference of one good over another. Basic microeconomic theory will formalize the concept of preferences. In this book, we have no intention to be formal about this construction. An important question one may want to consider is whether one can develop "reasonable" axioms which can define so-called "economic rationality"? We can say that a preference relation on objects to be consumed (from a so-called "consumption set" X) is rational if it possesses two essential properties (also called a pre-order):

$$\text{(i) } \forall x, y \in X : x \succeq y \quad \text{or } x \preceq y; \tag{9.22}$$

which is called "completeness" and

$$\text{(ii) } \forall x, y, z \in X : x \succeq y \quad \text{and} \quad y \succeq z \quad \text{then } x \succeq z; \tag{9.23}$$

which is the "transitivity" property.

An interesting property also indicates that preferences should not exhibit jumps, i.e., there should be continuity. If a rational preference relation $\succeq$ on a choice set is continuous, then one can say that there exists a continuous utility function $U(x)$ that represents $\succeq$. There are other issues to consider about the uniqueness and differentiability of the utility function, but this will not preoccupy us here.

The obvious question which is now appearing is: what is a utility function? In plain terms, it can be interpreted as a function which maps the quantity of a good onto a "degree" or "level" of satisfaction. Utility functions, $U(x, y)$, where x and y indicate quantities of good X and Y, map those levels of consumption onto a level of satisfaction (a level of "utility"). The key here is to consider levels of utility, in terms of a rank order. The interpretation of the number itself is senseless.

It is obvious that $U(x, y)$ has level curves. Imagine, we have a simple space configured by three axises X, Y, and Z. Assume the XY plane is horizontal. The image of $U(x, y)$ is read on the Z axis. We can imagine making a horizontal cut in $U(x, y)$, which indicates a level of utility (or satisfaction), and we can project that horizontal cut onto the XY plane. For a part of that projection, we will be able to measure combinations of quantities of goods X and Y for which the levels of utility are exactly the same. Part of the projections of those level curves onto the XY plane carry a name: they are called "indifference curves". Thus, if the coordinates (x_1, y_1) and (x_2, y_2) belong to the same indifference curve, it means that the level of satisfaction from consuming (x_1, y_1) is identically the same as the level of satisfaction from consuming (x_2, y_2): $U(x_1, y_1) = U(x_2, y_2)$.

The so-called demand function, which measures the inverse relationship between the price of a good and its quantity demanded, can be obtained via an optimization procedure, which involves maximizing a utility function subject to a so-called budget constraint. The budget constraint is a very simple object: it sets the expenditure (i.e., $p_x x + p_y y$, where p_x and p_y are denoting the prices of goods X and Y respectively) against a given income, I. The value of x and y which solve $\max U(x, y)$ subject to $p_x x + p_y y = I$ will constitute what is demanded of goods X and Y. The connection between the price of the good and the quantity demanded will yield the demand function. The situation is very similar to deriving the so-called supply function of a good, which essentially indicates that the higher the price, the more one wants to supply of a good.

The approach by Baaquie. A really poignant and successful approach which uses a formalism from statistical mechanics in economics is the contribution by Belal Baaquie. There are two good reasons to argue his approach is important:

(i) It argues for a physics formalism which can be *directly* used as a "model input" into a very fundamental building block of economic theory.
(ii) The approach has been empirically tested several times and the results are very promising.

To be able to successfully apply a physics formalism directly into a basic-building-block model in economics is a very challenging task. One needs to really show the economics model itself is *augmented* by doing so. Let us carefully weigh our words: the stress is on augmenting knowledge. Those applications are rare and we believe, the use of the quantum probability rule in DM is another example of such a type of successful application. We will briefly discuss DM in this part of the book but a much more advanced treatment is provided for in part III of the book.

Baaquie's paper is probably one of the first papers which looks at the very basics of micro-economic theory from a physics perspective. There is a lot of work where physicists approach problems in economics, but such work often focuses more on "symptoms" rather than on "models". We must keep this in mind.

In a nutshell, the approach by Baaquie revolves around:

• Defining a potential function $\mathcal{V}[\mathbf{p}]$ as a function, which *combines* supply and demand into a single entity,
• The emergence of stationary prices follows from the minimization of the microeconomic potential,
• Dynamics are added via the kinetic term,
• An expansion around the minimum of the potential is defined.

Following Baaquie [8], a demand function is proposed: $\mathcal{D}[\mathbf{p}] = \frac{m}{2}\sum_{i=1}^{N}\frac{d_i}{p_i^a}$; where a_i, $d_i > 0$ and a_i identifies the demand for a specific commodity; d_i is determined by the relative importance of quantity q_i in the demand for the total collection of N commodities. a_i and d_i affect respectively the slope and the location of the demand function (all *ceteris paribus*); m is budget income and p is the price of the commodity. The supply function is also proposed: $\mathcal{S}(\mathbf{p}) = \frac{m}{2}\sum_{i=1}^{N}s_i p_i^{b_i}$; where b_i; $s_i > 0$.

The key starting point in the approach by Baaquie is

$$\mathcal{V}[\mathbf{p}] \equiv \mathcal{D}[\mathbf{p}] + \mathcal{S}[\mathbf{p}]. \tag{9.24}$$

A key result is that

$$\left.\frac{\partial\mathcal{V}[\mathbf{p}]}{\partial p_i}\right|_{\mathbf{p}=\mathbf{p}_0} = 0 \Longrightarrow p_{0i} = \left(\frac{a_i d_i}{b_i s_i}\right)^{\frac{1}{a_i+b_i}}; \tag{9.25}$$

This is a result which augments the classical microeconomics result which yields: $p_i^* = (\frac{d_i}{s_i})^{1/(a_i+b_i)}$. For the case of $a = b$, the two approaches yield the same answer (a and b are shape parameters in respectively demand and supply functions). We note that a probability density function can be constructed, which indicates the highest likelihood of the price to occur at the minimum of the potential, i.e., when it is: $p_{0i} = (\frac{a_i d_i}{b_i s_i})^{\frac{1}{a_i+b_i}}$. More can be said though. The neighborhood around the minimum price can be parametrized. Baaquie [8] shows that if price grows at rate x, via $p = p_0 e^x$, one can write

$$\mathcal{L}(t) = \frac{m}{2}\left[L\left(\frac{\partial^2 x}{\partial t^2}\right)^2 + \tilde{L}\left(\frac{\partial x}{\partial t}\right)^2\right] + \frac{m}{2}\left[\frac{d}{p_0}e^{-ax} + sp_0 e^{bx}\right];$$

$$p = p_0 e^x > 0. \tag{9.26}$$

Baaquie shows that far away from equilibrium $x_i = \bar{x}_i + O(\sqrt{\frac{1}{m}})$. For a consumer with a large budget m, prices are very near $p_0\exp\{\bar{x}_i\}$ and fluctuate very little but as the budget becomes smaller and smaller, the fluctuations in the prices become larger and larger since the consumer now has to make (much harsher) choices. This leads to large changes in the uptake of certain commodities and hence leads to price fluctuations.

9.4. Option pricing and physics based partial differential equations

The theory of financial option pricing is most probably the most successful theory ever devised in finance. The so-called option pricing formulations provide for a fair price, in non-turbulent markets, of a so-called option contract. In the following section, we briefly introduce the idea of a financial option and we provide for a simple approach of pricing such an option. In a later section, we revisit the pricing with the help of the so-called stochastic approach.

9.4.1. *What are options?*

An option is a contract between a writer (seller) and a buyer. The contract will contain information on the exercise price; the time of exercise and the underlying asset. European call options give the holder of the contract the right to buy the underlying asset at a certain price (the strike price) at a precise time in the future (maturity date). European put options give the holder of the contract the right to sell the underlying asset at a certain price (the strike price) at a precise time in the future (the maturity date). American options can be exercised up to and including the maturity date. There are several factors affecting option prices, such as the (i) price of the underlying asset; (ii) strike price; (iii) time but also (iv) volatility and (v) the level of the risk free rate of interest. The so-called intrinsic value of an option is defined for the case of buying a "call" option as $\max(S - X, 0)$, where S is the price of the underlying asset and X is the strike price. For the buying of a "put" contract: $\max(X - S, 0)$.

One simple approach to derive a fair value of an option price is via the so-called binomial option pricing approach. The essential steps are as follows. We follow here Hull [60].[f]

---

[f]Many editions of the John Hull reference can be used.

We write the portfolio of long (buy) in shares and short (sell) in the option as: $S.u.\Delta - f_u$ for the case when the stock price goes up (with u the so-called up proportion; Δ some unknown quantity; f_u the value of the option when the price goes up). Similarly, we write the portfolio of long in shares and short in the option as: $S.d.\Delta - f_d$ for the case when the stock price goes down (with d the so-called down proportion; Δ some unknown quantity; f_d the value of the option when the price goes down). Remark the sign change: we have a minus sign because we have two opposing financial positions.

The objective now consists in finding an expression for Δ such that the portfolio is having the same return whether the price is up or down:

$$S.u.\Delta - f_u = S.d.\Delta - f_d, \qquad (9.27)$$

where from we can find that $\Delta = \frac{f_u - f_d}{Su - Sd}$. This quantity, Δ makes the portfolio to be risk free.

The expression above must equate with the cost of setting up the portfolio: $S.\Delta - f$ and hence one obtains then

$$\left(S.u.\Delta - f_u\right)e^{-rt} = S.\Delta - f. \qquad (9.28)$$

The option price at time $t = 0$ is denoted by f and by substituting Δ by $\frac{f_u - f_d}{Su - Sd}$ in $\left(S.u.\Delta - f_u\right)e^{-rt} = S.\Delta - f$, one obtains the price of the option:

$$f = e^{-rt}\left(pf_u + (1 - p)f_d\right). \qquad (9.29)$$

We note that p is the so-called risk neutral probability, which takes the form: $p = \frac{\exp(rt) - d}{u - d}$.

We will below come back on considering another pricing approach, using a so-called stochastic differential equation (SDE).

9.4.2. *Brownian motion and Einstein*

In the above development, we made the statement that the price of an asset, S (as quoted in the option contract) could go up or down; and we denoted this with respectively $S.u$ or also $S.d$. But this is a very vague statement. How can we be much more explicit, and maybe more precise, in detailing how S behaves over time? The academic finance community followed in the footsteps of Louis Bachelier [12], when it opted to use a version of the so-called Brownian motion to describe the evolution of S over time. In fact, it was Paul Samuelson, which we already mentioned in the introduction to this chapter, who picked up on the work of Bachelier in the 1960s (see [37, 38, 86]).

Option pricing theory will choose to use the so-called geometric version of Brownian motion, which we will begin to discuss in more detail below. Many articles have appeared on the topic of Brownian motion in both the physics and mathematics literature. A very accessible article is by Kac [64]. Using this beautiful article, we highlight some interesting issues relative to that stochastic motion. Kac's article treats the case of a so-called free particle. We note that forces are acting upon the particle from the surrounding molecules. When the motion of the free particle is projected upon the X-axis, Einstein[g] showed that the probability density function P which is found in $\int_{x_1}^{x_2} P(x|x_0; t) \mathrm{d}x$, where the integral indicates the probability the particle is between x_1 and x_2 at time t given the particle was at time $t = 0$ in position x_0, will solve the PDE:

$$\frac{\partial P}{\partial t} = L\frac{\partial^2 P}{\partial x^2}, \tag{9.30}$$

where L is a physical constant (more on this below). We note that the particle moves along the X-axis and it can move either to the right or to the left with 50% probability. We can make the remark that it is palatable to argue that such equal probabilities could be assumed if the position were to be substituted by for instance an asset price.

Under the usual probability conditions: probability must be nonnegative and the sum of all probabilities must add up to unity. The probability density function solving this PDE is the normal density: $P = \frac{1}{2\sqrt{\pi L t}} \exp(-(x - x_0)^2/4Lt)$. L can be shown to incorporate

---

[g]Einstein provided for the theory which showed that the so-called Brownian motion was a manifestation of molecular motion.

instantaneous velocity: if one thinks of a particle which moves left or right with distance Δ^h and it takes τ to make such a step then $L = \frac{\Delta^2}{2\tau}$. All of this is acceptable for a free particle, but with an outside force, which acts in the direction of the X-axis, a force factor needs adding

$$\frac{\partial P}{\partial t} = -\frac{1}{f}\frac{\partial (PF)}{\partial x} + D\frac{\partial^2 P}{\partial x^2}, \tag{9.31}$$

where F could denote gravity force for instance and f is a so-called friction coefficient. Kac [64] reports that it was Smoluchowski who showed the form of the above PDE.

The case of a so-called elastically bound particle is interesting. In fact, Kac [64, p. 380], reports that "It seems that Schrödinger and Kohlrausch [88] were the first to point out the connection between the Ehrenfest model and Brownian motion of an elastically bound particle." The force F in that case could be written as $F(x) = -bx$. Let us follow Kac [64, p. 379]. In a discrete setting, consider a particle which moves Δ steps to the left or to the right in a time period τ. Let R be an integer and let $k \in [-R, R]$. The probability of moving to the right is: $\frac{1}{2}(1 - \frac{k}{R})$ and the probability of moving to the left is: $\frac{1}{2}(1 + \frac{k}{R})$. As a simple example, let $R = 1$ and choose $k = 0.8$ then the probability to move to the right of 0.8 is $\frac{1}{10}$ while the probability of moving to the left is $\frac{9}{10}$. Now, the conditional probability that for a particle to be at position m, given a particle is at position n at time s, $p(n|m; s)$ will satisfy a difference equation but when one requires that $\Delta \to 0; \tau \to 0$ and $R \to \infty$ and[i] $\frac{\Delta^2}{2\tau} = D$ and $\frac{1}{R\tau} \to \gamma$, then $\frac{\partial P}{\partial t} = \gamma\frac{\partial(xP)}{\partial x} + D\frac{\partial^2 P}{\partial x^2}$ and the force $F(x) = -x/\gamma f$, where f is friction we hinted to already.

How is this now close to the Ehrenfest model? It is interesting to consider the Ehrenfest model, especially in light of the comment that the Brownian motion for an elastically bound particle is close

---

[h]Do not confuse this Δ with the "Δ" delta we mentioned as part of the elementary option price derivation.
[i]Kac [64] also mentions additional conditions.

to that model. The model is very intuitive. Consider two boxes, "box I" and "box II", and imagine that the *number* of balls indicate for instance the temperature. Consider an exchange of balls which is akin to an exchange of heat, assumed to be random. One can essentially think of isolated bodies with unequal temperatures. Assume there are a total of $2R$ balls in both boxes. The balls are all numbered. Draw a number between the number 1 and $2R$: pick up the ball and transfer it to the other box. Do this s times. The probability of getting $R + m$ balls given that you started with $R + n$ balls, after s times is: $p(R + n | R + m; s)$ and this can be seen as the same as $p(n|m; s)$.

This approach also has a very interesting other characteristic. Let us give an example. We still have our two boxes of balls. Assume "box I" has 10 balls and "box II" has 20 balls. Assume ball "3" is in "box I", so now move it to "box II". So now there are 9 balls in "box I" and 21 balls in "box 2". Repeat this process s times. Assume the time between drawings is τ. Then the total time this will take is $s\tau$. An interesting question is this: how long may it take to get to state n? In the context of our example, after s drawings, how long will it take to get back to 10 balls in "box I"? The answer is (see Kac [64, p. 386]): $\frac{\tau(R+n)!(R-n)!}{(2R)!} 2^{2R}$. Note that there is 100% certainty that there will be a point in time where we will reach again those 10 balls in "box I". As Kac [64, p. 386] indicates this certainty is the statistical analog of the "Wiederkehrsatz". The bigger the inequality in numbers between both boxes the longer it takes to revisit the state. Although there is no irreversibility here, i.e., there is a 100% certainty to revisit a state, the sheer length of time it may take may, of course, hint towards a degree of irreversibility of the process (see again Kac [64, p. 387], for more of a discussion).

We could formulate a Brownian motion as $dx = a dt + b dW$, where x is position; a is the drift parameter; dt is the infinitesimal change in time; b is the diffusion factor and dW is the Wiener process. We could also be a little more general in our definition and define the infinitesimal change in the value of x as $dx = a(x, t)dt + b(x, t)dW$ where $a(x, t)$ is now a drift function and $b(x, t)$ a diffusion function.

The concrete format $dx = adt + bdW$, can also be written, in discrete form as: $\Delta x = a\Delta t + b\epsilon\sqrt{\Delta t}$, where ϵ is a random variable taken from a normal density with mean zero and variance of unity.

We note[j] also that if we were to approximate dW^2, as ΔW^2 by a time interval Δt, then from an intuitive point of view, we could write $\lim_{\Delta t \to 0} \frac{\Delta W}{\Delta t}$ as: $\lim_{\Delta t \to 0} \frac{\Delta W}{\Delta t} = \lim_{\Delta t \to 0} \frac{\sqrt{\Delta t}}{\Delta t} = \infty$. What this shows, in a heuristic way, is that the ordinary time derivative on a stochastic path as defined by the above formalism, dx, is ill-defined. Hence, a different "differential formalism" is needed. Two well-known stochastic formalisms are either the calculus as defined by Itô or also the calculus defined by Malliavin.

We can graft the above development quite quickly onto a formal description of the evolution of an asset price process over time: if $x = S$ and S is a stock price, and we write the return $\frac{dS}{S} = \mu dt$ which yields when integrating over time: $S.\exp(\mu t)$, i.e., the asset price grows (in a continuously compounded fashion) with a rate μ. In fact, as is well known from high-school mathematics, $\lim_{n\to\infty}(1 + \frac{\mu}{n})^{nt} = \exp(\mu t)$, where n is the so-called frequency of compounding. Thus, in the absence of any Wiener process one can write: $\frac{dS}{S} = \mu dt$, while in the presence of such process one can write: $\frac{dS}{S} = \mu dt + \sigma dW$, where σ denotes the volatility (i.e., the variability of the return in percentage).

9.4.3. Exercises

Exercise 8. Is there a rationale in an asset pricing environment, to consider the equivalent of a "non-free" particle?

Exercise 9. Consider the one dimensional Brownian motion which describes the motion of a free particle. Explain (in words or in algebra) how in this context, the theory of Brownian motion as proposed by Einstein is closely related (or not) to the idea of using a Brownian motion in finance. From a financial perspective, name one argument

---

[j]This interesting heuristic argument comes out of Neftci [76].

which actually would invalidate (in a strict sense) the use of such a motion.

Exercise 10. Consider again the above question. In a finance environment, the assumed stock price path traced out by such motion poses a challenge for the use of ordinary derivatives. What is the main culprit for this problem? Briefly explain.

Exercise 11. Discuss how the Ehrenfest model does have potential relevance to finance. What is the analog of the Ehrenfest state in an asset price environment? Is there a feasible analog? Are those states recurrent within a financial context?

Exercise 12. Consider a SDE of the following format: $d\sigma = \alpha(\sigma) dt + \beta(\sigma) dW$; where $d\sigma$ denotes the infinitesimal change in the value of volatility, σ; $\alpha(\sigma)$ is some drift function of volatility; dt denotes the infinitesimal change in time; $\beta(\sigma)$ is some diffusion function of volatility; dW is a Wiener process. Now peruse the monograph by Wilmott [96] where it is shown that from empirical data you can estimate: $d\sigma = \alpha(\sigma) dt + v\sigma^\lambda dz$; with $v = 0.88$ and $\lambda = 1.05$. Describe how the author determines the form of the drift parameter. What assumptions are made?

9.4.4. *Some toolkit concepts which relate to stochastics*

If we want to heuristically define the concept of a so-called martingale within an asset pricing context, then in words, we might say that it will be the very last asset price observation which will serve as the best forecast for the unobserved, future asset price. If a martingale occurs in a financial environment, then we can write that the conditional expectation of the future asset price, S_{t+u} given all the information one has up to time t, i.e., I_t, is $E(S_{t+u}|I_t) = S_t$. The existence of a martingale implies there are no trends: $E(S_{t+u}|I_t) - E(S_t|I_t) = 0$. For continuous martingales, S_t: $E(S_t^2) < \infty$ (square integrability) and this has the important meaning that there is variability and there should be no jumps.

Following Neftci [76], we define the length of a trajectory as $V^1 = \sum_{i=1}^{n} |X_{t_i} - X_{t_{i-1}}|$ and the so-called "quadratic variation" as: $V^2 = \sum_{i=1}^{n} |X_{t_i} - X_{t_{i-1}}|^2$. Neftci [76], makes a nice heuristic argument which indicates that $V^2 \neq 0$ in a stochastic environment. The argument is quite straightforward: $\sum_{i=1}^{n} |X_{t_i} - X_{t_{i-1}}|^2 <$ $\max_i |X_{t_i} - X_{t_{i-1}}| \cdot \sum_{i=1}^{n} |X_{t_i} - X_{t_{i-1}}|$. If t_i gets very very close to t_{i-1}, then $\max_i |X_{t_i} - X_{t_{i-1}}| \to 0$ and this would mean that $V^2 \to 0$, unless $\sum_{i=1}^{n} |X_{t_i} - X_{t_{i-1}}|$ gets very large. We know though that a stochastic process must have a non-zero, finite, variance, therefore $V^2 \nrightarrow 0$ and $\sum_{i=1}^{n} |X_{t_i} - X_{t_{i-1}}| \to \infty$. Typically, one would also need to consider higher-order variations. Consider for instance:

$$V^3 = \sum_{i=1}^{n} |X_{t_i} - X_{t_{i-1}}|^3 < \max_i |X_{t_i} - X_{t_{i-1}}| \cdot \sum_{i=1}^{n} |X_{t_i} - X_{t_{i-1}}|^2,$$

and with the same argument that if t_i gets very very close to t_{i-1} then $\max_i |X_{t_i} - X_{t_{i-1}}| \to 0$, but now we know that $V^2 < \infty$ and therefore $V^3 \to 0$. We can make the same argument with higher order variations such as V^4, V^5, etc.

9.4.5. *Taylor series adapted for stochastic processes*

For a function $f(x)$ expanded around a value $x = x_0$ using Taylor series: $f(x) - f(x_0) = \frac{df}{dx}(x - x_0) + \frac{1}{2}\frac{d^2 f}{dx^2}(x - x_0)^2 + \frac{1}{6}\frac{d^3 f}{dx^3}(x - x_0)^3 + R$. If $\Delta x = x - x_0$ then we can rewrite this simply as: $f(x_0 + \Delta x) - f(x_0) = \frac{df}{dx}(\Delta x) + \frac{1}{2}\frac{d^2 f}{dx^2}(\Delta x)^2 + \frac{1}{6}\frac{d^3 f}{dx^3}(\Delta x)^3 + R$. If x is deterministic and Δx is very small, then Δx^2 will be even smaller. When x is random we can safely say that $E(\Delta x)^2$ will be non-zero but finite. Can we say anything about time? What about $E(\Delta t)^2$? Is time random? If it is not random, then it is reasonable to write that Δt^2 will go to zero if Δt is very small. A question which arises though is what happens for a random variable x when we need to consider Δx^3, Δx^4, Δx^5, etc. What about the cross terms (in the Taylor expansion): $\Delta x \Delta t$?

If we write a function f of two variables, S being the price of the asset and t is time, using the above expansion but now on two variables, we can write[k]

$$\Delta f = \frac{\partial f}{\partial S}\Delta S + \frac{\partial f}{\partial t}\Delta t + \frac{1}{2}\frac{\partial^2 f}{\partial S^2}(\Delta S)^2 + \frac{1}{2}\frac{\partial^2 f}{\partial t^2}(\Delta t)^2 + \frac{\partial^2 f}{\partial S \partial t}(\Delta S)(\Delta t) + R.$$

(9.32)

Neftci [76] provides for a "hands-on" rule, which says that if any part of the above expansion, denote it as $g(\cdot, \Delta t)$, when considered in ratio form as: $\frac{g(\cdot, \Delta t)}{\Delta t}$ disappears in the mean square sense then it can not be included in the expansion. If we assume the discrete change in the price of the asset S, ΔS, follows: $\Delta S = a\Delta t + \sigma \epsilon \sqrt{\Delta t}$, then let us number the terms above and apply the hands-on rule:

(1) $\lim_{\Delta t \to 0} \frac{\partial f}{\partial S}\frac{a\Delta t}{\Delta t} \neq 0$

(2) $\lim_{\Delta t \to 0} \frac{\partial f}{\partial S}\frac{\sigma \epsilon \sqrt{\Delta t}}{\Delta t} \neq 0$

(3) $\lim_{\Delta t \to 0} \frac{\partial f}{\partial t}\frac{\Delta t}{\Delta t} \neq 0$

(4) $\lim_{\Delta t \to 0} \frac{\partial^2 f}{\partial S^2}\frac{a^2 \Delta t^2}{\Delta t} = 0$

(5) $\lim_{\Delta t \to 0} \frac{\partial^2 f}{\partial S^2}\frac{\sigma^2 \Delta t}{\Delta t} \neq 0$

(6) $\lim_{\Delta t \to 0} \frac{\partial^2 f}{\partial S^2}\frac{(a\Delta t \sigma \epsilon \sqrt{\Delta t})}{\Delta t} = 0$

(7) $\lim_{\Delta t \to 0} \frac{\partial^2 f}{\partial t^2}\frac{(\Delta t)^2}{\Delta t} = 0$

(8) $\lim_{\Delta t \to 0} \frac{\partial^2 f}{\partial S \partial t}\frac{a\Delta t^2}{\Delta t} = 0$

(9) $\lim_{\Delta t \to 0} \frac{\partial^2 f}{\partial S \partial t}\frac{\sigma \epsilon \sqrt{\Delta t}\Delta t}{\Delta t} = 0$

As a result, for a process, $dS = adt + \sigma dW$, where S is the price of an asset, and a is the drift rate, while σ is the volatility and dW is the Wiener process, we would write: $df(S, t) = \frac{\partial f}{\partial S}(adt + \sigma dW) + \frac{1}{2}\frac{\partial^2 f}{\partial S^2}\sigma^2 dt + \frac{\partial f}{\partial t}dt$. This result is also the outcome of the so-called Itô lemma, which in effect can be seen as a Taylor series adapted for a stochastic environment.

It is interesting to also have a quick look at the meaning of a so-called Itô Integral. Here is a simple example, following Neftci [76]. Consider a function $f(W, t) = \frac{1}{2}W^2$. To find the Itô integral, $\int_0^t W dW$, one uses first the Itô lemma, assuming we are dealing with

---

[k]Note the use of continuous partial derivatives and the discrete change in the function f. We realize this is at best, heuristic.

a Wiener process, dW with a constant diffusion parameter of unity. We write: $df(W,t) = \frac{\partial f}{\partial W}dW + \frac{1}{2}\frac{\partial^2 f}{\partial W^2}dt + \frac{\partial f}{\partial t}dt$ and applying this onto: $f(W,t) = \frac{1}{2}W^2$, leads to: $df(W,t) = WdW + \frac{1}{2}dt + 0$. Then, $f(W,t) = \int_0^t WdW + \int_0^t \frac{1}{2}dt$ from where: $\int_0^t WdW = \frac{1}{2}W^2 - \frac{1}{2}t$.

9.4.6. *Exercises*

Exercise 13. Consider the function $f(l,t) = 17 + 2t + \exp(l)$. If we denote dl as the Wiener process, can you apply the above expansion to find an expression for $df(l,t)$?

Exercise 14. Differentiate the following function using Ito's lemma: $f(W_t,t) = e^{(\sigma W_t - \frac{1}{2}\sigma^2 t)}$, where W_t is a Wiener process.

9.4.7. *Option pricing: The stochastic approach*

In the binomial option pricing approach, we entered a portfolio which was long in shares and short in the option. A same portfolio is entered in the stochastic approach to option pricing. We follow again Hull [60]. The derivation is standard and can be found in many other basic option pricing textbooks.

We determine a portfolio value, Π, such that $\Pi = -F + \frac{\partial F}{\partial S}S$, where F is the option premium (or also the price of the option contract; or also the option pricing function); S is the price of the underlying asset; $\frac{\partial F}{\partial S}$ is the slope (towards S) of the option pricing function F.

The infinitesimal change in the value of the above portfolio, which we denote as $d\Pi$: $d\Pi = -dF + \frac{\partial F}{\partial S}dS$. The SDE, which underlines classical option pricing is the so-called geometric Brownian motion (it resists negative asset prices) and it is of the following form:

$$\bullet\ dS = \mu Sdt + \sigma SdW, \tag{9.33}$$

where μ is the expected return of the asset and σ the volatility. dW is the usual Wiener process. Recall our discussion of the Taylor expansion on two variables (adapted for a stochastic environment), which when applied using the above SDE, leads to

$$dF = \left(\frac{\partial F}{\partial S}\mu S + \frac{\partial F}{\partial t} + \frac{1}{2}\frac{\partial^2 F}{\partial S^2}\sigma^2 S^2\right) dt + \left(\frac{\partial F}{\partial S}\right)\sigma S dW. \quad (9.34)$$

If one substitutes the dF equation (see above) and the dS equation (see above) into $d\Pi = -dF + \frac{\partial F}{\partial S}dS$, then one obtains

$$d\Pi = -\left(\left(\frac{\partial F}{\partial S}\mu S + \frac{\partial F}{\partial t} + \frac{1}{2}\frac{\partial^2 F}{\partial S^2}\sigma^2 S^2\right) dt + \left(\frac{\partial F}{\partial S}\right)\sigma S dW\right)$$
$$+ \frac{\partial F}{\partial S}\left(\mu S dt + \sigma S dW\right). \quad (9.35)$$

Upon simplification, one obtains

$$d\Pi = \left(-\frac{\partial F}{\partial t} - \frac{1}{2}\frac{\partial^2 F}{\partial S^2}\sigma^2 S^2\right) dt. \quad (9.36)$$

Since we do not have the Wiener process, and if one assumes there is no possibility of realizing a risk free profit (i.e., one assumes the absence of arbitrage), then $\frac{d\Pi}{\Pi}\frac{1}{dt} = r_f$, where r_f is the risk free rate. Using this assumption,[1] one obtains:

$$\frac{\partial F}{\partial t} + r_f S\frac{\partial F}{\partial S} + \frac{1}{2}\sigma^2 S^2\frac{\partial^2 F}{\partial S^2} = r_f F. \quad (9.37)$$

This is the Black–Scholes PDE. This PDE is also known under the name of the backward Kolmogorov PDE[m] and it can be solved via the use of the heat equation approach.

Other ways exist to solving for the price of the option. In Haven and Khrennikov [49, p. 49–53], we provide for the relevant references and we go into quite some detail. The base of the approach is provided for in Neftci [76]. In a nutshell, we can provide for the following essential steps. An asset price: $S_t = S_0 \exp(Y_t)$ is proposed and Y_t follows a normal PDF with mean μt and variance $\sigma^2 t$. Then one can

---

[1]A discussion can also be had on the absence of the parameter μ. We do not pursue it here.
[m]The forward Kolmogorov PDE is also known as the Fokker–Planck PDE. This PDE plays a central role in statistical mechanics describing the time evolution of a probability density function (of the position of a particle).

consider: $E\left[S_t|S_u; u < t\right] = S_u \exp(\mu(t - u) + \frac{1}{2}\sigma^2(t - u))$, with S_u non-random at time u.

The possibility of using a risk free rate of interest (which can be objectively sourced via financial newspapers for instance) is of key importance in option theory. In option pricing theory, there is no dependence on preferences for risk. Such preferences for risk will vary from one decision maker to the other and hence can not be interpreted as objective. It can be shown that by introducing a new probability measure: "$\widetilde{P}$", one now could claim

$$E^{\widetilde{P}}\left[(\exp(-r_f t)S_t|S_u, u < t\right] = \exp(-r_f u)S_u, \qquad (9.38)$$

where r_f is the risk free rate of interest. To obtain a martingale, one writes:

$$E^{\widetilde{P}}[e^{-r_f(t-u)}S_t|S_u; u < t] = S_u. \qquad (9.39)$$

Note that the normal PDF has the form $N\left(\left(r_f - \frac{1}{2}\sigma^2\right)t, \sigma^2 t\right)$. The starting point for finding the pricing formula for the call contract (i.e., which thus provides an expression for F in the Black–Scholes PDE) is:

$$C_0 = \int_{-\infty}^{\infty} e^{-r_f T} \max[S_T - X, 0]\frac{1}{\sqrt{2\pi\sigma^2 T}}e^{-\frac{1}{2\sigma^2 T}(Y_T - (r_f - \frac{1}{2}\sigma^2)T)^2}\,dY_T.$$
$$(9.40)$$

9.4.8. *Exercises*

Exercise 15. Consider the so-called wealth approach in option pricing. Consult the paper of Bouchaud [20]. In that paper the average change of wealth is defined as $E(\Delta W) = E(\Theta(S - K))$, where $\Theta(.)$ is the Heaviside function. (a) describe precisely why a Heaviside function is employed; (b) describe precisely the meaning of the ϕ parameter in the set up of the wealth approach.

Exercise 16. Consult the paper by Cox, Ross and Rubinstein [36] and provide for the essential arguments which explain how the binomial pricing formula converges to the Black–Scholes equation.

Exercise 17. Denote, $E(S_T|F_t) = S_t(pu + (1-p)d)$ where F_t contains all information up to time t, $t < T$; where S_i is the price of the asset at time i; p is a probability and u is a number, which when multiplied with S_t gives the asset price when it moves up and d is a number, which when multiplied with S_t gives the asset price when it moves down. Explain what is a necessary and sufficient condition to obtain a martingale?

Exercise 18. Consider the Black–Scholes PDE. In basic option pricing the volatility is assumed to be constant. Is this a reasonable assumption? Discuss.

Exercise 19. Explain in your own words, why we cannot find an ordinary mathematical derivative of a Brownian motion path (when position is on the Y-axis and time is on the X-axis)

Exercise 20. In the derivation of the backward Kolmogorov PDE for option pricing, discuss what will be the issue if $\frac{d\Pi}{\Pi}\frac{1}{dt} \neq r_f$.

Chapter 10

Modeling Information with
an Operational Formalism

In the former chapter, we took a step back, by considering the classical mechanics framework and potential uses of that framework in a social science environment. Note the "step back" relative to the first part of the book, where we actually used second quantization, but in a way which is almost divorced from physics.

10.1. Elementary quantum mechanics

Part I of the book has informed us that there is, in fact, nothing un-natural to start using ideas from second quantization in social science. We believe that the interesting message we get out of Part I of the book is that we actually can avoid tying a physics formalism to social science. The formalism which Part I of the book presents is for a large part, "physics-free". As explained previously (at the beginning of this part of the book), Part II of the book centers on using first quantization and we attempt to apply formalisms from that stage of quantum physics to social science. We have been careful to provide also for a transition. Classical and statistical mechanical concepts are already embedded in some of the existing and very successful theories in finance, such as financial option pricing. There are also concepts which operate within both classical and quantum mechanics. Examples of this are the Hamiltonian framework which we discussed and also the idea of stationary action. The so-called quantum-like paradigm, does take a step back though (relative to the first part of the book) in that it really rationalizes the use of the formalism from the area of first quantization into social science, via the argument that the quantum mechanical wave function is a carrier of information.

In Chapter 3 of the first part of the book, we informed the reader about some of the basic mathematical elements of the quantum mechanical representation of a system. (i.e., not necessarily a physical system). Let us now enumerate some essential differences which distinguish quantum mechanics from classical mechanics:

- Position *and* momentum cannot be simultaneously determined.
- The state does not determine the value of the measurement performed on a system in this state.
- Quantum mechanics uses a complex[a] Hilbert space of states.
- Observables in quantum mechanics are represented by *Hermitian* operators (and this is also connected to the time evolution of states).
- Probabilities are defined as squared absolute values of complex amplitudes — Born's rule.[b]
- Quantum interference: quantum probability violates[c] the basic laws of classical probability theory; in particular, the law of total probability (see [66] for details).

---

[a]We note that the appearance of complex numbers in quantum theory is one of its mysteries. On first sight, there is no reason to expect that states have to be vectors with complex coordinates (i.e., values of physical observables are real and so are the probabilities of their realization).

[b]The Born rule determines quantum probabilities and establishes the basic relation between theory and experiment. Experimenters can calculate relative frequencies of occurrence of various values of an observable in a long-run measurements. The experience of thousands of experiments demonstrated the perfect matching of these frequencies with the theoretical prediction given by Born's rule. The latter is also one of the quantum mysteries. In spite of the tremendous efforts of experts working in quantum foundations (during the last hundred years), there is still no natural derivation of this rule (see [66] for details and discussion)

[c]In the quantum formalism, the violation of the law of total probability is expressed in the form of quantum interference. The latter can be observed in the famous two-slit experiment as well other interference experiments. Quantum interference is not interference of physical waves moving in space, cf. with interference of classical light. But this is interference of probabilities; so to say, probabilistic waves.

- Results of measurements are the eigenvalues of the operator which represents the observable.
- Quantum mechanics has entanglement.[d]
- Conservation rules involving important quantities like energy and momentum are still applicable in both classical mechanics and quantum mechanics. We must be careful though. One might have the impression that the notion of energy is the same in classical and quantum physics. However, we cannot assign to a quantum system in an arbitrary state the concrete value of energy, it can be in superposition. There is conservation of energy for eigenstates of the energy observable. See [65].

10.2. Elementary quantum mechanics in social science

A very intuitive idea which brings us almost immediately in connection with very basic quantum mechanics is the approach of "superposed" thoughts in which thoughts or ideas are formulated as kets. This idea was already formulated by Baaquie and Martin [11]. See also [49]. The superposed ideas can be written in this simple form:

$$|a\rangle = c_1|\text{idea}_1\rangle + c_2|\text{idea}_2\rangle + c_3|\text{idea}_3\rangle + \cdots \qquad (10.1)$$

with of course: $|c_i|^2$ = probability of each idea to occur in the superposed thought. Similarly, we could think of "values" versus the "price" of an asset, by simply writing that $|p\rangle = a_1|\text{value}_1\rangle + a_2|\text{value}_2\rangle + a_3|\text{value}_3\rangle + \cdots$; with, of course, $|a_i|^2$ =probability of each value to occur. We insist this is not an un-natural formulation. Most of us will, while reading a book, have other ideas "flashing" through our mind. We note that the price/value formulation above was also mentioned by Øksendal [80] where he very correctly observes that the stock price of a company only emerges when there is an

---

[d]Nowadays, entanglement is often considered as the main distinguishing and even characterizing feature of quantum theory. Such an exciting quantum effect as instantaneous action at a distance confirmed by the Bell test is a consequence of entanglement. In this book, we shall not pay much attention to entanglement (do not forget that this is a first course!). See [66] for details.

interaction with the market. Björk [16, p. 209], in relation to the paper by Øksendal [80], mentions that "In that paper the S process is no longer interpreted as the observed stock price. Instead, it is given the interpretation of an unobserved 'value' process, and the actual stock price is then produced through an 'observer' in a quantum mechanical fashion."[e]

Of course, to a large degree, this above equation, which symbolizes the superposition of idea or value states is an analogy. If one wants to "fine-tune" the above idea, then we could interject (in a critical way!) with questions such as

- how does the collapse of the wave function occur in this setting? Or also,
- "should we worry about the Copenhagen interpretation in this context?"

We can add "more oil on the fire". In Haven [51], we mentioned that, as is well known from basic quantum mechanics, orthogonal states remain orthogonal over time. Thus, if $\langle s_1(0)|s_2(0)\rangle = 0$ is valid, then at any other later time: $\langle s_1(t)|s_2(t)\rangle = 0$. This requires that the operator $\mathbb{U}(t)$, which acts on the ket at time zero, and the operator $\mathbb{U}^{\dagger}(t)$, which acts on the bra at time zero, must be unitary. As is well known, the non-unitarity of $\mathbb{U}$ would make the Hamiltonian (if there is one) non-Hermitian. Finally, since we talk about a Hamiltonian, we may well ask what the meaning is of the eigenvalues of the matrix of the Hamiltonian?

Let us go back to the simple "price-value" idea we mentioned above. If we think that "value states"[f] were an ingredient of the price of an asset, then there is no explicit good reason to claim that it must always be the case that orthogonal value states remain orthogonal over time. As we mentioned above, we could think of values versus

---

[e]Both the papers by Björk [16] and Øksendal [80] also refer back to a concept, known in quantum mechanics, by the name of the "Wick product".

[f](i.e., the value (as opposed to the price) we accord to an object).

price of assets: $|p\rangle = a_1|\text{value}_1\rangle + a_2|\text{value}_2\rangle + a_3|\text{value}_3\rangle + \cdots$ with of course $|a_i|^2$ = probability of each value to occur. Some other immediate queries arise such as

(i) Are the kets: $|\text{value}_1\rangle$; $|\text{value}_2\rangle$; $|\text{value}_3\rangle \cdots$ linearly independent?

(ii) Are those kets a basis for a space?

(iii) What is the meaning of the additive inverse: $|\text{value}_1\rangle + |-\text{value}_1\rangle = 0$?

These questions are answerable, but only in open-ended ways. Is this a problem? We need to make it clear that we do not use such a simple formalism to imply that superposed thoughts (as in the example above) *is* quantum mechanical in nature. This is not our claim and in fact we reiterate the idea of the so-called quantum-like paradigm, which we mentioned in the introduction to this part of the book. We maintain that the quantum wave function is informational in nature and the quantum formalism itself, becomes useful to model processes which are steered by "information". As we mentioned before, we stress that the quantum-like paradigm does NOT imply that macroscopic processes outside of the quantum physical scale exhibit quantum mechanical features. Such a position, like the quantum-like paradigm, does not carry seeds of destruction! As long as we can augment knowledge by using this formalism, we remain in a strong position. The deeper philosophical and/or physics meaning of what is behind the simple examples we just listed should *not* pre-occupy us. We take a very pragmatic stance to the use of the quantum formalism. In essence, we do "pick and choose" but as one will see, especially after reading Part III of the book, there is more depth in our approach than just plain pragmatism. Furthermore, let us not forget, Part I of our book! There a formalism was developed, which is essentially physics-free. Is there a contradiction to argue first, for a physics-free formalism and then to revert back to a "physics-bound" formalism in Parts II and III of this book? The essence of the quantum-like paradigm is such that it is not, *per sé*, "physics-bound".

10.2.1. *An example from finance*: *State prices*

In the example above, the kets were examples of states which are not observable. As is well known from basic quantum mechanics, quantum states do not have the usual coordinates we assign when we consider classical mechanically bound particles. Of course, from a quantum physical point of view, we may wonder whether the quantum state contains all the information. Again, this is a very deep debate which we will not enter in this book.

In finance, we have an interesting object, called the "state price", which is in effect also unobservable. The state prices form a major input in, what we could call, a non-event based probability. This type of probability we already discussed in the section on financial options. To get a feel that the probability definition which we used in the binomial option pricing model is in fact, arguably, non-event based, we can just consider how a risky asset price may evolve over time when we use such a probability measure. The usual argument, which is then formulated, is very simple. Consider the expected value of this risky asset, A, as $E(A) = pAu + (1 - p)Ad$ where u is the up proportion, which when multiplied with the price A, yields the price when the market is up; while the price when the market is down will be Ad. The alert reader may wonder where the values of u and d can possibly, objectively, come from. An argument can be made that such values depend on the past volatility of prices (see [60]). We do not expand on it in this book. If we now substitute the non-event based probability, which we mentioned in the section on what options are, i.e., $p = \frac{\exp(rt) - d}{u - d}$ in $E(A)$ above, we simply obtain $A \exp(rt)$, where r is the risk free rate of return. This is a very non-intuitive result: why is the return on a risky asset, with price A, to be risk free? We note that the risk free rate of interest is equivalent to the rate of return on a risk free asset. The rate is a variable, which to a large degree, is objectively determinable from any major financial publication. In effect, this is probably a variable which is closest to, what is being used in the sciences, an objectively measurable variable. Of course, prices of asset are also objectively determinable, but the argument we make here is slightly different: rates of return on *risky* assets are very difficult to determine. In other words, if a model needs as input, the return on a risky asset, then such a model has an immediate weakness. This is actually the beauty of the Black–Scholes model, which we covered before. No return rate of a risky asset needs to be included in that model.

To highlight the real character of unobserved states, as they occur in theoretical finance, we follow Neftci [76, p. 20–22]. We take the simple case of three assets and two states of nature.[g] As an example of the states of nature,[h] we could use say, for instance, "a good economy", which is state 1, and "a bad economy", which is state 2.

Assume, a bond[i] with a current price of 1 unit of currency, and a rate of return of $1 + r$ in both states, where r is the risk-free rate of interest. Consider then:

1. A risky asset which costs, now, $S(t)$ and will cost, in the future, at time $t + 1$, either $S_1(t + 1)$ or $S_2(t + 1)$; where the index i in S_i indicates the state of the economy.
2. A financial option which costs now, $O(t)$ and will cost in the future, at time $t + 1$, either $O_1(t + 1)$ or $O_2(t + 1)$.

The "non-arbitrage" theorem then says that if we have positive constants, c_1, c_2 so that the system of equations:

$$1 = (1 + r)c_1 + (1 + r)c_2$$
$$S(t) = S_1(t + 1)c_1 + S_2(t + 1)c_2 \qquad (10.2)$$
$$O(t) = O_1(t + 1)c_1 + O_2(t + 1)c_2;$$

is satisfied, then there are no arbitrage possibilities (and vice versa). The meaning of the existence of those non-arbitrage conditions is as follows. Essentially, an arbitrage opportunity is equivalent to an opportunity which gives rise to a riskless profit (i.e., a profit for

---

[g]See Part III of our book for the quantum-like representation of such states.
[h]We are not yet discussing state prices.
[i]A bond is a financial instrument which promises to pay a certain amount, x, in the future upon receipt of payment to own the bond (by the investor), now, of an amount y, and $y < x$ (if the interest rates a strictly positive). Many different types of bonds exist but this does not concern us in this book.

which no risk has been taken). In academic finance, to make sure we provide for asset price models which yield a benchmark price, we must assume they are free of arbitrage.

In the setting of such a non-arbitrage theorem, the quantities $(1 + r)c_1$ and $(1 + r)c_2$ will be equated to the so-called risk-neutral probability values, which we can denote as respectively, $\tilde{p}_1$ and $\tilde{p}_2$. We note the un-natural ingredients of those probability values: i.e., a risk free rate and *unobserved* state prices. We could easily make the argument that

$$|\text{state price}\rangle = a_1|c_1\rangle + a_2|c_2\rangle + \cdots \qquad (10.3)$$

with of course $|a_i|^2 =$ probability of each value to occur.

If we now go back to the idea of the quantum-like paradigm, the centerpiece argument is that the wave function is the carrier of information. In physics, this corresponds to the information interpretation of quantum mechanics, which was developed by several authors. We should mention first of all, Brukner and Zeilinger [21–26], Kofler [70], Zeilinger [97, 98], Chiribella *et al.* [31, 32], d'Ariano [2, 3] and Plotnitsky [81]. Those papers are fundamental for the position we take in arguing for the use of quantum-like methods.

This is a very interesting idea, which, in some sense, we can quite naturally embed in this non-arbitrage context. In order to spot the so-called arbitrage opportunities within very complex financial markets, the need for information is essential. We could make the following argument. Let the wave function, $\psi(.)$, be the carrier of information and let the probabilities values $\tilde{p}_1$ and $\tilde{p}_2$ be drawn (for given values of the integral) from the usual $\|\psi\|^2 = \int_{\mathbb{R}} |\psi(q)|^2 dq$. Let this information function, $\psi(q)$ correspond to the situation where there is no arbitrage. Assume now that information leads to the existence of an arbitrage opportunity. Hence, consider now an information wave function $\eta(q)$, which has a different functional form from $\psi(q)$. The probability values, $\tilde{p}_1^*$ and $\tilde{p}_2^*$, which now occur will trigger the existence of arbitrage and those values could be argued to be drawn from $\|\eta\|^2 = \int_{\mathbb{R}} |\eta(q)|^2 d(q)$. See [49] and also [52] for much more precise details.

In conclusion, we have a simple example here which shows that the change in the information wave function from $\psi(q)$ to $\eta(q)$ could trigger arbitrage.

10.2.2. *Quantum mathematics and finance*

So far in Parts I and II of the book, we have used two approaches that say: (i) we can develop, starting from second quantization, a formalism which is largely physics-free (Part I of the book); and (ii) the quantum-like paradigm which revolves centrally around the idea that the wave function is the carrier of information, and the formalism emerging from this approach can be used in social science. Belal Baaquie [7] provides for an approach which is quite closely allied to the second approach, i.e., the one of using so-called quantum mathematics in social science. The use of such mathematics is possible because, as per Baaquie [7, p. 1666] "... the interpretation of the symbols of quantum mechanics in such disciplines have no fixed prescription..."

We discussed option pricing theory in a former section of this part of the book. We can actually introduce quantum mathematics in this context. Baaquie [6, 7] interprets the option pricing function in an analogous way to the wave function in quantum mechanics, but the option pricing function is observable. A very interesting finding is that the so-called Black–Scholes Hamiltonian (in the no-arbitrage (martingale) formulation) which Baaquie [7, p. 1668] formulates:

$$H_{\mathrm{BS}} = \left[-\frac{\sigma^2}{2} + \left(\frac{\sigma^2}{2} - r \right) + r \right] \exp(x) = 0, \qquad (10.4)$$

where σ is stock price volatility; r is the risk free rate; and x is the growth rate of stock S (a typical underlying variable of an option contract). The key issue here is that H_{BS} is *not Hermitian* and the non-Hermiticity is intimately linked with the requirement of non-arbitrage.

10.3. Non-Hermitian Hamiltonians in modern quantum physics

As we mentioned before and also in Part I of the book (see Chapter 3), Hermiticity is an important property of quantum physics. Can we think of *non-Hermitian* Hamiltonians in quantum physics?

The standard presentation of quantum mechanics is fundamentally based on the consideration of *Hermitian Hamiltonians* (HH). We can safely say that "Hermiticity" belongs to the quantum physics "establishment".[j] We use the word "establishment" in the sense that any *departure* from the use of HH is treated as a departure from physics.

At the same time, in quantum mechanics, it is clearly stated that the dynamics with HH (given by the Schrödinger equation) describes only the evolution of *isolated systems*. If a system is not isolated and, for example, its exchange of energy with an environment leads to dissipation, then the dynamics of the system's state cannot be modeled with the aid of the Schrödinger equation. What can one do in such a case? It seems that the consideration of non-HHs would be the most natural step to solve this problem. However, mainstream physics did not choose this way, because of a few serious objections. We point to two of them:

- The eigenvalues of non-HH cannot be real, so one has to handle energies given by complex numbers.
- The law of conservation of probability can be violated,[k] so the probabilistic interpretation of the state of a quantum system is impossible.

Those objections resulted in making that the quantum physics of open systems evolved in a totally different way, i.e., without questioning the HH-postulate. The theory of open quantum systems is

---

[j]In Part I, we learned about some of the concepts which are part of that establishment (see Chapter 3).

[k]For HH-dynamics, the conservation of probability is the direct consequence of the unitarity of the evolution operator.

based on the quantum master equation, which we already briefly discussed before. See [79]. This equation does not preserve so to say "the wave representation" of a quantum state, as the vector of the complex Hilbert space. This theory handles generalized quantum states, which are mathematically represented by density operators, also called mixed quantum states (see Part III of this book). One of the main problems of the master equation approach is that typically it is difficult (if at all possible) to determine its coefficients on exact physical grounds. These coefficients contain the contribution of the environment, which is very complex. In physics, the majority of quantum master equations are of the phenomenological nature. The same can be said about the quantum(-like) master equations used in decision making (DM) and political science. See for instance, [4, 5, 68, 69].

Finally, we remark that the quantum master equation is derived as the trace (with respect to the environment's degrees of freedom) of the HH-dynamics of the compound system, unifying a physical system under study and its environment. Thus, in principle, the quantum master equation approach does not question the HH-paradigm.

Recent years have been characterized by the revolutionary change of the HH-paradigm of quantum mechanics (see [13]) and it started from a purely mathematical curiosity ("what would happen if we reject this assumption?"). Researchers elaborated extremely interesting and novel physical models based on non-HHs. Moreover, these models led to new exciting experimental studies. This revolution is based on the mathematical observation that even non-HHs can have real eigenvalues for some interesting examples (see below), and they are even non-negative. Moreover, important and physically interesting dynamics with non-HHs preserve probability and provide the possibility for the probabilistic interpretation of the quantum state. Thus, the non-HH generalization of Schrödinger's equation can lead to the state evolution having the basic features of the physically meaningful dynamics given by the standard Schrödinger equation. At the same time (at least in some cases), the non-HH generalization of Schrödinger's equation has a clearer relation to the physical phenomena than the corresponding quantum master equation. We remark that during recent years, non-HH modeling in quantum physics is flowering (more than two thousands publications and around ten conferences), see [13].

The possibility to model real physical phenomena with the non-HH dynamics can be very well illustrated by the following simple (but very important for applications) example (see [14, 15, 39]). Consider the Hamiltonian

$$H = p^2 + x^2(ix)^\epsilon, \qquad (10.5)$$

where $\epsilon > 0$ is a real number. This is a non-HH and one may think that the dynamics with such a Hamiltonian are physically totally meaningless. However, the dynamics have the aforementioned two basic properties of standard quantum mechanics: the energy levels are all real and positive if the parameter ϵ is positive and probability is conserved in time.

This recent non-Hermitian revolution in quantum mechanics stimulates the use of non-HHs outside of physics as well, e.g., in economics and finance.

10.4. Bohmian mechanics and social science?

The history of science will inform us that within the foundations of quantum mechanics several viewpoints exist. The interested reader may want to peruse key texts such as [63, 82, 83]. We will however, briefly discuss an approach, here, which is due to David Bohm and Basil Hiley. The main references about this approach are [17–19, 49, 59] for a discussion of the applications in social science, especially finance.

Bohmian mechanics is intimately associated with a formal object known as the "quantum potential". The interpretation of this object in terms of how it relates to the real potential, as used, for instance, in the second law of Newton is a topic of discussion in the literature.

See [59] for an excellent discussion. Here are a couple of interesting ideas which relate to this approach of quantum mechanics:

- An ensemble of trajectories exist if the "quantum potential" is non-zero.
- The ensemble of trajectories collapses to a unique trajectory when the "quantum potential" is zero.

The so-called quantum potential is very easy to obtain. One classical way of deriving it as follows. See, for instance, [59] for much more detail or also [49]. We follow below some of the steps in [33].

The wave function in polar form $\psi(q, t) = R(q, t)e^{i\frac{S(q,t)}{h}}$ where $R(q, t) = |\psi(q, t)|; S(q, t)/h$ is the argument of the complex number. Note that q is position and t is time. The wave function $\psi(q, t)$ is inserted into the Schrödinger equation:

$$ih\frac{\partial\psi}{\partial t} = -\frac{h^2}{2m}\frac{\partial^2\psi}{\partial q^2} + V(q, t)\psi(q, t). \tag{10.6}$$

Separating in real and imaginary parts, one obtains — two important equations,

$$\frac{\partial R^2}{\partial t} + \frac{1}{m}\frac{\partial}{\partial q}\left(R^2\frac{\partial S}{\partial q}\right) = 0, \tag{10.7}$$

called the continuity equation, and also

$$\frac{\partial S}{\partial t} + \frac{1}{2m}\left(\frac{\partial S}{\partial q}\right)^2 + \left(V - \frac{h^2}{2mR}\frac{\partial^2 R}{\partial q^2}\right) = 0. \tag{10.8}$$

For the latter equation, if $\frac{h^2}{2m} \ll 1$ and letting $\frac{h^2}{2mR}\frac{\partial^2 R}{\partial q^2}$ be small then this equation collapses to the Hamilton–Jacobi equation. We note that the term:

$$-\frac{h^2}{2mR}\frac{\partial^2 R}{\partial q^2}, \tag{10.9}$$

is called the quantum potential.

A Newton-like equation can now be written as

$$m\frac{d^2q(t)}{dt^2} = -\frac{\partial V(q,t)}{\partial q} - \frac{\partial Q(q,t)}{\partial q}, \qquad (10.10)$$

where $Q(q,t)$ is the quantum potential which depends on the wave function and the wave function evolves according to the Schrödinger PDE. The initial conditions are $q(t_0) = q_0$ and $q'(t_0) = q'_0$ (momentum).

An interesting question may be whether the state prices which we discussed above can be modeled to follow a path derived from $m\frac{d^2q(t)}{dt^2} = -\frac{\partial V(q,t)}{\partial q} - \frac{\partial Q(q,t)}{\partial q}$? In Haven and Khrennikov [49], we provide for some idea of the possible paths which can occur using the above extended second Newtonian law. In some sense, we could claim that the absolute value of the slope of V could be an indicator of the tightness (i.e., the likelihood) of the equilibrium price to be unique. In Haven and Khrennikov [49, p. 185], we argue for $-\nabla Q$ to be a so-called pricing rule.

We also note that, in recent work, Tahmasebi *et al.* [90] have estimated a quantum potential using real financial data. In effect, they estimate the quantum potential for the Standard and Poor's[1] index. One can estimate the quantum potential from the PDF on return data, for instance, by isolating the R function from the PDF and using it in the quantum potential. They do observe that the walls of potential widen with the time scale (from "daily" to longer time scales). The infinite high walls of the empirically estimated quantum potential do not allow for high variation in returns on short time scales.

It needs to be remarked that Bohmian mechanics has the characteristic to be non-local. This essentially means that the outcome of a measurement on one particle is instantaneously noticeable on another particle. Particles may be located in other galaxies. Distance does not matter. There is substantial literature available on the connection between non-locality and hidden variables. See the recent work of Hensen [58], which discusses the existence of non-locality

---

[1] The Standards and Poor's index is a major stock index. Other major indices are the Dow Jones index for instance.

as independent of hidden variables. For our macroscopic applications, non-locality of Bohmian mechanics is not so disturbing as non-locality in quantum physics. Non-locality of the financial market can be imagined in the following way. There are two time scales: (a) a very fine time scale corresponding to the rapid exchange of information (via computers and optical fibers) in the financial market; (b) a coarser time scale of DM at which traders of the financial market operate. Bohmian mechanics can be used to describe the process of DM. Formally such a model is non-local, but this is "coarse grained" non-locality. At the level of physical communications, the financial market is completely local.

We also need to mention an issue which revolves around the concept of factorizing the wave function. If one can claim that a wave function is writable as

$$\psi(x_1, x_2) = \psi_A(x_1).\psi_B(x_2), \tag{10.11}$$

where particle x_1 which is associated with ψ_A follows its own Schrödinger PDE, and similarly for particle x_2. Hence, particle x_1 and x_2 are in some sense independent, since they evolve according to their Schrödinger PDEs. Hence, we could claim that factorizability is akin to locality. In Bohmian mechanics, factorizability does not obtain; i.e., we must write that

$$\psi(x_1, x_2) \neq \psi_A(x_1).\psi_B(x_2). \tag{10.12}$$

10.4.1. *Smooth trajectories?*

Let us recall again the Newton-like PDE, which we also could term as the Newton–Bohm–Hiley equation:

$$m\frac{d^2q(t)}{dt^2} = -\frac{\partial V(q,t)}{\partial t} - \frac{\partial Q(q,t)}{\partial t}$$

and $Q(q,t)$ depends on the wave function and the wave function evolves according to the Schrödinger PDE. We can now make the argument that if $q(t)$ were to make up a trajectory such that $\sum_{i=1}^{n} |q(t_i) - q(t_{i-1})|^2 > 0$, then we have so-called non-zero quadratic variation. A stochastic process has non-zero quadratic variation. We discussed this already.

It is well known that the Bohmian trajectories exhibit smoothness, which does not allow for non-zero quadratic variation. This can surely call into question then to what degree such paths can then be used to reflect the dynamic evolution of prices?

In Choustova [33] and Khrennikov [66], a proposal is made to randomize the Newton–Bohm–Hiley equation in the following way:

$$m\frac{d^2q(t,\omega)}{dt^2} = -\frac{\partial V(q(t,\omega),t)}{\partial t} - \frac{\partial Q(q(t,\omega),t)}{\partial t} \qquad (10.13)$$

and $Q(q,t)$ is as before and the initial conditions are now different:

$$q(0) = q_0(\omega); p(0) = p_0(\omega) \text{ (momentum)}, \qquad (10.14)$$

but the initial conditions are now random variables (they give the initial distribution of prices and price changes) and ω is a chance parameter. Remark that $q(t,\omega)$ is a stochastic process. However, even with this randomization, one does *not* obtain non-zero quadratic variation. A subtle issue arises where one may wonder how the randomness in the Bohmian model would actually occur? Choustova [33, p. 31], makes the argument that "Bohmian randomness is not reduced to randomness of initial conditions...". She adds that (p. 31) "A really new impact is given by the essentially quantum randomness which is encoded in the pilot-wave function." See also [66].

One can make m (emission of number of shares) to become: $m(t,\omega)$ in the Newton–Bohm–Hiley equation and if mass can become zero at times, non-zero quadratic variation will occur. See also [34].

10.4.2. *Fisher information?*

Let us consider:

$$x_{\text{obs}} = x_0 + x \qquad (10.15)$$

and x_{obs} is an observed value; and let x_0 be the "true" value and x is the noise. Fisher information I can be defined as

$$\int \frac{1}{P}\left(\frac{dP}{dx}\right)^2 dx, \qquad (10.16)$$

where $P(.)$ is the PDF on noise "x". Consult [42] for much more on the topic of Fisher information.

When $P(.)$ is peaked around "x", it means there are little fluctuations and thus a lot of information. I relates to a measure of error and the error can be described as the (squared) distance between the estimate of the true value and the true value. The Cramer–Rao inequality is observed — $e^2 I \geq 1$, which indicates a trade-off between large error and little information (and vice versa).

It can be shown that the quantum potential has a proportional relationship to Fisher information. Reginatto [84] provides for the essential arguments. One can also look at the relationship between the quantum potential and Fisher information from the point of view of the "hydrodynamical approach" to quantum mechanics. The origins of this approach can be traced back to the work of Madelung [74]. The protagonist in the development of this theory (which generates a quantum potential) is by Nelson [77, 78]. It is straightforward to show that the osmotic velocity term in that theory can be related to Fisher information, which is itself related to the quantum potential. See [44, 45, 50, 71, 72] for more details.

It has been shown by Hawkins and Frieden [55, 56] that by optimizing Fisher information, one can establish links with a Schrödinger-like PDE. The minimum Fisher information solution, we mean thus the solution of the Lagrangian minimization, can be shown to follow, using real amplitudes $q(x)$ in $q^2(x) = P(x)$:

$$\frac{\mathrm{d}^2 q(x)}{\mathrm{d}x^2} = \frac{1}{4}\left[\lambda_0 + \sum_{n=1}^{N} \lambda_n f_n(x)\right] q(x). \qquad (10.17)$$

This follows a Schrödinger-like differential equation. See [57]. We note that $\lambda_n f_n(x)$ is a potential. The wave function within its format of a probability amplitude is now acquiring a macroscopic identity as a device, which can be used to formalize information.

Recall the discussion we had on state prices in the section on elementary quantum mechanics and social science. From a finance and purely non-arbitrage perspective, we could say a little more about the "probabilities" found from $q^2(x) = P(x)$ in the above Schrödinger-like differential equation. In a purely non-arbitrage context, the best we really could do is to formulate, "kets", as we mention in the section on state prices. We could write $\sqrt{s_1}|$ state1$\rangle + \sqrt{s_2}|$state2$\rangle + \sqrt{s_3}|$ state3$\rangle + \sqrt{s_4}|$ state4$\rangle +$ ....and state 1, state 2, etc... are states of the world. Financially, we could say one is willing to pay s_2 units of currency for say "1" unit of currency if state 2 occurs and nothing else if another state occurs.[m] We could make the statement: the more one is willing to pay — the higher one thinks the probability s_2 will be. In some sense, this is a subjective probability, which says that "my degree of belief that the next measurement will yield state 2 will be given by s_2".

Using our discussion on the quantum potential and the extended Newtonian law, we could actually provide for a simple example, which highlights the use of Fisher information. Recall the extended Newtonian law, with the quantum potential:

$$m\frac{\mathrm{d}^2 q(t)}{\mathrm{d}t^2} = -\frac{\partial V(q,t)}{\partial q} - \frac{\partial Q(q,t)}{\partial q}, \tag{10.18}$$

where Q is the so-called quantum potential. Assume an amplitude function[n]:

$$R(q) = c(q^2 + d), \tag{10.19}$$

$c, d > 0$; then:

$$Q(q) = \frac{-2}{q^2 + d}, \tag{10.20}$$

and the "force":

$$\frac{-\partial Q}{\partial q} = \frac{-4q}{(q^2 + d)^2}. \tag{10.21}$$

The price trajectory $q(t)$ can be found as the solution of the second law equation with initial condition $q(t_0) = q_0, q'(t_0) = q_0'$.

---

[m]This is an interpretation which can be found in Neftci [76] (albeit without any reference to the superposition of kets).

[n]See Khrennikov [66, p. 163] for this and another example.

The argument we can make is that the above does really have a link with Fisher information, since the quantum potential is closely related to Fisher information. Thus:

1. A pricing rule can be derived using the quantum potential as input.
2. The pricing rule forms part of the second law.
3. We can derive trajectories from that second law.
4. Within this mechanism sketched here: Fisher information and price trajectories coexist.

10.4.3. *Beyond analogies*

The former section introduced some examples by which we wanted to show that analogies with the formal frameworks, which interpret quantum mechanics from a Bohmian mechanics or also hydrodynamical approach, are usable. We note however the word "analogies".

The Bohmian approach has recently been put to the test in a macroscopic environment. Before any misunderstanding may occur, the results so far do not show that the macroscopic world is quantum mechanical. However, there are very interesting features which need mentioning. We remark those new results are accompanied by experimental testing. The key work in this regard is by Bush [29, 30]; Eddi *et al.* [40]; Fort *et al.* [41]; Hardesty [47].

In Haven [50], we provide for some of the details. In a nutshell, the model creates a so-called walking droplet and most importantly it exhibits the well-known wave–particle duality, a concept, every beginner student in quantum physics knows well. Bush [29, p. 274] mentions that "the guiding wave passes through both slits and the walker droplet "feels" the second slit by virtue of its pilot wave."

As we have remarked in Haven [50], the setup is interesting also especially because it embeds a memory property, i.e., the past behavior of the walking droplet will affect the current trajectory. In non-behavioral finance for instance, memory properties are often shunned and the martingale (which we defined previously) is a formal tool, which very explicitly indicates there is no memory. In Haven [50], we also provided for an example on an analogy of how the surface slope of the liquid "platform" will influence how the walking droplet behaves. Given the availability of very specific parameters that are present in the formal model, one may wish to think that such parameters can possibly be directly imported within a financial/economics setting.

10.4.4. *Exercises*

Exercise 21. Consider the quantum potential and the real potential. Describe the salient differences between both potentials.

Exercise 22. Assume stock prices could be modeled via the use of a Bohmian trajectory. What will be a major difference between such trajectory and a Brownian motion trajectory? What are the financial implications of this major difference?

Exercise 23. Using concepts from physics in a social science environment does require prudence. Discuss the problems which may occur when one wants to use the following concepts in social science (you can surely give an example as part of your discussion): Unitary operators; Conservation of energy; Non-locality.

Exercise 24. We saw several examples of how potential functions could be applied within a finance setting. Discuss the role of such potential function in the following cases (an example will aid greatly in your discussion): a time-dependent potential; a potential which is defined as the sum of demand and supply.

Exercise 25. Consider the following statement: "modern finance ...has not yet provided us with either the appropriate concepts or measures for the bounds on the minimal overall uncertainty that have to be present in an economy." (Shubik, M. (1999). Quantum economics, uncertainty and the optimal grid size. *Economics Letters*, 64(3), 277–278). Do you agree or do you not agree with this statement. Explain your decision.

Exercise 26. From a social science point of view, what is the difference in interpretation between the real potential and the quantum potential?

Exercise 27. How would you go about estimating the quantum potential when considering real financial data?

Exercise 28. Refer back to the non-arbitrage model. Can you explain how one can argue that a change in the information wave function can trigger arbitrage?

Chapter 11

Decision Making and Quantum Probability

11.1. Ellsberg paradox and elementary quantum mechanics

Decision making (DM) formalisms are very important within social science, since they provide for a platform upon which much more specialized theories can be constructed on. In economics, the various theories of expected utility are an example of such a platform. Given the enormous complexity of formalizing a DM process, it is certainly not surprising that some paradoxes may exist, which can weaken the formalism in question. See, for more details, [49, 66, 91, 92].

Consider the following scenario. Imagine participants who take part in an experiment on DM. Two activities are proposed, and participants need to decide which activity they prefer. This ranking of activities is conditioned upon the absence or presence of a precise piece of information (which can be deemed to be relevant to the ranking of the alternatives). This experiment (in various guises) has been repeated many times. In a quite consistent way, the following general result will emerge (see [91]):

- Experiment participants prefer to do activity "X" over activity "Y" if they KNOW that an event E_A has occurred.

- Experiment participants *continue* to prefer to do activity "X" over activity "Y" if they KNOW that an event E_A has NOT occurred.

- However: experiment participants prefer to do activity "Y" over activity "X" if they DO NOT KNOW whether the event E_A has occurred or not.

The above effect (also known as the "disjunction effect") violates the so-called "sure-thing" principle in the Savage expected utility framework (see [87]). The Savage expected utility framework uses subjective probabilities to calculate expected utility. This is a different framework from the so-called von Neumann-Morgenstern [95] framework, which uses objective probability in expected utility calculations.

Let us now bring in the so-called Ellsberg paradox (an example of the disjunction effect). For more background, see [49, 53, 66]. The Ellsberg paradox can be explained in the following way,[a] by simply using a two-stage gamble. You gamble the first time and then you decide to gamble a second time on the basis of you being told: (i) you won in the first gamble; (ii) you lost in the first gamble; *or* (iii) you have no information on how you did in the first gamble. The so-called sure-thing principle in economics says that:

(i) if you prefer to gamble the second time, knowing you won the first gamble and

(ii) you are preferring to gamble the second time, given you know, you lost in the first gamble,

then you should not object to gamble the second time even if you have *no information* whether you lost or won in the first gamble. This is intuitively appealing.

Tversky and Shafir [91] study finds that 69% of experiment participants will want to participate in a second gamble if they know they won in the first gamble. Almost 60% of experiment participants will want to gamble a second time if they know they lost in the first gamble. A really interesting observation is then as follows: 36% of the experiment participants will *not* opt for a second gamble if they have *no information* on either having won or lost in the first gamble.

---

[a]Many different ways exist to present this paradox.

Busemeyer and Wang [27, p. 92] (see also [28]) argue that in a Markovian model, one should find that "the probability of gambling in the unknown case must be the average of the probabilities of gambling in the two known cases". This is not the case when we consider the 36% relative to the 69% and the almost 60% gambling rates. The Markovian approach, which is described in Busemeyer and Wang [27, p. 91–92], revolves around the framework where there are (i) two states of belief on the outcome of the first gamble; and (ii) there are also two states of action ("gamble" or "not gamble").

In what we could call, the quantum-like approach, Busemeyer and Wang [27, p. 91–92], define basis states with the use of the following kets:

- $|WG\rangle$; (you simultaneously believe you won in the first gamble and you will undertake a second gamble);
- $|WN\rangle$; (you simultaneously believe you won in the first gamble and will not gamble);

and similarly for the basis states: $|LG\rangle$; $|LN\rangle$. The corresponding probability amplitudes are: $\psi_{WG}; \psi_{WN}; \psi_{LG}; \psi_{LN}$.

If there exists an initial state vector ψ and one gets the information you lost or won, then Busemeyer and Wang [27] propose that a unitary operator U is applied on $U.\psi$. Thus, as an example if you are informed you lost the gamble, then the initial state is transformed from $[\psi_{WG}; \psi_{WN}; \psi_{LG}; \psi_{LN}]$ to: $[0, 0, \psi_{LG}, \psi_{LN}]$ and an unknown state will be a superposition of the lost and win states.

As has been shown by many authors (see [49, p. 152–154] for many references), the quantum-like model can accommodate observed percentages by using the probability interference term. This, of course, also leads us into the difficult debate of what a "quantum probability" is as opposed to a non-quantum probability. We tackle some of those fundamental issues in Haven and Khrennikov [54].

In the well-known double-slit experiment, the so-called law of total probability is violated (see [49, p. 122–123]). The violation of the sure thing principle is narrowly related to the violation of this law. See [53]. The law of total probability can be easily illustrated as follows (see [49, pp. 122–123]). Let $a = +1$: "the democrats will win", $a = -1$ and "the negation", $a = +1$. An example for the b-variable: "you buy a condominium in midtown Manhattan", $b = -1$ and "the negation", $b = +1$.

The law of total probability is then

$$\mathbf{P}(b=j) = \mathbf{P}(a= +1)\mathbf{P}(b=j|a= +1) + \mathbf{P}(a = -1)\mathbf{P}(b=j|a= -1),$$

$$where\ j = +1\ or\ j = -1. \qquad (11.1)$$

For a rigorous treatment of total probability, see Part III of the book.

11.1.1. *Exercises*

Exercise 29. Consider the assertion that quantum mechanical techniques have aided in understanding better DM paradoxes. Given an example (and describe) one such DM paradox.

Exercise 30. Precisely explain what concept of quantum mechanics can aid in better understanding the paradox you described in the exercise above.

References — Part II

[1] Aoki, M. (1994). New macroeconomic modelling approaches: Hierarchical dynamics and mean field approximations. *Journal of Economic Dynamics and Control* 18, 865–877.

[2] d' Ariano, G.M. (2007). Operational axioms for quantum mechanics. In: Adenier, G., Fuchs, C. and Khrennikov, A. (Eds.). *Foundations of Probability and Physics-4*, 889, AIP, Melville, New York, pp. 79–105.

[3] d' Ariano, G.M. (2011). Physics as information processing. In: Jaeger, G., Khrennikov, A., Schlosshauer, M. and Weihs, G. (Eds.). *Advances in Quantum Theory*, 1327, AIP, Melville, New York, pp. 7–16.

[4] Asano, M.; Ohya, M.; Tanaka, Y.; Khrennikov, A.; Basieva, I. (2011). On application of Gorini–Kossakowski–Sudarshan–Lindblad equation in cognitive psychology. *Open Systems and Information Dynamics* 18, 55–69.

[5] Asano, M.; Khrennikov, A.; Ohya, M.; Tanaka, Y.; Yamato, I. (2015). *Quantum Adaptivity in Biology: From Genetics to Cognition*. Springer, Heidelberg.

[6] Baaquie, B. (2004). *Quantum Finance*. Cambridge University Press, Cambridge.

[7] Baaquie, B. (2013). Financial modelling and quantum mathematics. *Computers and Mathematics with Applications* 65, 1665–1673.

[8] Baaquie, B. (2013). Statistical microeconomics. *Physica A* 392(19), 4400–4416.

[9] Baaquie, B.; Du, X.; Tanputramana, W. (2015). Empirical microeconomics action functionals. *Physica A* 428, 19–37.

[10] Baaquie, B.; Du, X.; Bhanap, J. (2014). Option pricing: Stock price, stock velocity and the acceleration Lagrangian. *Physica A* 416, 564–581.

[11] Baaquie, B.; Martin, F. (2005). Quantum psyche: Quantum field theory of the human psyche. *Neuroquantology* 1, 7–42.

[12] Bachelier, L. (1900). Théorie de la spéculation. *Annales scientifiques de l'Ecole Normale Supérieure* 17, 21–86.

[13] Bender, C.M. (2016). PT symmetry in quantum physics: From a mathematical curiosity to optical experiments. *Europhysics News* 47(2), 18–2.

[14] Bender, C.M.; Boettcher, S. (1998). Real spectra in non-Hermitian Hamiltonians having PT symmetry. *Physical Review Letters* 80, 5243.

[15] Bender, C.M.; Brody, D.C.; Jones, H.F. (2002). Complex extension of quantum mechanics. *Physical Review Letters* 89, 270401.

[16] Björk, T.; Hult, H. (2005). A note on Wick products and the fractional Black–Scholes model. *Finance and Stochastics* 9(2), 197–209.

[17] Bohm, D. (1952). A suggested interpretation of the quantum theory in terms of hidden variables. *Physical Review* 85, 166–179.

[18] Bohm, D. (1952). A suggested interpretation of the quantum theory in terms of hidden variables. *Physical Review* 85, 180–193.

[19] Bohm, D.; Hiley, B. (2005). *The Undivided Universe*. Routledge, London.

[20] Bouchaud J.P. (2002). An introduction to statistical finance. *Physica A* 313, 238–251.

[21] Brukner, C.; Zeilinger, A. (1999). Malus' law and quantum information. *Acta Physica Slovaca* 49, 647–652.

[22] Brukner, C.; Zeilinger, A. (1999). Operationally invariant information in quantum mechanics. *Physical Review Letters* 83, 3354–3357.

[23] Brukner, C.; Zeilinger, A. (2009). Information invariance and quantum probabilities. *Foundations of Physics* 39, 677–689.

[24] Brukner, C. (2015). On the quantum measurement problem. arXiv:1507. 05255 [quant-ph]. Cornell University Library, New York.

[25] Brukner, C.; Zeilinger, A. (2005). Quantum physics as a science of information. In: Elitzur, A., Dolev, S. and Kolenda, N. (Eds.). *Quo Vadis Quantum Mechanics?* Springer, Berlin.

[26] Brukner, C.; Zeilinger, A. (2003). Information and fundamental elements of the structure of quantum theory. In: Castell, L. and Ischebeck, O. (Eds.). *Time, Quantum and Information*. Springer, Berlin.

[27] Busemeyer, J.; Wang, Z. (2007). Quantum information processing: Explanation for interactions between inferences and decisions. In: Quantum Interaction (Stanford University). *Papers from the AAAI Spring Symposium*. Technical Report SS-07-08. Bruza P. D.; Lawless, W.; van Rijsbergen, K.; Sofge, D. (Eds.); pp. 91–97.

[28] Busemeyer, J.R.; Bruza, P.D. (2012). *Quantum Models of Cognition and Decision*. Cambridge University Press, Cambridge.

[29] Bush, J.W.M. (2015). Pilot wave hydrodynamics. *Annual Review of Fluid Mechanics* 47, 269–292.

[30] Bush, J.W.M. (2015). The new wave of pilot-wave theory. Available at: http://math.mit.edu/~bush/?p=3087.

[31] Chiribella, G.; d'Ariano, G.M.; Perinotti, P. (2010). Probabilistic theories with purification. *Physical Review A* 81, 062348.

[32] Chiribella, G.; d'Ariano, G.M.; Perinotti, P. (2012). Informational axioms for quantum theory. In: d'Ariano, M; Fei, Sh.-M.; Haven, E.; Hiesmayr, B.; Jaeger, G.; Khrennikov, A. and Larsson, J.-A. (Eds.). *Foundations of Probability and Physics - 6*, 1424, AIP, Melville, New York, pp. 270–279.

[33] Choustova, O. (2007). *Quantum Bohmian Model for Financial Market.* Department of Mathematics and System Engineering. International Center for Mathematical Modeling. Växjö University, Sweden.

[34] Choustova, O. (2008). Quantum model for the price dynamics: The problem of smoothness of trajectories. *Journal of Mathematical Analysis and Applications* 346, 296–304.

[35] Cohen, R. (2013). Comments made upon a talk made by one of the authors (E. Haven) at Imperial College, London.

[36] Cox, J.; Ross, S.; Rubinstein, M. (1979). Option pricing: A simplified approach. *Journal of Financial Economics* 7, 229–263.

[37] Davis, M.H.A.; Ehtheridge, A. (2006). *Louis Bachelier's Theory of Speculation: The Origins of Modern Finance.* Princeton University Press, New Jersey.

[38] Davis, M.H.A. (2016). Model-free methods in valuation and hedging of derivative securities. In: Haven, E. *et al.*: *The Handbook of Post-Crisis Financial Modelling*; pp. 168–189. Palgrave-MacMillan Publishers, UK.

[39] Dorey, P.E.; Dunning, C.; Tateo, R. (2001). Spectral equivalences, Bethe ansatz equations, and reality properties in PT symmetric quantum mechanics. *Journal of Physics A* 34, 5679–5704.

[40] Eddi, A. *et al.* (2011). Information stored in Faraday waves: The origin of a path memory. *Journal of Fluid Mechanics* 674, 433–463.

[41] Fort, E., Eddi, A. *et al.* (2010). Path-memory induced quantization of classical orbits. *Proceedings of the National Academy of Sciences of the U.S.A.* 107(41), 17515–17520.

[42] Frieden, B. (2002). *Science from Fisher Information.* Cambridge University Press, Cambridge.

[43] Gallegati, M.; Keen, S.; Lux, T.; Ormerod, P. (2006). Worrying trends in econophysics. *Physica A* 370, 1–6.

[44] Gondran, M.; Lepaul, S. (2012). Indiscernability and mean field: A base for quantum interaction. *Lecture Notes in Computer Science* (LNCS) 7620, 218–226.

[45] Guéant, O. (2009) (quoted in Gondran and LePaul). A reference case for mean field game models. Cahier de la Chaire Finance et Développement Durable, 10.

[46] Haken, H. (1983). *Synergetics.* Springer-Verlag, New York.

[47] Hardesty, L. (2014). Fluid mechanics suggests alternative to quantum orthodoxy. M.I.T News Office. Available at: http://news.mit.edu/2014/fluid-systems-quantum-mechanics-0912

[48] Haven, E.; Khrennikov, A. (2016). *The Palgrave Handbook of Quantum Models in Social Science.* Palgrave-McMillan Publishers, UK.

[49] Haven, E.; Khrennikov, A. (2013). *Quantum Social Science.* Cambridge University Press, Cambridge.

[50] Haven, E. (2016). Links between fluid mechanics and quantum mechanics: A model for information in economics? In: Special Issue: *"Quantum*

Foundations: Information approach"; G.M. d'Ariano and A. Khrennikov (Eds.). *Philosophical Transactions of the Royal Society A* 374, 20150237.

[51] Haven, E. (2015). Why you want to borrow from my discipline? In: *Advanced Series on Mathematical Psychology*, Vol. 6 (*Contextuality from Quantum Physics to Psychology*). E. Dzhafarov; S. Jordan; R. Zhang; V. Cervantes (Eds.). World Scientific, Singapore, pp. 367–377.

[52] Haven, E. (2008). The variation of financial arbitrage via the use of an information wave function. *International Journal of Theoretical Physics* 47, 193–199.

[53] Haven, E.; Sozzo, S. (2016). A generalized probability framework to model economic agents' decisions under uncertainty. *International Review of Financial Analysis*. doi:10.1016/j.irfa.2015.12.002.

[54] Haven, E.; Khrennikov, A. (2016). Statistical and subjective interpretations of probability in quantum-like models of cognition and decision making. *Journal of Mathematical Psychology*. doi:10.1016/j.jmp.2016.02.005.

[55] Hawkins, R.; Frieden, R. (2012). Asymmetric information and quantization in financial economics. *International Journal of Mathematics and Mathematical Sciences* 1–11.

[56] Hawkins, R.; Frieden, R. (2015). Quantization in financial economics: An information theoretic approach. In: E. Haven and A. Khrennikov, (Eds.). *The Palgrave Handbook of Quantum Models in Social Science: Applications and Grand Challenges*. Palgrave-MacMillan Publishers.

[57] Hawkins, R.; Frieden R. (2014). *Fisher Information and Quantization in Financial Economics*. ESRC Seminar Series: Financial Modelling Post 2008: Where Next? (University of Leicester, UK).

[58] Hensen, B. *et al.* (2015). Loophole-free Bell inequality violation using electron spins separated by 1.3 kilometers. *Nature* doi:10.1038/nature.15759.

[59] Holland, P. (2000). *The Quantum Theory of Motion: An Account of the de Broglie–Bohm Causal Interpretation of Quantum Mechanics*. Cambridge University Press, Cambridge.

[60] Hull, J. (2012). *Options, Futures, and Other Derivatives*. 8th Edition. Pearson Publishers, London.

[61] Ilinski, K. (2001). *Physics of Finance: Gauge Modelling in Non-Equilibrium Pricing*. John Wiley and Sons, New York.

[62] Jammer, M. (2000). *Concepts of Mass*. Princeton University Press, Princeton.

[63] Jammer, M. (1974). *The Philosophy of Quantum Mechanics*. John Wiley and Sons, New York

[64] Kac, M. (1947). Random walk and the theory of Brownian motion. *American Mathematical Monthly* 54(7), 369–391.

[65] Khrennikov, A. (1999). Classical and quantum mechanics on information spaces with applications to cognitive, psychological, social and anomalous phenomena. *Foundations of Physics* 29(7), 1065–1098.

[66] Khrennikov, A. (2010). *Ubiquitous Quantum Structure: From Psychology to Finance*. Springer, New York.

[67] Khrennikov, A.; Haven, E. (2009). Quantum mechanics and violations of the sure-thing principle: The use of probability interference and other concepts. *Journal of Mathematical Psychology* 53(5), 378–388.

[68] Khrennikova, P.; Haven, E.; Khrennikov, A. (2014). An application of the theory of open quantum systems to model the dynamics of party governance in the US political system. *International Journal of Theoretical Physics* 53(4), 1346–1360.

[69] Khrennikova, P.; Haven, E. (2015). Instability of political preferences and the role of mass media: A dynamical representation in a quantum framework. *Philosophical Transactions of the Royal Society A* 378(2058) 20150106.

[70] Kofler, J.; Zeilinger, A. (2010). Quantum information and randomness. *European Review* 18, 469–480.

[71] Lasry, J.M.; Lions, P.L. (2006). Jeux à champs moyen: I. le cas stationnaire. *Comptes Rendus de l'Académie des Sciences de Paris* 343(9), 619–625.

[72] Lasry, J.M.; Lions, P.L. (2006). Jeux à champs moyen: II. horizon fini et contrôle optimal. *Comptes Rendus de l'Académie des Sciences de Paris* 343(10), 679–684.

[73] Lux, T. (1997). Time variation of second moments from a noise trader/infection model. *Journal of Economic Dynamics and Control* 22(1), 1–38.

[74] Madelung, E. (1926). Quantentheorie in hydrodynamischer form. *Zeitschrift fur Physik* 40, 322.

[75] Matson, J. (2009). Benoit Mandelbrot and the wildness of financial markets. *Scientific American,* NewsBlog (March 13, 2009).

[76] Neftci, S. (2000). *An Introduction to the Mathematics of Financial Derivatives.* Academic Press, Oxford.

[77] Nelson, E. (1966). Derivation of the Schrödinger equation from Newtonian mechanics. *Physical Review* 150, 1079.

[78] Nelson, E. (2013). Stochastic mechanics of particles and fields. In: Quantum Interaction (7th International Conference). Atmanspacher, H.; Haven, E.; Kitto, K.; D. Raine, (Eds). *Lecture Notes in Computer Science* (LNCS) 8369; 1–6. Springer, Berlin.

[79] Ohya, M.; Volovich, I. (2011). *Mathematical Foundations of Quantum Information and Computation and its Applications to Nano- and Bio-systems.* Springer, Heidelberg.

[80] Øksendal, B. (2007). Fractional Brownian motion in finance. In: Jensen, B.S. and Palokangas, T. (Eds.). *Stochastic Economic Dynamics.* CBS Press, Copenhagen.

[81] Plotnitsky, A. (2002). Quantum atomicity and quantum information: Bohr, Heisenberg, and quantum mechanics as an information theory. *Quantum Theory: Reconsideration of Foundations.* Växjö University Press, Växjö.

[82] Plotnitsky, A. (2012). *Niels Bohr and Complimentarity.* Springer, New York.

[83] Plotnitsky, A. (2002). *The Knowable and the Unknowable: Modern Science, Non-Classical Thought, and the "Two Cultures".* University of Michigan Press, Ann-Arbor, MI.

[84] Reginatto, M. (1998). Derivation of the equations of nonrelativistic quantum mechanics using the principle of minimum Fisher information. *Physical Review A* 58(3), 1775–1778.

[85] Samuelson, P. (1977). *A Quantum Theory Model of Economics*. In: Collected Scientific Papers, Vol. 4; H. Nagatani and K. Crowley. M.I.T. Press, Cambridge, Massachusetts.

[86] Samuelson, P. (1965). Rational theory of warrant pricing. *Industrial Management Review* 6, 13–39.

[87] Savage, L.J. (1954). *The Foundations of Statistics*. John Wiley and Sons, New York.

[88] Schrödinger, E.; Kohlrausch, F. (1926). Das Ehrenfestsche model der H-kurve. *Physikalische Zeitschrift* 27, 306–313.

[89] Susskind, L.; Hrabovsky, G. (2013). *The Theoretical Minimum*. What You Need to know to Start Doing Physics. Basic Books. New York.

[90] Tahmasebi, F. *et al.* (2015). Financial market images: A practical approach owing to the secret quantum potential. *Europhysics Letters* 109(3), 30001.

[91] Tversky, A.; Shafir, E. (1992). The disjunction effect in choice under uncertainty. *Psychological Science* 3, 305–309.

[92] Tversky, A.; Kahneman, D. (1983). Extensional versus intuitive reasoning: The conjunction fallacy in probability judgment. *Psychological Review* 90(4), 293–315.

[93] van Kampen, N.G. (1981). *Stochastic Processes in Physics and Chemistry*. North-Holland.

[94] Verhulst, F. (1998). *The Validation of Metaphors*. Mathematisch Instituut (Utrecht, The Netherlands).

[95] von Neumann, J.; Morgenstern, O. (1947). *Theory of Games and Economic Behavior*. Princeton University Press, Princeton.

[96] Wilmott P. (1998). *Derivatives: The Theory and Practice of Financial Engineering*. John Wiley and Sons, New York.

[97] Zeilinger, A. (1999). A foundational principle for quantum mechanics. *Foundations of Physics* 29, 631–641.

[98] Zeilinger, A. (2010). *Dance of the Photons: From Einstein to Quantum Teleportation*. Farrar, Straus and Giroux, New York.

Part III

The Quantum-Like Paradigm with Advanced Applications

Chapter 12

Basics of Classical Probability

12.1. Introduction

This part of the book is devoted to the quantum-like operational representation of the process of decision making (DM) by cognitive systems, in particular, by humans. From the outset, we stress that this approach is *not* about deriving cognition from genuine quantum physical processes in the brain. In our approach, the brain is treated as a black box such that its information processing cannot be described classically. We shall proceed under the conjecture that information processing in the brain can be better modeled by using the mathematical formalism of quantum probability (QP), although the brain is a macroscopic system whose physical functioning is well described by classical physics. This conjecture is (at least partially) justified by the presence of plenty of experimental statistical data in cognitive psychology, psychophysics, game theory, and DM. This is data which does not match the basic laws of classical probability (CP).

In short, CP's approach to conditional probability generates strong constraints to the process of DM. The use of the QP model provides a possibility to relax these constraints. Thus, the main point consists in transiting from the CP conditioning given by the Bayes formula, $P(B|C) = P(B \cap C)/P(C), P(C) > 0$ (see below), to the QP conditioning defined with the aid of the von Neumann projection postulate (or more generally theory of quantum instruments).

We remark that in classical DM, the *rationality* of agents is defined as following from the Bayesian updating of probabilities. Thus, classical rationality is Bayesian rationality. Hence, by using QP conditioning, instead of CP Bayesian conditioning, the notion of rationality of decision makers will be generalized.

We start this part of the book with a brief introduction to CP and QP by emphasizing the role of conditional probabilities. Then, we proceed to a comparison of classical and quantum approaches to common knowledge and related problems of DM.

12.2. Classical probability

In the nineteenth century, George Boole wrote the book *An Investigation of the Laws of Thought on Which are Founded the Mathematical Theories of Logic and Probabilities* (see [20]). This was the first mathematical model of the process of thinking based on the laws of reasoning which nowadays are known as *Boolean logic*. This logic, also known as classical logic, plays a crucial role in information theory, DM, computer science and artificial intelligence and digital electronics.

Boolean logic serves as the basis of the modern (measure theoretic) probability model, which was formalized by Kolmogorov in 1933 [74]. We remark that the process of axiomatization of probability was very long, a few hundred years. Probability theory (as a mathematically rigorous formalism) is very young compared with geometry for instance. A variety of probability models preceded the modern Kolmogorov model. The main competitor of the Kolmogorov model was the frequency model of von Mises [95] (see also [65]), in which probabilities are per definition limits of relative frequencies for realizations of events in infinite sequences of trials — collectives (random sequences). The main problem of the von Mises approach was that he did not separate two notions, probability and randomness. To define probability, he needed to define properly randomness of an individual sequence of trials. The latter is a very difficult problem that has not yet been solved. von Mises' attempt to solve this problem is commonly treated as unsuccessful. However, it generated a wave of interest to the problem of the mathematical formalization of the notion of randomness (see [65]). We can mention three main streams in the modern development of the theory of randomness (see [65]): (a) randomness as unpredictability (the original von Mises approach which was developed by Church[a]); (b) randomness as algorithmic complexity (Kolmogorov, Solomonoff, Chaitin); (c) randomness as typicality (Martin–Löf stimulated by Kolmogorov's lectures in Moscow in the 1960s). This attempt to combine from the very beginning probability and randomness as well as treating probability not as a purely mathematical theory, but similarly to a physical theory (e.g., as hydrodynamics), led to an extensive critique of the frequency probability theory of von Mises and stimulated the spreading of the Kolmogorov theory. The latter handles solely probability without direct relevance to randomness and this makes life much easier. Finally, we remark that the final period of the formalization of CP theory (von Mises and Kolmogorov activities) overlapped with the initial period of the creation of QP (see [96]). Thus, one should not consider CP as something old and well established and QP as very young and shaky. As formal mathematical theories, they appeared practically at the same time.

Now, we briefly discuss the Kolmogorov model. We remark that in discussions about quantum foundations, this model is typically mentioned as 'classical probability' (CP) and nowadays von Mises' "classical probability" is practically forgotten. The Kolmogorov model is based on the representation of events by sets, subsets of some set Ω, the *sample space*, or *space of elementary events*. The system of sets representing events, say $\mathcal{F}$, matches with the operations of Boolean logics; $\mathcal{F}$ is a so-called σ-algebra of sets.[b] It is closed with respect to the (Boolean) operations of (countable) union, intersection, and complement (or in logical terms "and, or, not"). Thus, by applying any theorem of probability theory, e.g., the central

---

[a]In fact, Church started to work on the theory of the algorithm where he attempted to formalize mathematically von Mises' collectives.

[b]Here the symbol σ encodes "countable". In American terminology, such systems of subsets are called σ-fields.

limit theorem, we use classical Boolean logic. We remark that at the beginning, Kolmogorov played a lot with possible structures of the system of events (see [65] for discussion and references). Thus even for him, the creator of the present model of probability, the structure of a σ-algebra was not something absolute. Kolmogorov pointed out that it may happen that, e.g., the intersection of two events cannot be treated as an event. However, finally he fixed the structure of a σ-algebra on the set of events, mainly by keeping in mind mathematical simplicity.

Mathematical formalism. The set-theoretic model of probability is based on the following two natural (from the viewpoint of classical logic) axioms:

- (AK1) events are represented as elements of a σ-algebra and operations for events are described by Boolean logic.
- (AK2) probability is represented as a probability measure.

For the convenience of the reader, we present the definition of a probability measure: p is a (countably) additive function on a σ-algebra $\mathcal{F}$:

$$p(\cup_{j=}^{\infty} A_j) = \sum_{j=}^{\infty} p(A_j),$$

for $A_j \in \mathcal{F}, A_i \cap A_j = \emptyset, i \neq j$, which is valued in $[0, 1]$ and normalized by 1, $p(\Omega) = 1$. A triple $\mathcal{P} = (\Omega, \mathcal{F}, p)$ is called the (Kolmogorov) *probability space*.

We also remind the definition of a *random variable* as a *measurable function*, $a: \Omega \rightarrow \mathbb{R}$. To define measurability, we have to introduce one special σ-algebra of subsets of the real line, the Borel σ-algebra $\mathcal{B}$. This is the minimal σ-algebra containing all possible intervals, $I = [a, b], (a, b], [a, b), (a, b)$. Then the function a is measurable if, for any set $B \in \mathcal{B}$, its pre-image $a^{-1}(B) = \{\omega \in \Omega: a(\omega) \in B\}$ belongs to the σ-algebra of events $\mathcal{F}$. Measurability can be (equivalently) defined in a simpler way. For measurability, it is sufficient that the inverse image of any interval belongs to $\mathcal{F}$, i.e., $\{\omega \in \Omega: a(\omega) \in I\} \in \mathcal{F}$. Moreover, it is sufficient to consider the intervals of the form $(-\infty, a)$, i.e., $\{\omega \in \Omega: a(\omega) < \alpha\} \in \mathcal{F}$ for any real number α.

Discrete random variables, i.e., variables taking finite or a countable number of real values, $a = \alpha_1, \ldots, \alpha_n, \ldots$, are simpler to handle and they are useful in many applications. A discrete function is measurable if all α_j-slices of Ω, the sets $\{\omega \in \Omega: a(\omega) = \alpha_i\}$, are events, i.e., they belong to $\mathcal{F}$.

In applications, random variables represent observables. This functional representation of observables is widely used in classical models of physics, biology, economics, finance, cognitive science, and psychology, but not in quantum physics (and novel quantum-like models outside of physics).

The following question deserves some attention: "should all physical observables be represented by *measurable functions?*" Since the Kolmogorov model is typically considered as "given by God" (as so it was during thousands of years with the Euclidean model in geometry), and since the property of measurability is firmly associated with the notion of a random variable, this question is practically never asked. It seems that only one person, Pitowsky [86], paid attention to this question. His answer was negative. Pitowsky assumed that some physical observables can be immeasurable and in this way he was able to construct a functional ("classical") representation of quantum observables. However, his proposal was totally ignored by the physics community and nowadays it is completely forgotten.

Finally, we remark that, for the same set Ω, we can consider various σ-algebras. Therefore, by considering measurability we always point to the fixed σ-algebra $\mathcal{F}$.[c] In particular, when Pitowsky considered the immeasurability of functions representing quantum observables, this was immeasurability with respect to the largest σ-algebra used in measure theory, the so-called Lebesgue σ-algebra (see e.g., [75]).

---

[c]We remark that even for the real line, one can consider not only the Borel σ-algebra. However, the definition of a random variable is rigidly coupled to the Borel σ-algebra.

12.2.1. *Bayes formula, conditional probability, and formula of total probability*

In the Kolmogorovian model, conditional probability is not derived in any way from the "usual probability". Conditional probability is *per definition* given by the *Bayes formula*:

$$P(B|C) = P(B \cap C)/P(C), \quad P(C) > 0. \tag{12.1}$$

By Kolmogorov's interpretation, it is the *probability of an event B to occur under the condition that an event C has occurred.* One can immediately see that this formula is one of the strongest exhibits of the Boolean structure of the model: one cannot even assign a conditional probability to an event without using the Boolean operation of intersection. Let us consider a countable family of disjoint sets H_k belonging to $\mathcal{F}$ such that their union is equal to Ω and $P(H_k) > 0$, $k = 1, \ldots$ Such a family is called a *partition* of the space Ω.

Theorem 1 (Formula of total probability (FTP)). *Let* $\{H_k\}$ *be a partition. Then, for every set* $B \in \mathcal{F}$*, the following FTP holds*

$$p(B) = \sum_k p(H_k)p(B|H_k). \tag{12.2}$$

To prove this theorem, one has to represent conditional probabilities in the right-hand side with the aid of the Bayes formula (so just using their definition) and then to use the (countable) additivity of probability.

This formula (FTP) plays a crucial role in classical DM based on the Bayesian procedure for *probability update* (PU). The events H_k are treated as hypotheses and the probabilities $p(H_k)$ as prior probabilities. Especially interesting for us is the case where a partition is induced by a discrete random variable a taking values $\{\alpha_k\}$. Here,

$$H_k = \{\omega \in \Omega : a(\omega) = \alpha_k\}.$$

Let b be another discrete random variable. It takes values $\{\beta_j\}$. For any β_j, we have

$$p(b = \beta_j) = \sum_k p(a = \alpha_k)P(b = \beta_j | a = \alpha_k). \tag{12.3}$$

Here, $p(a = \alpha_k) = p(H_k)$.

12.2.2. *Interpretation of probability: Statistical, subjective and their mixing*

Any scientific theory is a combination of the mathematics and its interpretation. We have briefly presented the mathematical structure of Kolmogorov's probability theory. Now we turn to its interpretation, the Kolmogorov's interpretation of probability (see [74]):

"[...] we may assume that to an event A which may or may not occur under conditions Σ, is assigned a real number $P(A)$, which has the following characteristics:

- (a) one can be practically certain that if the complex of conditions Σ is repeated, a large number of times, N, then if n is the number of occurrences of event A, the ratio n/N will differ very slightly from $P(A)$;
- (b) if $P(A)$ is very small, one can be practically certain that when conditions Σ are realized only once, the event A would not occur at all."

The (a)-part of this interpretation is nothing else than the frequency interpretation of probability, see the above discussion on the von Mises model of probability [95]. This is the essence of the *"statistical interpretation of probability"*, which is mathematically justified by the law of large numbers (a theorem in the Kolmogorov measure-theoretic mathematical model): frequencies converge to probabilities for almost all elementary events.

Before we analyze the (b)-part of Kolmogorov's interpretation, we recall the *subjective interpretation of probability* (see [38]). Instead of assigning to events objective weights, subjectivists assign to events personal weights, and each agent assigns to an event A her/his own degree of belief. This is personalization of probability.

The analysis of the (b)-part is more complicated. The referring to "to be practically certain" that "the event A would not occur at all" can be treated as a subjective element of Kolmogorov's interpretation of probability (see also the discussion below on Cournot's principle and Bernoulli's *moral certainty*). Since "practically" depends on the viewpoint of a decision maker, this is a step, although small (since here probability is treated objectively with objectification through calculation of frequencies), toward the subjective interpretation of probability by de Finetti [38]. For Kolmogorov, the objectivity of statistical probability is encoded in the complex of conditions (context) Σ, it is its objective property, determined by its repeatability.

We remark that, although the mathematical structure of the Kolmogorov model is commonly accepted, his interpretation of probability cannot be considered as the canonical one. Other authors by using the same notion of probability space may operate with different interpretations of probability. The situation is similar to quantum theory, where the same mathematical formalism based on the theory of operators in complex Hilbert space has a variety of very different interpretations. In fact, the majority of the probabilistic community uses either the statistical (frequency) interpretation of probability or the subjective interpretation and not the Komogorovian mixture of the statistical interpretation and Cournot's principle.

Cournot's principle. The (b)-part of Kolmogorov's interpretation of probability is also known as *Cournot's principle*. Its first version is due to Bernoulli (1713) who related mathematical probability to moral certainty/impossibility. "Something is morally certain if its probability is so close to certainty that the shortfall is imperceptible." (see [93, p. 4]). And, "Something is morally impossible if its probability is no more than the amount by which moral certainty falls short of complete certainty" (see [93, p. 4]). In spite of our above remark that there is a subjective element in the (b)-part of Kolmogorov's interpretation (and Cournot's principle (i.e., setting the level of moral impossibility)), those who used this principle treated probability objectively. Subjectivists, such as de Finetti, rejected it.

12.2.3. *Contextuality of Kolmogorov theory*

This reference to Σ is very important for our further considerations. Kolmogorov pointed out that each probability space is determined by its own complex of conditions (*context*) Σ. For example, he definitely would not be surprised if statistical data collected for a few different experimental contexts, $\Sigma_1, \ldots, \Sigma_n$, would violate one of the laws of probability; for example, the FTP. For him, in general, each of these contexts determines its own probability space

$$\mathcal{P}_{\Sigma_j} = (\Omega_{\Sigma_j}, \mathcal{F}_{\Sigma_j}, p_{\Sigma_j}).$$

Since the FTP was proven by working in a single Kolmogorov probability framework (the same probability measure was used to define all conditional probabilities in the right-hand side of FTP), the possibility of its violation in a multispace framework is not surprising. Unfortunately, this contextuality dimension of the CP model (which was so strongly emphasized in Section 2 of Kolmogorov's book (see [74]) has be washed out in the process of the further development of CP. Therefore, by seeing a violation of FTP, some people often make fundamental philosophic conclusions such as, e.g., the "death of realism". The latter means the impossibility to assign definite values of observables to chance parameters $\omega \in \Omega$ (in physics one speaks about hidden variables and one uses the symbols $\lambda \in \Lambda$.), i.e., the impossibility to construct the functional representation of observables $\omega \to a(\omega)$. Kolmogorov would defend realism, but at the same time emphasize its contextuality, i.e., the dependence on the experimental context. For Kolmogorov, one cannot speak about probability and random variables before the concrete experimental context is fixed. In quantum physics, people often do this. This started from Heisenberg and Bohr. We remark that, in fact, the Heisenberg uncertainty relation can be coupled to interference and violation of the FTP, as was shown by Feynman [44]. Thus, their anti-realistic attitude based on the uncertainty relation and the analysis of interference was partially a consequence of informally operating with probability. And the latter is explainable, since, as we pointed out, at that time, in the 1920s, the mathematical theory of probability had not yet been developed.

12.2.4. *Exercises*

Exercise 31. Consider the random experiment of n-times tossing of a symmetric coin, where n is a fixed number. Construct the probability space (denote it $\mathcal{P}_n$) for this experiment: the space of elementary events Ω, the σ-algebra of events $\mathcal{F}$ and the probability measure P.

Exercise 32. Consider on the probability space $\mathcal{P}_n$ the set of random variables $\xi_k, k = 1, 2, \ldots, n$, defined as $\xi_k(\omega) = 1$ if the result of the kth coin tossing is head and $\xi_k(\omega) = 0$ if the result is tail. Check that these are measurable functions. Find the conditional probabilities $p_{k|m}(\beta|\alpha) \equiv P(\xi_k = \beta|\xi_m = \alpha)$, where $\alpha, \beta = 0, 1$ and $k, m \leq n$. Are "acausal probabilities" $p_{k|m}(\beta|\alpha), k < m$, well defined?

Exercise 33. Write the FTP for the random variables $a = \xi_m$ and $b = \xi_k$. Is it useful for "acausal predictions", $k < m$?

Exercise 34. Solve the above exercises for the tossing of an asymmetric coin.

Exercise 35. Try to solve the analogs of the above exercises for the experiments with infinitely long coin tossing. [Note: this is a more complicated problem, especially the construction of the sigma-algebra and the proof of the σ-additivity of the probability measure.]

Exercise 36. Prove the FTP for the general probability space. [Note: this is an abstract, but simple task.]

Exercise 37. What would happen with the Kolmogorov interpretation of probability if its a-part were excluded? Would such an interpretation still be useful?

Exercise 38. What would happen with the Kolmogorov interpretation of probability if its b-part (Cournot's principle) were excluded? Would such an interpretation still be useful?

12.3. Classical decision making through the Bayesian probability update

The classical scheme of DM is based on the Bayesian PU. There is a set of states of nature $\Theta = \{\theta_1, \ldots, \theta_m\}$ (or "states of mind" in applications to cognition and psychology); a random variable A is given and it is taking values from the set $X = \{x_1, \ldots, x_m\}$; and for each state of nature θ one can get the probability distribution $\pi(x|\theta)$, $x \in X$.

As a starting point, say Alice assigns the probabilities to possible states of nature, $\pi(\theta)$. It can be considered as the probability distribution of a random variable B.

Alice then measures the random variable and updates the prior probability distribution on the basis of information gained from this concrete result of measurement. The classical PU is based on the Bayes rule which is a direct consequence of the Bayes formula defining conditional probability:

$$\pi(\theta|x) = \frac{\pi(x|\theta)\pi(\theta)}{p(x)}, \quad p(x) = \sum_{\theta} \pi(\theta)\pi(x|\theta), \tag{12.4}$$

where the last equality is the FTP (12.2).

In the formalism of PU and DM, instead of a collection Θ of states of nature (mind), we can consider a collection of *hypotheses* (H_k) forming the disjoint partition of the sample space Ω. The Bayesian PU can be used to update the probabilities of these hypotheses as the evidence $A = x$ appears:

$$\pi(H_k|x) = \frac{\pi(x|H_k)\pi(H_k)}{p(x)}, \quad p(x) = \sum_{k} \pi(H_k)\pi(x|H_k). \tag{12.5}$$

12.3.1. *Subjective and frequentist interpretations of classical Bayesian inference*

Bayesian inference is mathematically simple. However, its interpretation reflects the diversity of interpretations of probability. Originally (by Bayes) all probabilities in (12.4) were interpreted as *subjective probabilities* (see [38]). The prior probabilities $\pi(\theta)$ represent Alice's degrees of belief that the real state of nature (mind) is θ, prior to information about the value x of A. The same is valid for the conditional probabilities $\pi(x|\theta)$, i.e., likelihoods. These are degrees of Alice's belief that A would take the value x if the state θ were realized. The output $\pi(\theta|x)$ of PU (12.4) is the degree of belief that the state of nature is θ, in light of the information that $A = x$. This subjective probability viewpoint on the Bayesian PU is widely used and is known as Bayesianism.

However, the mathematical formula (12.4) can be interpreted in a totally different way, in the frequentist framework (see [95]). Here probabilities are assigned not to individual events, but rather they represent frequencies of realization of parameters in a long series of experiments. The values of the prior probabilities $\pi(\theta)$ as well as the likelihoods $\pi(x|\theta)$ are estimated on the basis of statistical data available before the measurements of A. The output of (12.4), $\pi(\theta|x)$, gives the probability that the state of nature is θ conditioned on the result $A = x$, i.e., in a long sequence of experiments, the frequency of realization of θ conditioned on the value x of A approaches $\pi(\theta|x)$ (see [95]).

For a subjective Bayesian, the probability distribution given by (12.4) reflects knowledge about the present state of nature (mind) after collecting data. For a frequentist, (12.4) does not reflect such knowledge: it is not about the "present state", as this state is the only unknown parameter, and $\pi(\theta|x)$ is its probability distribution.

The subjective approach can be used in DM to make an *individual decision*. Suppose that the parameter θ is dichotomous, $\theta = \theta_1, \theta_2$. The odds in favor of an event is given by the ratio of the probability it will occur to the probability that it will not, so one sets

$$O(\theta_1) = \frac{\pi(\theta_1|x)}{\pi(\theta_2|x)} = \frac{\pi(x|\theta_1)\pi(\theta_1)}{\pi(x|\theta_2)\pi(\theta_2)}. \qquad (12.6)$$

If

$$O(\theta_1) > 1 \qquad (12.7)$$

then Alice decides that the state $\theta = \theta_1$. In the opposite case she takes $\theta = \theta_2$.

The frequentist approach can be used in DM as well, but for decisions which can be repeated for many trials (in theory for infinitely many trials). Here, the odds-function (12.6) is used not for the individual DM, but for estimating the frequency of realization of the state of the world (mind) θ_1 compared to the state of the world (mind)

θ_2. Of course, not every DM can be embedded into the frequentist framework.

12.3.2. *Cromwell rule*

We point to one important feature of the classical PU and, hence, the classical DM model. For some state of nature (including the mind): if a decision maker, Alice, assigned to some state θ the prior probability zero, then any PU would lead again to a zero posterior probability. In this case, the Bayesian PU simply idles. It can thus be argued that such PU excludes any possibility to come to novel creative decisions. In the same way if $\pi(\theta) = 1$, then $p(x) = \pi(x|\theta)$ and $\pi(\theta|x) = 1$. Here again the Bayesian PU simply idles.

To escape Bayesian idling, one has to follow the so-called *Cromwell rule* (see [78]). In relation to what is mentioned above, Lindley [78, p. 104] indicates "...It is inadvisable to attach probabilities of zero to uncertain events, for if the prior probability is zero so is the posterior, whatever be the data." And the same author also indicates to steer away from probabilities which equal unity. In conclusion, "So never believe in anything absolutely, leave some room for doubt: as Oliver Cromwell told the Church of Scotland, '*I beseech you, in the bowels of Christ, think it possible that you may be mistaken.*'" (see [37, p. 448], [78, p. 104]).

Using the same symbols as above, the so-called *Cromwell rule* says that (see [78, p. 104]), $\pi(x|\theta) < 1$ ($\pi(x|\theta) > 0$) unless θ implies x is true (unless θ implies x is false).

Following the Cromwell rule is really important. As was pointed out, in classical Bayesian analysis departures from this rule can lead to paradoxical conclusions. Thus, all possibilities (even those which are "practically impossible") have to be taken into account by assigning them, although very small but nevertheless, non-zero probabilities $\epsilon > 0$. However, the use of the Cromwell rule leads to huge lists of possible states of nature (mind), which all have to be taken into account in the process of PU. It generates incredible computational difficulties. In the situation when a decision has to be made as quickly as possible, the applicability of the Bayesian PU is really questionable. Therefore, it would be attractive to proceed without this rule and at the same time to escape Bayesian idling. Such a possibility is provided by the quantum scheme of DM which is based on a generalization of the Bayesian PU.

Thus, a big enough state space is an important first step in the Bayesian approach to DM. From the start, we have to account even for the most inconceivable possibilities by considering the corresponding states of nature (e.g., that the moon is made of green cheese[d]).

In the quantum model, though, we are free to assign to them zero priors. Of course, the invariance of the extreme probabilities, zero and one, with respect to the Bayesian PU is just one of the symptoms of classical Boolean logic in the process of DM when modeled with the aid of CP.

---

[d]See Lindley [78, p. 104]: *"So leave a little probability for the moon being made of green cheese; it can be as small as 1 in a million, but have it there since otherwise an army of astronauts returning with samples of the said cheese will leave you unmoved."*

Chapter 13

Quantum Probability

13.1. Quantum probability: Pure states

The state space of a quantum system is based on a complex Hilbert space H. This is a complex linear space endowed with a scalar product, a positive definite non-degenerate Hermitian form. Denote the latter by $\langle \cdot | \cdot \rangle$. It determines the norm on H,

$$\|\phi\| = \sqrt{\langle \phi | \phi \rangle}. \tag{13.1}$$

This norm determine the metric $d(x, y) = \|x - y\|$ on H. This metric and the corresponding convergence of sequences (more generally topology) play the important role in mathematical models for quantum systems whose states are represented in infinite-dimensional Hilbert spaces. However, in the following considerations, we shall proceed with *finite dimensional Hilbert spaces*. Here, we shall not use convergence based on the distance d, and the norm is used just to denote the right-hand side of (13.1).

A reader who does not feel comfortable with the abstract framework of functional analysis can simply proceed with the Hilbert space $H = \mathbb{C}^n$, where $\mathbb{C}$ is the set of complex numbers, and the scalar product

$$\langle u | v \rangle = \sum_i u_i \bar{v}_i, u = (u_1, \ldots, u_n), v = (v_1, \ldots, v_n).$$

Instead of linear operators, one can consider matrices.

Pure quantum states are represented by normalized vectors, $\Psi \in H$: $\|\Psi\| = 1$. Two vectors Ψ_1 and Ψ_2 such that $\Psi_1 = \lambda \Psi_2$, where $\lambda = e^{i\theta}$, represent the same pure state. Thus, in fact, a state is determined by a normalized vector up to complex scalars with unit absolute value. In Section 13.3, we shall introduce a more general class of quantum states, mixed states. Therefore, it is now useful to underline the type of quantum states under consideration.

In standard quantum mechanics (QM), a quantum observable A is represented by a Hermitian operator, which we denote by the same symbol A. Since we work in the finite-dimensional case, any quantum observable has the spectral decomposition

$$A = \sum_i a_i P_i, \tag{13.2}$$

where a_i are eigenvalues of A and P_i are orthogonal projectors onto the corresponding eigen-subspaces. The system of mutually orthogonal projectors (P_i) is known as the *orthogonal partition of the unit operator*:

$$\sum_i P_i = I, P_i \perp P_k, i \neq k.$$

The reader who likes matrices and dislikes abstract operators can just use the theorem from linear algebra that any Hermitian matrix can be diagonalized, its eigenvalues are real and eigenvectors corresponding to different eigenvalues are orthogonal.

We remark that by the *spectral postulate* of QM, in any measurement of A, one can get only one of its eigenvalues a_i. In many physical considerations, the magnitudes of the eigenvalues of A play the crucial role. For example, they determine the energy levels of atoms and, hence, the spectrum of radiation. However, in quantum information, the magnitudes are not important. Here (a_i) are just labels. The latter viewpoint is very useful for our applications to DM (see Section 13.2).

Let there be given a state Ψ and a quantum observable A. By the basic probabilistic law of QM, *Born's rule*, the probability to get the number a_i as the result of a measurement is equal to

$$p(A = a_i) \equiv p(A = a_i|\Psi) = \langle \Psi|P_i|\Psi \rangle = \|P_i\Psi\|^2. \tag{13.3}$$

If after a measurement of the A-observable, one plans to perform a measurement of another observable B, represented by the Hermitian operator

$$B = \sum_i b_i P_i',$$

then one needs to know the output state resulting from the first measurement (through the feedback reaction of the measurement to the initial state). This post-measurement state is determined by the *projection postulate* of QM:

$$\Psi_i = \frac{P_i \Psi}{\|P_i \Psi\|}. \tag{13.4}$$

This is nothing else than the quantum analog of the classical rule for probability update (PU), which is now a transformation of a state and not a probability. As we pointed out, in QM it is known as the projection postulate and measurements inducing feedbacks of such a type are called *von Neumann–Lüders measurements*. We remark that the projection-type feedback to the state is only a special type of feedback considered in quantum theory. In general, quantum measurements are formalized via the theory of *quantum instruments* (see [85]). In this book, we shall not use this theory and restrict our considerations to von Neumann–Lüders measurements.

For the B-measurement following the A-measurement, the state Ψ_i plays the same role as the state Ψ has played for the A-measurement. By applying Born's rule to the initial state Ψ_i we obtain the following quantum rule for conditional probability:

$$p(B = b_j | A = a_i) = \langle \Psi_i | P_j' | \Psi_i \rangle = \frac{\langle P_i \Psi | P_j' | P_i \Psi \rangle}{\|P_i \Psi\|^2}. \tag{13.5}$$

We note that the conditional probability $p(B = b_j | A = a_i)$ also depends on the initial state Ψ: $p(= b_j | A = a_i) \equiv p(B = b_j | A = a_i, \Psi)$.

13.1.1. *Exercises*

Consider the Pauli matrices:

$$\sigma_1 = \begin{pmatrix} 0 & 1 \\ 1 & 0 \end{pmatrix}, \quad \sigma_2 = \begin{pmatrix} 0 & -i \\ i & 0 \end{pmatrix}, \quad \sigma_3 = \begin{pmatrix} 1 & 0 \\ 0 & -1 \end{pmatrix}. \tag{13.6}$$

These matrices are named after the physicist Wolfgang Pauli and they play an important role in quantum mechanics.

Exercise 39. Are the Pauli matrices Hermitian? Are they unitary? [Note: see Part I for the corresponding definitions.]

Exercise 40. Check the basic algebraic relations for the Pauli matrices:

$$\sigma_1^2 = \sigma_2^2 = \sigma_3^2 = -i\sigma_1\sigma_2\sigma_3 = \begin{pmatrix} 1 & 0 \\ 0 & 1 \end{pmatrix} = I$$

and (anti-commutation relations)

$$\{\sigma_a, \sigma_b\} = 2\delta_{ab}\,I,$$

check also that

$$[\sigma_1, \sigma_2] = 2i\sigma_3$$
$$[\sigma_2, \sigma_3] = 2i\sigma_1$$
$$[\sigma_3, \sigma_1] = 2i\sigma_2$$

Exercise 41. Find their eigenvalues and eigenvectors and construct the spectral decompositions, see (13.2).[a]

Exercise 42. Take the pure state given by the vector $\psi = \frac{1}{\sqrt{2}}(1,1)$. Find the conditional probabilities (13.5) for the observables $A = \sigma_2$ and $B = \sigma_3$ and then for $A = \sigma_3$ and $B = \sigma_2$. Do these conditional probabilities coincide?

---

[a]Eigenvalues can be obtained, e.g., from one of the above algebraic relations or directly by using linear algebra. We remark that here projectors from the spectral decomposition are one dimensional and correspond to projections onto the eigenvectors. Thus, each sum (13.2) contains only two summands.

Exercise 43. Now consider three observables $A = \sigma_1, B = \sigma_2, C = \sigma_3$ and the state $\psi = \frac{1}{\sqrt{2}}(1,1)$. By using the same machinery of the state update as for the definition of the quantum conditional probability (13.5), define the sequential-conditional probability $p(C = \gamma | A = \alpha, B = \beta)$. Is it equal to the probability $p(C = \gamma | B = \beta, A = \alpha)$?

We remark that in quantum physics the Pauli matrices represent the spin-$\frac{1}{2}$ observables (up to scaling by the constant factor). We also remark that this coupling with physics of spin is not important for our purpose, i.e., the applications to decision making and cognition. Nevertheless, it is useful to explore the mathematical formalism of quantum physics. In this way, we get to know a lot about the properties of the borrowed operator algebras. This is a good place to point out that our approach is of a phenomenological nature. In contrast to genuine quantum mechanics, in quantum-like modeling, we cannot start with a kind of "classical theory" analogous to classical phase space physics. Therefore, we simply borrow quantum operator algebras to match formally the features of observables used to describe the process of decision making. The spin operator algebras are excellent tools for such a purpose.

Now we move to the matrices representing the spin-1 observables (up to scaling by the constant factor). They have the following form:

$$\Sigma_1 = \frac{1}{\sqrt{2}} \begin{pmatrix} 0 & 1 & 0 \\ 1 & 0 & 1 \\ 0 & 1 & 0 \end{pmatrix}, \quad \Sigma_2 = \frac{1}{\sqrt{2}} \begin{pmatrix} 0 & -i & 0 \\ i & 0 & -i \\ 0 & i & 0 \end{pmatrix},$$

$$\Sigma_3 = \begin{pmatrix} 1 & 0 & 0 \\ 0 & 0 & 0 \\ 0 & 0 & -1 \end{pmatrix}. \tag{13.7}$$

Exercise 44. For spin-1 matrices, solve the analogs of exercises 39, 41–43 formulated for the Pauli matrices; use the state $\psi = \frac{1}{\sqrt{3}}(1,1,1)$.

Exercise 45. To work in the three-dimensional state space, one has to perform sufficiently long, although simple computations. Those who can use calculation software packages can try to write a program to compute quantum conditional probabilities for arbitrary pairs of

Hermitian matrices of any size. If such a program were written (and tested by calculations for the Pauli matrices), it would be easy to generalize it to compute sequential-conditional quantum probabilities of the form $p(B = \beta | A_1 = \alpha_1, \ldots, A_n = \alpha_n)$, where $B, A_j, j = 1, \ldots, n$ are arbitrary Hermitian matrices.

Exercise 46. By using the program discussed in the previous exercise, one can solve the analogs of the above exercises for the matrices representing the spin-3/2 observables:

$$\Sigma_1 = \begin{pmatrix} 0 & \sqrt{3} & 0 & 0 \\ \sqrt{3} & 0 & 2 & 0 \\ 0 & 2 & 0 & \sqrt{3} \\ 0 & 0 & \sqrt{3} & 0 \end{pmatrix}, \quad \Sigma_2 = \begin{pmatrix} 0 & -i\sqrt{3} & 0 & 0 \\ i\sqrt{3} & 0 & -2i & 0 \\ 0 & 2i & 0 & -i\sqrt{3} \\ 0 & 0 & i\sqrt{3} & 0 \end{pmatrix},$$

$$(13.8)$$

$$\Sigma_3 = \begin{pmatrix} 3 & 0 & 0 & 0 \\ 0 & 1 & 0 & 0 \\ 0 & 0 & -1 & 0 \\ 0 & 0 & 0 & -3 \end{pmatrix}.$$

From these considerations, the reader can see that a slight increase in the state space dimension makes the quantum calculations essentially more complicated.[b]

13.2. Quantum decision making through update of the belief state

We now apply quantum probability to model the process of PU and DM. We are interested in applications outside of physics, e.g., to cognition as well as DM in economics and finance (e.g., by agents of

---

[b]Thus, if the human brain really uses the quantum algebra (which is simply the linear space algebra), then it should have very powerful computational resources. However, there are no reasons to assume that the brain processes information as a digital computer. It may use other computational methods. For example, it can work as a quantum computer. But, for the moment, the latter assumption is not so well justified. The brain can essentially speed up information processing by working as a classical wave "device" (see [68]).

the market). Here it is natural to proceed with a subjective interpretation of probability, i.e., a probability expressing the degree of belief of a decision maker, say Alice. We remark that nowadays the subjective interpretation of probability is heavily debated in physics. At the end of the last century [46–50] elaborated a novel interpretation of QM based on this interpretation of probability, known as *quantum Bayesianism* (QBism). However, QBism cannot be considered as a commonly accepted interpretation of QM. At the same time, in applications to DM in psychology, economics, and finance the use of subjective probability is commonly accepted. Thus, one can say that we use QBism as the basis of a general theory of DM (see [57] for details).

There is given a complex Hilbert space H representing belief states of Alice. There are two given observables $B = \theta_1, \ldots, \theta_m$ and $A = x_1, \ldots, x_m$. The first one corresponds to the determination of the state of nature (of mind) and the second one to the collection of additional information (which will be used for PU). Denote the corresponding Hermitian operators by the same symbols, A and B. Here,

$$A = \sum_x x E_x^a \quad \text{and} \quad B = \sum_\theta \theta E_\theta^b,$$

where (E_θ^b) and (E_x^a) are orthogonal projectors corresponding to eigen-subspaces of these operators.

We consider the following PU-scheme. Alice creates an initial mental representation of the situation given by a pure quantum state $\Psi_0 \in H$, a *belief state* (thus here $\|\Psi_0\| = 1$). With the aid of this state, she assigns the subjective probability to the "states of nature" by performing direct measurements of B and she gets the prior probabilities:

$$\pi(\theta) = \langle \Psi_0 | E_\theta^b | \Psi_0 \rangle = \|E_\theta^b \Psi_0\|^2. \tag{13.9}$$

This observation is a process of DM about possible probabilities for θ.

In principle, we can proceed without the explicit assignment of the prior probabilities $\pi(\theta)$ given by (13.9). Thus, the prior measurement of the B-observable can be eliminated from the quantum scheme of PU. So, we can start simply with the preparation of the initial belief state Ψ_0 and its update resulting from gaining information with the aid of the A-observable (see below).

Now Alice wants to update the probabilities of θ on the basis of additional information from the measurement of A. By using the quantum rule for conditional probabilities, we get

$$\pi(\theta|x) = \frac{\langle E_x^a \Psi_0 | E_\theta^b | E_x^a \Psi_0 \rangle}{\|E_x^a \Psi_0\|^2}. \tag{13.10}$$

This is the basic quantum PU rule corresponding to observables of the von Neumann–Lüders type.

In the formalism of quantum PU and DM, instead of a collection Θ of states of nature (mind), we can consider a collection of *hypotheses* (H_k), which are represented by projectors forming a mutually orthogonal partition of the unit operator, $\sum_k H_k = I$.

As for the classical PU, the probabilities in (13.10) can be interpreted not only as subjective, but also as frequency based. This leads to two basic interpretations of the quantum state; (i) the subjective one structured as QBism (see the discussion at the beginning of this section), or; (ii) the statistical one represented by a variety of interpretations in the "spirit of Copenhagen" or in the spirit of the Einstein ensemble interpretation (see [65, 67, 87]).

By the subjective interpretation, Ψ_0, represents the belief state of Alice (i.e., representing her private beliefs). She first updates this state by measuring the A-variable (in general, this is a self-measurement performed unconsciously) and on the basis of this update, she assign new degrees of belief to the values of the parameter θ. We can speculate[c] that Alice's brain really uses the quantum-like representation of probabilities and that she makes decisions by using odds given by the quantum analog of the classical Bayesian odds (again in the case of the dichotomous θ):

$$O(\theta_1) = \frac{\pi(\theta_1|x)}{\pi(\theta_2|x)} = \frac{\langle E_x^a \Psi_0 | E_{\theta_1}^b | E_x^a \Psi_0 \rangle}{\langle E_x^a \Psi_0 | E_{\theta_2}^b | E_x^a \Psi_0 \rangle}. \tag{13.11}$$

---

[c]But just speculate, because quantum-like modeling cannot provide us with deeper insights to the brain's functioning. The brain is treated as a black box.

Thus, we can speculate that Alice's brain really computes (unconsciously) the quantity $O(\theta_1)$ and if it is larger than 1, she makes the decision that $\theta = \theta_1$.

By the statistical interpretation, (13.10) is not about the internal structure of the process of DM, but it describes the statistical distribution in a long series of DM-experiments.

The use of the subjective interpretation, in particular, of QBism, is more attractive from the viewpoint of modeling of cognition (see [57]). The statistical interpretation can be used to model statistical data obtained in experimental studies in psychology and psychophysics.

Proposition 1. *Quantum PU coincides with classical Bayesian PU iff operators representing observables commute.*

Proof. (a) Suppose that $[\widehat{A}, \widehat{B}] = 0$. In general (regardless of commutativity), by using the quantum rule for conditional probabilities, we get

$$p(x|\theta) = \frac{\langle E_\theta^b \Psi_0 | E_x^a | E_\theta^b \Psi_0 \rangle}{\|E_\theta^b \Psi_0\|^2}; \qquad (13.12)$$

we also have

$$p(x) = \langle \Psi_0 | E_x^a | \Psi_0 \rangle = \|E_x^a \Psi_0\|^2. \qquad (13.13)$$

For the quantum PU commutativity of projectors implies:

$$\pi(\theta|x)p(x) = \langle E_x^a \Psi_0 | E_\theta^b | E_x^a \Psi_0 \rangle = \langle \Psi_0 | E_x^a E_\theta^b E_x^a | \Psi_0 \rangle$$
$$= \langle \Psi_0 | E_\theta^b (E_x^a)^2 | \Psi_0 \rangle = \langle \Psi_0 | E_\theta^b E_x^a | \Psi_0 \rangle. \qquad (13.14)$$

In the same way,

$$p(x|\theta)p(\theta) = \langle E_\theta^b \Psi_0 | E_x^a | E_\theta^b \Psi_0 \rangle = \langle \Psi_0 | E_\theta^b E_x^a E_\theta^b | \Psi_0 \rangle$$
$$= \langle \Psi_0 | E_x^a (E_\theta^b)^2 | \Psi_0 \rangle = \langle \Psi_0 | E_x^a E_\theta^b | \Psi_0 \rangle. \qquad (13.15)$$

By using commutativity once again we obtain that $\pi(\theta|x)p(x) = p(x|\theta)p(\theta)$.

(b) Suppose that, for any state Ψ_0, PU is given by the Bayes rule. This means that

$$\langle\Psi_0|[E_x^a, E_\theta^b]|\Psi_0\rangle = 0 \tag{13.16}$$

for any pure state Ψ_0. For a complex Hilbert space, this necessarily implies that $[E_x^a, E_\theta^b] = 0$.

From the quantum PU rule (13.10), it is clear that this PU does not idle for $\pi(\theta) = 0, 1$. Thus, a quantum agent can ignore the Cromwell rule. This is a very important feature of PU in the QP-framework. Quantum PU can lead to novel creative decisions (as opposed to the classical PU, which idles for states θ with zero prior probability).

We remark that in the previous considerations, the initial belief state is a pure state. This assumption is quite natural from the psychological viewpoint: i.e., to start with a superposition of possibilities represented by a pure state. However, the scheme works as well for any initial belief state represented as a most general quantum state, a so-called mixed state, given by a density operator ρ (see Section 13.3). Observables A and B also can be of the most general form given by quantum instruments.[d]

A comparison of the classical Bayesian and quantum rules for PU is a novel and interesting topic for experimental research (see [57, 73], for the first steps in this direction).

13.2.1. *Exercises*

Exercise 47. For observables A and B given by the Pauli matrices, see (13.6), σ_2 and σ_3 and for the pure state given by the vector $\psi = \frac{1}{\sqrt{2}}(1, 1)$, find the output, see (13.10), of the quantum PU.

---

[d]Here, instead of Hermitian operators, observables are represented by so-called positive operator valued measures (POVMs). Such generalization is especially important for QBism, where the A-observable has to be an informationally complete POVM (see [49]).

Exercise 48. Do the same for A and B given by σ_3 and σ_2, respectively. Do the outputs of the PUs coincide? Can one find a pure state such that these updates would coincide?

Exercise 49. Give an example of a pair of observables and a state ψ for which quantum PUs coincide.

Exercise 50. For observables A and B given by the Pauli matrices σ_2 and σ_3 and for the pure state given by the vector $\psi = \frac{1}{\sqrt{2}}(1, 1)$, find the odds given by (13.11). Apply this to quantum decision making.

Exercise 51. For the same observables as in the previous problem, consider another state, say $\psi = (\sqrt{1/3}, \sqrt{2/3})$, find the odds given by (13.11). Apply this to quantum decision making. Modify this state and proceed with the state $\psi = (\sqrt{1/3}, i\sqrt{2/3})$. Is there a difference in decision making?

Exercise 52. Consider the analogs of the above exercises for the spin-1 and spin-3/2 matrices, see (13.7), (13.8).

The latter calculations are long and one may try to write a computer programme of the quantum PU for arbitrary matrices.

13.3. Quantum probability: Mixed states

As was remarked, pure states form a special class of quantum states. We now introduce quantum states of the most general type, mixed states. Start with a pure state, let $\Psi \in H, \|\Psi\| = 1$. Then Ψ determines an operator of the orthogonal projection on it, denote it P_Ψ. As with any projector, this operator is Hermitian and positive definite, $\langle \phi | P_\Psi | \phi \rangle = \|P_\Psi \phi\|^2 \geq 0$, for any $\phi \in H$. It is also idempotent, i.e., $P_\Psi^2 = P_\Psi$. As a one-dimensional projector, it has the trace equal one: $\mathrm{Tr} P_\Psi = 1$. To define the general class of quantum states (to extend the class of pure states), we relax one of these constraints: an operator representing a quantum state need not be idempotent, i.e., a quantum state is represented by any Hermitian (positive definite and trace one) operator ρ. Such operators are called *density operators*.

We remark that, since such a ρ is Hermitian, in the basis of its eigenvectors (e_k) it can be represented by the diagonal matrix

$\rho = \text{diag}(p_1, \ldots, p_n)$. Since ρ is positive definite, all p_j are non-negative and, since its trace equals to one, $\sum_j p_j = 1$. Thus the state-operator ρ can be represented in the form:

$$\rho = \sum_j p_j P_{e_j}. \tag{13.17}$$

This expansion can be considered as the probabilistic mixture, with probabilities p_j, of the pure states (e_j). Thus the state ρ represents an ensemble of quantum (or quantum-like systems) prepared in one of the pure states e_j. This is the motivation to call such states *mixed quantum states*.

There is given a state ρ (represented by a density operator) and an observable A (represented by a Hermitian operator $A = \sum_i a_i P_i$, where (a_i) are its eigenvalues and (P_i) are projectors onto corresponding eigensubspaces).

Then, by quantum theory, the probability to obtain the concrete value a_i as the result of measurement, is given by the Born rule; and for mixed states, it has the form:

$$p(A = a_i) \equiv p(A = a_i | \rho) = \text{Tr} \rho P_i. \tag{13.18}$$

This rule is the consequence of the Born rule for pure states (see (13.3), and the representation (13.17) for density operators).

However, if after measurement of the A-observable one plans to perform the measurement of another observable B (represented by a Hermitian operator $B = \sum_i b_i P_i'$), then one needs to know not only the result of the A-measurement, but even the output state ρ_{a_i}. This state is determined (for measurements of the von Neumann–Lüders type) by the projection postulate; and for mixed states, it has the form:

$$\rho_i = \frac{P_i \rho P_i}{\text{Tr} P_i \rho P_i}. \tag{13.19}$$

In fact, although we call this rule a postulate, it can be derived from the projection postulate for pure states (13.4) and the representation (13.17) for density operators.

For the B-measurement following the A-measurement, the state ρ_i plays the same role as the state ρ played for the A-measurement. In particular, by applying the Born rule (13.18) once again, we obtain

$$p(B = b_j | A = a_i) \equiv p(B = b_j | A = a_i, \rho) = \text{Tr}\rho_{a_i}P'_j = \frac{\text{Tr}P_i\rho P_i P'_j}{\text{Tr}P_i\rho P_i}.$$

(13.20)

In quantum theory, this probability is treated as the conditional probability. In the future, we shall often denote this probability as $p(P'_j | P_i)$, see the next section on quantum logic for a motivation.

13.3.1. *Exercises*

Consider the two-dimensional state space with the fixed orthonormal basis, say (e_1, e_2). Thus states can be represented as 2×2 density matrices.

Exercise 53. Let $\psi = (a, b)$, where $|a|^2 + |b|^2 = 1$. Represent this pure state by a density matrix. For which ψ is this matrix diagonal?

Exercise 54. Give examples of diagonal and non-diagonal density matrices which do not correspond to pure states.

Exercise 55. For the quantum states given by the density matrices from the previous exercise and the observables given by a pair of Pauli matrices, say σ_1 and σ_2, find quantum conditional probabilities (see (13.20)).

Exercise 56. Generalize the quantum PU scheme (Section 13.2) to a prior state given by a density operator. Take the states represented by the matrices which you found from Exercise 55 and consider for them all problems about PU and decision making from Section 13.2.1.

13.4. Events in quantum logic

Following von Neumann [96]; Birkhoff and von Neumann [19], we represent *events, propositions,* as orthogonal projectors in complex Hilbert space H.

For an orthogonal projector P, we set $H_P = P(H)$, its image, and vice versa, for a subspace L of H, the corresponding orthogonal projector is denoted by the symbol P_L.

The set of orthogonal projectors is a *lattice* with the order structure: $P \leq Q$ iff $H_P \subset H_Q$ or equivalently, for any $\Psi \in H$, $\langle \Psi | P\Psi \rangle \leq \langle \Psi | Q\Psi \rangle$. This lattice is known as *quantum logic*. Thus, in classical Boolean logic, events are represented by sets and in quantum logic events are represented by orthogonal projectors.

We recall that the lattice of projectors is endowed with operations "and" ($\wedge$), conjunction, and "or" ($\vee$), disjunction. For two projectors P_1, P_2, the projector $R = P_1 \wedge P_2$ is defined as the projector onto the subspace $H_R = H_{P_1} \cap H_{P_2}$ and the projector $S = P_1 \vee P_2$ is defined as the projector onto the subspace H_R defined as the minimal linear subspace containing the set-theoretic union $H_{P_1} \cup H_{P_2}$ of subspaces H_{P_1}, H_{P_2}: this is the space of all linear combinations of vectors belonging to these subspaces. The operation of negation is defined as the orthogonal complement:

$$P^\perp = \{y \in H \colon \langle y | x \rangle = 0 \colon \text{for all } x \in H_P\}.$$

In the language of subspaces, the operation "and", conjunction, coincides with the usual set-theoretic intersection, but the operations "or", disjunction, and "not", negation, are non-trivial deformations of the corresponding set-theoretic operations. It is natural to expect that such deformations can induce deviations from classical Boolean logic.

Consider the following simple example. Let H be a two dimensional Hilbert space with the orthonormal basis (e_1, e_2) and let $v = (e_1 + e_2)/\sqrt{2}$. Then $P_v \wedge P_{e_1} = 0$ and $P_v \wedge P_{e_2} = 0$, but $P_v \wedge (P_{e_1} \vee P_{e_2}) = P_v$. Hence, for quantum events, in general *the distributivity law is violated*:

$$P \wedge (P_1 \vee P_2) \neq (P \wedge P_1) \vee (P \wedge P_2) \qquad (13.21)$$

As can be seen from our example, even mutual orthogonality of the events P_1 and P_2 does not help to save the Boolean laws.

Thus, quantum logic relaxes some constraints set by classical Boolean logic, in particular, the distributivity between the operations of conjunction and disjunction.

As we have already seen in the previous chapters, the mathematical formalism of QM provides the novel and theoretically solid base for a variety of applications to cognition, and social science (e.g., economics and finance) (see [59] for one of the pioneering studies). Especially decision making is characterized by a high wave of interest to quantum-like modeling. We can point to a few recent monographs and reviews and references herein: [1–9, 13, 14, 24, 26–34, 39–42, 55, 56, 61–64, 67, 70–73, 76, 92, 97, 98] and see also [66] up to and including [90].[e] Since in these works the quantum-like approach to decision making was presented in high detail, we will not exert much effort to discuss this approach in general. We just remark that in quantum-like decision making, belief-states of decision makers are represented as quantum states (pure or more generally mixed) and the processes of decision making are modeled as quantum measurements. In the simplest models, these are measurements of the projection (von Neumann–Lüders) type (see [89–90]). More generally, these are quantum instruments which represent observables (decision operators) and measurements feedback onto the input state (transformations of the belief states resulting from decision making (see [70]). In particular, these instruments can be represented on the basis of decoherence type dynamics, see [5–9].

In this book, we concentrate on the quantum-like treatment of one concrete problem of decision making, namely, Aumann's theorem [15] where agents search on agreement of their decisions (see [69] for the quantum-like model).

The celebrated Aumann theorem states that if two agents have common priors, and their posteriors for a given event E are common knowledge, then their posteriors must be equal, i.e., *agents with the same priors and common knowledge cannot agree to disagree.* Our

---

[e]We remark that the framework of quantum(-like) decision making has interesting applications not only in psychology, cognitive science, and social science, but even in molecular biology, where a cell is considered as a kind of decision maker (see [9] up to and including [18]). In principle, such an approach can be interpreted as the first step towards the mathematical modeling of the cell's cognition.

aim is to show that in some contexts, agents using a quantum probability scheme for decision making can agree to disagree even if they have the common priors, and their posteriors for a given event E are common knowledge. We also point to sufficient conditions guaranteeing the impossibility to agree on disagree even for agents using quantum(-like) rules in the process of decision making.

A quantum(-like) analog of the knowledge operator is introduced; its basic properties can be formulated similarly to the properties of the classical knowledge operator defined in the set-theoretical approach of the representation of the states of the world and events (Boolean logic). However, this analogy is just formal, since quantum and classical knowledge operators are endowed with very different assignments of truth values. A quantum(-like) model of common knowledge naturally generalizing the classical set-theoretic model will be presented.

We illustrate our approach by a few examples; in particular, on attempting to escape the agreement on disagree for *two agents performing two different political opinion polls*. We restrict our modeling to the case of the information representation of an agent given by a single quantum question-observable (of the projection type). A scheme to extend our model of knowledge/common knowledge to the case of an information representation of an agent based on a few (in general incompatible) question-observables is also presented and possible pitfalls will be discussed.

Chapter 14

Common Knowledge

The notion of *common knowledge* plays a crucial role in various problems of coordination of actions in philosophy, economics (including accounting and capital market research), game theory, statistics, computer science, and artificial intelligence. Surprisingly, this notion was elaborated not so long ago, in the 1950s, starting with the works of Littlewood [79], Schelling [91], Harsanyi [51–53], Nozick [84], and culminating in a detailed account of common knowledge by Lewis [77]; see also [45] for the first mathematical account of the common knowledge problem.

We remark that the impact of common knowledge studies is not reduced to concrete (in particular, aforementioned) areas of research. These studies have the strong multi disciplinary dimension, since researchers from different areas have to debate about this notion by emphasizing commonalities and differences in its usage.

Common knowledge is a generalization of a simpler notion *mutual knowledge*: everybody in a group of people is aware about some fact or event. The role of this notion in coordination was discussed long ago (see [54]). However, as we pointed out above, the step from a mutual to a common knowledge perspective took a few hundred years.

Now we present a few illustrative examples for the notion of common knowledge:

Example 1 (Earthquake, Japan, 11 March 2011). At the time of this earthquake, one of the authors of this book (A.K.) was participating in a quantum bio-information workshop at the Noda-city campus of Tokyo University of Science (on the fourth floor of the

195

conference building). Around 3 p.m., the building started to first shake and then strongly shake.[a] This shaking of the building and that it was a sign of a strong earthquake was mutual knowledge for the workshop participants. However, people did not try to escape from the building until somebody loudly said: "This is a very strong earthquake". Immediately, people left the building. This announcement, of a fact known to everybody in the conference room, made the mutual knowledge, common. This crucially changed the workshop participant's behavior. After this announcement, each workshop participant knew that "each participant knows that each participant knows that earthquake is very strong" and so on, *ad infinitum.*

However, this was not the end of the story! After a half-hour stay at some distance from the conference building, and seeing that there were no more signs of an earthquake, the workshop participants decided to return to the conference room and continue the workshop. In the middle of the session, the building started to shake again and sufficiently strongly. However, nobody, this time, said publicly that shaking was strong. The session continued. Maybe the participants expected such an announcement from the session's chairman who may have expected it from the conference organizers.[b]

Thus common knowledge is an essentially stronger assumption than simply mutual knowledge. To have *common knowledge means not only that everybody knows some information E, but even that everybody knows that everybody knows E and that everybody knows that everybody knows that everybody knows E and so on, ad infinitum.*

---

[a]Earthquakes nearby Tokyo happen often. During some periods of the year, objects in rooms will shake practically everyday. Amplitudes vary from day to day. Of course each time one could estimate the strength of the shake, but this is difficult to do subjectively.

[b]A collaborator of one of the authors of this book (A.K.) who was the last speaker of this session indicated that she was really scared during her talk and very angry when people started to ask questions after she finished.

Remark (*ad infinitum*). The definition of common knowledge is based on the *infinite* hierarchy of levels of knowing. This presence of infinity might give the impression that this notion is not useful for concrete applications in which the infinite level of commonality is unapproachable. However, this is not the case. Of course, common knowledge is an ideal notion, but its role in science is similar to the role of other ideal notions, such as, e.g., "a point", "a straight line", or irrational numbers. We cannot proceed mathematically without such ideal notions. This exhibits the transcendental structure of human reasoning.

Example 2. "Blue eyes paradox" (see [45, 94]. We follow here "common knowledge" [98]). There is an island populated by people with blue and green eyes, say k people have blue eyes, others have green eyes. (The island's inhabitants do not know the number k.) At the beginning, nobody knows the color of her/his eyes. There is a very strict rule: if a person finds that she/he has blue eyes, that person must move away from the island before sunrise. On this island, everybody knows the eye colors of others. It is forbidden to discuss eye colors and there are no mirrors or similar devices.

A stranger comes to the island and announces to all the people: "At least one of you has blue eyes". Thus it becomes common knowledge. The problem: what is the eventual outcome of this public announcement?

Consider first, the simplest case, $k = 1$. Some person will recognize that she/he alone has blue eyes (by seeing only green eyes in the others) and leaves at the first sunrise. Let now $k = 2$. At the first sunrise, nobody leaves the island. Then two people having blue eyes by seeing only one person with blue eyes, and that no one left on the first sunrise, understand that $k > 1$. They leave at the second sunrise. And so on, by using the inductive argument. The paradox is that if $k > 1$, then the stranger told the people on this island what they already knew: there are blue-eyed people. However, without the stranger's announcement, this fact was not common knowledge. The "becoming" of common knowledge has dramatic consequences for the inhabitants of the island.

For $k = 2$, it is first-order knowledge. Each person having blue eyes knows that there is someone with blue eyes, but she/he does not know that the other blue-eyed person has this same knowledge. For $k = 3$, it is second-order knowledge. After 2 days, each person having blue eyes knows that a second blue-eyed person knows that a third person has blue eyes, but no one knows that there is a third blue-eyed person with that knowledge, until the third day arrives. And so on. . . .

14.1. General discussion on Aumann's theorem for classical and quantum agents

Aumann's approach [15,16] to common knowledge and his "no agreement on disagree theorem" played an important role in the creation of a proper mathematical model of common knowledge (see also [21, 43, 58, 80, 81, 83], for generalizations).

The main puzzle raised by Aumann's theorem and its generalizations is that people often 'agree on disagree'; so the natural question arises: *How to explain differences in beliefs?* (see, e.g., [15, 94] for a discussion). The simplest solution is to deny the possibility that decision makers are able to set common priors. However, in many situations, the common prior assumption is very natural, since the assignment of common priors is based on sharing common information. As was pointed out in Vanderschraaf and Sillari [94], "Another way Aumann's result might fail is if agents do not have common knowledge that they update their beliefs by Bayesian conditionalization. Then clearly, agents can explain divergent opinions as the result of others having modified their beliefs in the 'wrong' way."

Of course, the latter explanation is based on the consideration of Bayesian updating as the "right" way of updating. The reduction of rationality to "Bayesian rationality" is an important assumption of classical decision theory. As we shall discuss later in more detail, this assumption is equivalent to the assumption that human beings process information by using the rules of *Boolean logic*.

We will show that agents using more general logic, so-called quantum logic, in information processing (see [62] for a discussion), can "agree on disagree" (see [69]). They would not update their beliefs in the "wrong" way, since they all apply (at least heuristically) another common rule for probability update (PU), based on the laws of quantum information and probability.

We remark that from the logical point of view, the use of the quantum formalism implies the violation of the laws of classical (Boolean) logic. This viewpoint was presented already in the pioneering monograph of von Neumann [96] (see [19] for the detailed presentation). Thus, from this viewpoint, cognitive systems can violate the laws of Boolean logic and follow the laws of more general "quantum logic".

How can one find evidence of violations of classical logic? Since classical probability theory (Kolmogorov's measure-theoretic axiomatics, 1933) is based on Boolean logic, then possible departures from classical logic can be seen in the violations of the basic laws of classical probability theory (see [64] for an extended discussion). One of such laws is the *law of total probability.* Its violation has been found to occur in various sets of statistical data, e.g., for the recognition of ambiguous figures (see [35, 36, 67]). In the case of the disjunction effect (which refers to violations of Savage's sure-thing principle and, hence plays an important role in economics), we mention the work by Busemeyer *et al.* [27–32]; Pothos and Busemeyer [89, 90]; Khrennikov [66, 67]; Asano *et al.* [5–9]; Haven and Khrennikov [55, 56]; Aerts *et al.* [3]. See also [64, 73] for other theoretical and experimental studies of violations of the law of total probability outside of physics.

We will show that the quantum generalization of the Bayesian updating leads to violation of the celebrated *Aumann theorem* which states (we have already mentioned it before) that *if two agents have the common priors, and their posteriors for a given event E are common knowledge, then their posteriors must be equal; agents with the same priors cannot agree to disagree.* We will show that in *some contexts*, agents using quantum logic can *agree to disagree* even if they have the common priors, and their posteriors for a given event E are common knowledge.

One of the departures from the classical Aumann's model is the existence of *incompatible information representations of the world* by different agents. Instead of the set-theoretical (Boolean) partitions of the space of the states of the world Ω, we consider partitions of the unit operator in complex Hilbert space H (the space of the quantum states of the world) consisting of the mutually orthogonal projectors. In general, these partitions can be incompatible, i.e., the corresponding question-operators of different agents need not commute. We note that here we proceed with the simplest mathematical model of quantum measurements based on the projection operators (measurements of the von Neumann–Lüders type). The generalization to measurements represented as quantum instruments seems to be possible, but technically non-trivial.

We point out that the incompatibility of information representations of different agents is not the only quantum feature of the model generating the possibility to agree on disagree. We will show (in Chapter 16 (Section 16.2)) by an example that has non-trivial cognitive and psychological (as well as sociological) content, that the Aumann theorem can be violated even for commuting question-operators of agents. This example was motivated by Moore's [82] political poll studies on the honesty of Bill Clinton and Al Gore. Moore studied the order effect. As was shown in Wang and Busemeyer [97], the corresponding statistical data exhibits non-classical features and can be represented with the aid of incompatible observables (see also [32] for a general discussion on quantum representation of order effects in psychology).

We would like to make compatible these question-observables: $A^{(1)}$ = "Is Bill Clinton honest and trustworthy?" and $A^{(2)}$ = "Is Al Gore honest and trustworthy?". To do this, we associate them with two different agents who perform two different political polls. The first one is based (solely) on the question $A^{(1)}$ and the second one, on the question $A^{(2)}$. Here, the order effect disappears and the question-observables $A^{(i)}, i = 1, 2$, can be represented by commuting operators, $[A^{(1)}, A^{(2)}] = 0$. In Chapter 16, Section 16.2 we demonstrate that even in this situation quantum(-like) decision makers can agree on disagree.

In short, the main reason for this is that the basic quantum element introducing violations into Aumann's theorem is the use of a more general rule of updating of probabilities, the quantum analog of the Bayesian updating (see [73] for the general discussion). A few different sources of incompatibility are combined in this rule. Besides the most evident source, namely, possible incompatibility of information representations of trading agents, two other sources also play important roles. These are possible incompatibilities of information representations with quantum events and common prior states. They both can contribute nontrivially to the interference term, perturbing the matching of posterior probabilities (even in contexts with common prior states and non-trivial common knowledge). These two latter sources of quantumness of decision making were not considered in previous studies on quantum cognition and psychology.

We also point out that the model we will be presenting is just the first step toward the quantum modeling of the process of (dis)agreeing on disagree. One interesting possibility is to extend the generalization of the present model briefly presented in Chapter 15 (Section 15.6). In this generalized model, even each individual agent creates her/his information representation by using a group of, in general, incompatible questions. It is also interesting to find new mental phenomena in which quantum(-like) interference is not a consequence of solely incompatibility of observables, but where the aforementioned additional contributions to the interference term also play their roles.

Our study is closely coupled to theory of *rationality*. In the conventional theory of decision making (based on the classical probability theory and Boolean logic), a decision maker is per definition rational if and only if she/he uses the Bayesian rule for probability updating. Thus, in fact, conventional rationality is *Bayesian rationality*. In general, quantum agents by updating probabilities violate the Bayes rule. From the conventional viewpoint, they are irrational. However, we can generalize the notion of rationality: per definition agents using the quantum rule for PU, see (13.10), Section 13.2, are rational (*quantum-rational*). This viewpoint on rationality, in fact, matches with Bayesian rationality. The latter can also be treated as a particular case of quantum rationality (see Section 13.2, Proposition 1). Thus, agents processing information by using the quantum rule for PU are not "crazy" or improperly behaving. They proceed rationally but they have a more complex representation of the world.

Finally, we remark that quantum rationality is not the only possible generalization of classical (Bayesian) rationality, since the quantum model of probability is not the only possible generalization of classical (Boole–Kolmogorov) probability (see, e.g., [67] for hyperbolic probability, Khrennikov [65] for negative probability and more generally p-adic probability (covering, in particular, negative probability); Khrennikov [60] for probability valued in noncommutative algebras). Each such non-Kolmogorovean model generates its own PU and, hence, its own notion of rationality. One of the main advantages of the quantum model is that it is simple (even compared to the classical measure-theoretic model) and well elaborated.

We will now start with the classical mathematical formalization of the problem of common knowledge and searching agreement between "classical agents" who are processing information by using the rules of Boolean logic (and as a consequence use the Bayesian updating of probabilities).

14.2. Classical probabilistic approach
to common knowledge

Aumann's considerations are applicable to a finite number of *agents*, call them $i = 1, 2, \ldots, N$. These individuals are about to learn the answers to various multiple choice *questions* so to make observations.

Mathematically, the situation is represented with the aid of a classical probability space (based on the Kolmogorov axiomatics, 1933), see Chapter 12. Typically, it is assumed that the state space Ω representing all possible states of the world is finite (see [21, 83] for the general measure-theoretic framework). Events are subsets of Ω.

Each agent creates its *information representation* for possible states of the world based on its own possibilities to perform measurements, i.e., "to ask questions to the world". Mathematically, these representations are given by partitions of Ω: $\mathcal{P}^{(i)} = (P_j^{(i)})$, where, for each agent i,

$$\cup_j P_j^{(i)} = \Omega \quad \text{and} \quad P_j^{(i)} \cap P_k^{(i)} = \emptyset, \; j \neq k.$$

Thus, an agent cannot get to know the state of the world ω precisely: she/he can only get to know to which element of its information partition $P_j^{(i)} \equiv P^{(i)}(\omega)$ this ω belongs. In this set-theoretic model of knowledge, by definition, the agent i knows an event E in the state of the world ω if the element of his information partition containing this ω is contained in E:

$$P^{(i)}(\omega) \subset E. \tag{14.1}$$

In logical terms, this can be written as $P^{(i)}(\omega) \Rightarrow E$, the event $P^{(i)}(\omega)$ implies the event E; we also remark that $\{\omega\} \Rightarrow P^{(i)}(\omega)$.

It is assumed that on Ω, there is defined a probability p, *the common prior* of all agents. In accordance with the measure-theoretic model of probability theory (Kolmogorov, 1933), there is given a σ-algebra, say $\mathcal{F}$, of subsets of Ω, its elements represent events ("propositions" in some interpretations), and there is given a probability measure p defined on $\mathcal{F}$. In the knowledge models, it is typically assumed that $\mathcal{F}$ is generated by agents' partitions, i.e., this is the minimal σ-algebra containing all systems of a set $\mathcal{P}^{(i)}, i = 1, \ldots, N$. It is important to point out that, in particular, such a σ-algebra contains all subsets of the form $P_{j_1}^{(1)} \cap \cdots \cap P_{j_N}^{(N)}$. Hence, in the classical knowledge model, the prior probability is assigned not only to the individual elements of the agents' information representations, i.e., $P_j^{(i)} \to p(P_j^{(i)})$, but even to more complex events

$$P_{j_1}^{(1)} \cap \cdots \cap P_{j_N}^{(N)} \to p_{j_1 \cdots j_N} \equiv p(P_{j_1}^{(1)} \cap \cdots \cap P_{j_N}^{(N)}). \tag{14.2}$$

Thus, by agreeing on the prior, the agents have to agree on numerous conjunctive probabilities. These probabilities present a much more detailed information picture of the world than simply probabilities for individual information representations. We shall see that this is not the case for quantum agents.

Thus, already the classical framework is based on the analysis of uncertainty in knowing the states of the world. The probabilistic part of quantum formalism is also a tool to describe uncertainties. Roughly speaking, "quantum uncertainty" represented by superpositions of states is deeper than "classical uncertainty". There is a very strong opinion that only quantum randomness is genuine randomness (already von Neumann wrote about "irreducible quantum randomness" (see [96])).

We consider the systems of sets $\tilde{\mathcal{P}}^{(i)} = \{\cup_m P^{(i)}_{j_m}\}$ consisting of finite unions of the elements of the systems $\mathcal{P}^{(i)}$ and the system $\tilde{\mathcal{P}} = \cap_i \tilde{\mathcal{P}}^{(i)}$. A set O belongs to the system $\tilde{\mathcal{P}}$ if it belongs to any $\tilde{\mathcal{P}}^{(i)}$. Thus, for each i, it can be represented as

$$O = \cup_m P^{(i)}_{j_m}, \tag{14.3}$$

for some finite set of indices (depending on i).

We now repeat the definition of common knowledge, for two agents (and we continue to proceed with two agents):

ACN. *An event E is common knowledge at the state of the world ω if 1 knows E, 2 knows E, 1 knows 2 knows E, 2 knows 1 knows E, and so on.*

In the theory of common knowledge, the basic role is played by the set of all states of the world for which E is common knowledge. It is denoted by the symbol κE. As was shown by Aumann [15], this set of states of the world belongs to $\tilde{\mathcal{P}}$ and, hence, for each i, it can be represented (in the case $\kappa E \neq \emptyset$) in the form (see (14.3)):

$$\kappa E = \bigcup_m P^{(i)}_{j_m}. \tag{14.4}$$

Let E be an event. For a state of the world ω, each agent i updates the common prior $p(E)$ on the basis of the observation of the element $P^{(i)}(\omega)$ of its information partition. (For this agent, it means that the state of the world ω is contained in $P^{(i)}(\omega)$.) This update is given by the conditional probability

$$\mathbf{q}_i(\omega) = p(E \cap P^{(i)}(\omega))/p(P^{(i)}(\omega)).$$

We remark that the conditional probability $\mathbf{q}_i(\omega)$ is defined to be the same for all states of the world ω in a given element of the partition. Thus, in fact,

$$\mathbf{q}_i(\omega) \equiv \mathbf{q}_{ik},$$

where $\omega \in P_k^{(i)} = P^{(i)}(\omega)$.

Now, Aumann's theorem states that if both

$$\mathbf{q}_1(\omega) = q_1 \quad \text{and} \quad \mathbf{q}_2(\omega) = q_2 \tag{14.5}$$

are common knowledge and prior probabilities are the same, then necessarily $q_1 = q_2$ — simply because

$$q_i = p(E|\kappa C_{q_1 q_2}) = p(E \cap \kappa C_{q_1 q_2})/p(\kappa C_{q_1 q_2}), \tag{14.6}$$

where $C_{q_1 q_2}$ is the event (14.5): "the first agent by updating the prior probability of the event E assigns the value q_1 and the second agent the value q_2".

To prove (14.6), we use the Aumann representation (14.4) in which $C_{q_1 q_2}$ plays the role of an event, i.e., for each agent i, $\kappa C_{q_1 q_2}$ can be "sliced" into elements of the information partition of this agent:

$$\kappa C_{q_1 q_2} = \cup_m P_{jm}^{(i)}. \tag{14.7}$$

If $\omega \in \kappa C_{q_1 q_2}$, then, in particular, both agents know this event $C_{q_1 q_2}$ (the knowledge of the first order), i.e., $P^{(i)}(\omega) \subset C_{q_1 q_2}, i = 1, 2$. Thus, for any $P_{jm}^{(i)}$ in (14.7), we have that $P_{jm}^{(i)} \subset C_{q_1 q_2}$; hence,

$p(E|P_{jm}^{(i)}) = q_i$. Now, for each i, we have

$$p(E|\kappa C_{q_1 q_2}) = p(E \cap \kappa C_{q_1 q_2})/p(\kappa C_{q_1 q_2})$$

$$= p(E \cap \cup_m P_{jm}^{(i)})/p(\kappa C_{q_1 q_2})$$

$$= \frac{1}{p(\kappa C_{q_1 q_2})} \sum_m p(E|P_{jm}^{(i)}) p(P_{jm}^{(i)})$$

$$= q_i \sum_m p(P_{jm}^{(i)})/p(\kappa C_{q_1 q_2}) = q_i. \qquad (14.8)$$

In order to avoid confusion concerning the conditioning on *posterior probabilities being common knowledge*, we can reformulate Aumann's theorem as: given the common priors, posterior probabilities may be common knowledge only when they are equal.

The most convenient approach for applications to common knowledge is the operator (hierarchic) approach based on the operator of common knowledge (see [17, 81, 94] and references herein).

In the quantum case, the operator approach, although very useful, generates additional technical issues. To simplify the reading of the next chapters, we present a quantum analog of the operator formalism for common knowledge in Chapter 17. In the main part, we shall only use the fact that the standard definition of common knowledge **ACN** combined with the quantum definition of knowing of an event (cf. with Equation (14.1) of the present chapter), implies a quantum analog of Aumann's representation ((14.4), see Lemma 1, Chapter 15 (Section 15.3) and in Chapter 17).

Quantum(-like) Formalization of Common Knowledge

15.1. Quantum representation of the states of the world

In our quantum-like model, the *"states of the world"* are given by pure states. Thus, the unit sphere $S_1(H)$ in a complex Hilbert space H represents (up to phase factors) all possible states of the world.[a] Questions posed by agents are mathematically described by Hermitian operators, say $A^{(i)}$. We state again that events (propositions) are identified with orthogonal projectors. For the state of the world Ψ, an event P *occurs* (takes place with probability 1) if Ψ belongs to H_P.

To simplify considerations, we proceed in the case of the finite[b] dimensional state space of the world, $m = \dim H < \infty$. Here, each Hermitian operator can be represented as a linear combination of orthogonal projectors to its eigen-subspaces. In particular, the questions of agents can be expressed as

$$A^{(i)} = \sum_j a_j^{(i)} P_j^{(i)}, \qquad (15.1)$$

---

[a]We remark that the set $S_1(H)$ is uncountable, cf. with the original Aumann framework [15] in which the state space is countable. Nevertheless, we can, in fact, proceed similarly to the original Aumann approach. In this sense, the quantum framework is simpler than the classical, since in the case of an uncountable state space, the latter is quite complicated as the result of using the measure-theoretic model. See [21, 83] for details.

[b]Generalization to the infinite dimensional case needs to be explored with more advanced methods of functional analysis.

where $(a_j^{(i)})$ are real numbers, all different eigenvalues of $A^{(i)}$, and $(P_j^{(i)})$ are the orthogonal projectors onto the corresponding eigen-subspaces. Here, (a_j) encode possible answers to the question of the ith agent.[c] The system of projectors $\mathcal{P}^{(i)} = (P_j^{(i)})$ is the spectral family of $A^{(i)}$. Hence, for any agent i, it is a "disjoint partition of unity":

$$\bigvee_k P_k^{(i)} = I, \quad P_k^{(i)} \wedge P_m^{(i)} = 0, \ k \neq m. \tag{15.2}$$

We remark that (15.2) is simply the lattice-theoretical expression of the following operator equalities:

$$\sum_k P_k^{(i)} = I, \quad P_k^{(i)} P_m^{(i)} = 0, \ k \neq m. \tag{15.3}$$

This spectral family can be considered as an *information representation* of the world by the ith agent. In particular, "getting the answer $a_j^{(i)}$" is the event which is mathematically described by the projector $P_j^{(i)}$.

If the state of the world is represented by Ψ and, for some k_0, $P_\Psi \leq P_{k_0}^{(i)}$, then

$$p_\Psi(P_{k_0}^{(i)}) = \mathrm{Tr} P_\Psi P_{k_0}^{(i)} = 1 \text{ and, for } k \neq k_0, \ p_\Psi(P_k^{(i)}) = \mathrm{Tr} P_\Psi P_k^{(i)} = 0.$$

Thus, in this case, the event $P_{k_0}^{(i)}$ occurs with the probability one and other events from an information representation of the world by the ith agent, have zero probability.

However, in opposition to the classical case, in general Ψ need not belong to any concrete subspace[d] $H_{P_k^{(i)}}$. Nevertheless, for any

---

[c]Although in quantum physics, the magnitudes of these numbers play an important role, in quantum information theory, the eigenvalues are merely formal labels encoding, information which can be extracted from a state with the aid of an observable. In the case of dichotomous answers, we can simply use zero to encode "no" and one to encode "yes".

[d]We state again that in the classical probability model, the states of the world are encoded by points of Ω. Take one fixed state ω. Since the information

pure state Ψ, there exists the minimal projector $Q_\Psi^{(i)}$ of the form $\sum_m P_{jm}^{(i)}$ such that $P_\Psi \leq Q_\Psi^{(i)}$. This projector can be constructed in the following way. Each state Ψ determines the set of indices

$$O_\Psi^{(i)} = \{j : P_j^{(i)} \Psi \neq 0\}. \tag{15.4}$$

Then the minimal projector corresponding to the state Ψ has the form:

$$Q_\Psi^{(i)} = \sum_{j \in O_\Psi^{(i)}} P_j^{(i)}. \tag{15.5}$$

The projector $Q_\Psi^{(i)}$ represents the ith agent's knowledge about the Ψ-world. We remark that $p_\Psi(Q_\Psi^{(i)}) = 1$.

15.2. Knowing events, quantum representation

Consider the system of projectors $\tilde{\mathcal{P}}^{(i)}$ consisting of sums of the projectors from $\mathcal{P}^{(i)}$:

$$\tilde{\mathcal{P}}^{(i)} = \{P = \sum_m P_{jm}^{(i)}\}. \tag{15.6}$$

Then

$$Q_\Psi^{(i)} = \min\{P \in \tilde{\mathcal{P}}^{(i)} : P_\Psi \leq P\}, \tag{15.7}$$

see (15.4), (15.5) for the constructive definition.

---

representation of each agent is a partition of Ω, for each i, there exists an element of partition, say $P_j^{(i)}$, containing this ω. For this state of the world, the ith agent should definitely get the answer $a_j^{(i)}$ corresponding to the element $P_j^{(i)}$. Thus, any agent is able to resolve uncertainty at least for her/his information representation (although she/he is not able to completely resolve uncertainty about the state of the world). In the quantum case, an agent is not able to resolve uncertainty even at the level of her/his information representation. And the prior probability is updated in this uncertainty context.

Definition 1. For the Ψ-state of the world and the event E, the ith agent knows E if

$$Q_{\Psi}^{(i)} \leq E. \tag{15.8}$$

It is evident that if, for the state of the world Ψ, the ith agent knows E, then $\Psi \in H_E$. In general, the latter does not imply that E is known (for the state Ψ).[e] However, if $\Psi \in E = P_j^{(i)}$, then this event is known for i. The same is valid for any event of the form $E = P_{j_1}^{(i)} \vee \cdots \vee P_{j_k}^{(i)} (= P_{j_1}^{(i)} + \cdots + P_{j_k}^{(i)})$; if $\Psi \in H_E$, then such E is known for i.

We remark that the straightforward analog of the classical definition, see (14.1), would be based on the condition $P_j^{(i)} \leq E$ for

$$P_{\Psi} \leq P_j^{(i)}, \tag{15.9}$$

instead of the more general condition (15.8). However, it would trivialize the class of possible states of the world, because condition (15.9) is very restrictive.[f]

Definition 1 is natural generalization of the classical definition. A more detailed analysis of the meaning of knowing an event from the viewpoint of quantum probability theory is presented in Chapter 17, Section 17.1.1.

We remark that Definition 1 can be considered as the quantum analog of *knowing with probability* 1 and it will generate the quantum analog of *common knowledge with probability* 1 (compare with the corresponding classical studies [21, 43, 58, 80, 81, 83]). In principle,

---

[e]For example, the state space H is four dimensional with the orthonormal basis (e_1, e_2, e_3, e_4), the projectors P_1 and P_2 project H onto the subspaces with the bases (e_1, e_2) and (e_3, e_4), respectively. Here (P_1, P_2) is the information representation of an agent. Let E be the projector onto the subspace with the basis (e_1, e_4) and let $\Psi = (e_1 + e_4)/\sqrt{2}$. Then $Q_{\Psi} = I$, the unit operator. Hence, E is not known for this agent, although it belongs to H_E.

[f]For example, let for some player, all projectors to be one dimensional and let $(e_j^{(i)})$ be the corresponding orthonormal basis in H. Then only states of the world of the form $\Psi = e_j^{(i)}$ would bring knowledge about some event for this agent. For agents having incompatible information representations, the set of the states of the world which can bring knowledge about some event for both would be empty.

we can develop a more general approach based on knowing an event with some probability $p < 1$. However, even quantum agents can have common knowledge with probability 1 and we would like to model this situation. We shall see that already "quantization" of the notion of common knowledge with probability 1 generates non-trivial departures from Aumann's classical theorem.[g]

15.2.1. *Exercises*

Consider the two-dimensional state space and fix some orthonormal basis, say $(e_1, e_2,)$. Consider three agents whose information representations are encoded in the observables represented (in this basis) by Pauli matrices $\sigma_j, j = 1, 2, 3$, see (13.6).

Exercise 57. Let the state of the world be given by the pure state $\Psi = e_1 = (1, 0)$ and let the event E correspond to this state, i.e., it is represented by the projector P_{e_1} on this vector. Who does know this event?

Exercise 58. Let, for the same state of the world $\Psi = e_1$, the event E be given by the projector on the vector $\phi = \frac{1}{\sqrt{2}}(1, 1)$. Who does know this event?

Consider the three-dimensional state space and fix some orthonormal basis, say (e_1, e_2, e_3). Consider agents whose information representations are encoded in the observables represented in this basis by spin-1 matrices $\Sigma_j, j = 1, 2, 3$, see (13.7).

Exercise 59. Let the state of the world be given by the pure state $\Psi = e_2 = (0, 1, 0)$ and let the event E correspond to this state, i.e., it is represented by the projector P_{e_2} on this vector. Who does know this event?

Exercise 60. Let the state of the world be given by the pure state $\Psi = \frac{1}{\sqrt{3}}(1, 1, 1)$ and let the event E correspond to this state, i.e., it

---

[g]We shall present a quantum model for common knowledge with $p < 1$ in a future paper.

is represented by the projector P_Ψ on this vector. Who does know this event?

15.3. Common knowledge, quantum representation

We shall use the standard definition of common knowledge (see **ACN**), but based on the quantum representation of knowing an event (see Definition 1). The detailed presentation in the framework of the hierarchic operator approach can be found in Chapter 17, Section 17.1. As in the classical case, we have that: "Where something is common knowledge, everybody knows it."

We recall that in the classical case, for each event E, the set of all states of the world is considered for which E is common knowledge. It is denoted by the symbol κE.

This definition is naturally generalized to the quantum case. Here κE is defined as the projector on the subspace consisting of all states of the world for which E is common knowledge, see Chapter 17, Section 17.1.

Similar to the set-theoretic framework, we introduce the system of projectors

$$\tilde{\mathcal{P}} = \cap_i \tilde{\mathcal{P}}^{(i)}.$$

We remark that (by definition) a projector $P \in \tilde{\mathcal{P}}$ if and only if, for each $i = 1, \ldots, N$, it can be represented in the form

$$P = \sum_m P^{(i)}_{j_m}. \tag{15.10}$$

As in the set-theoretic case, we obtain (see Chapter 17, Section 17.1), the following result about the common knowledge projectors:

Lemma 1. *If $\kappa E \neq 0$, then $\kappa E \in \tilde{\mathcal{P}}$.*

We postpone the presentation of examples of applications illustrating how this knowledge structure works, to the next chapter (Sections 16.1 and 16.2). In principle, the reader can jump to these sections and by ignoring the problem of the violation of the Aumann theorem, just look at the knowledge/common knowledge structures presented in these examples.

15.4. Quantum state update, projection postulate

In the classical Aumann scheme, the update of the prior probability distribution on the basis of information representations of agents plays the crucial role. Therefore, the quantum analog of the Aumann scheme is based on the quantum procedure of the state update as the result of measurement.

15.5. Quantum(-like) viewpoint on the Aumann's theorem

15.5.1. *Common prior assumption*

Suppose now that both agents assign to possible states of the world the same quantum probability distribution given by the density operator ρ, a prior state. Thus they do not know exactly the real state of the world (the latter is always a pure state) and, in general, a possible state of the world appears for them as a mixed quantum state ρ. Of course, in some contexts, ρ can correspond to a pure state, i.e., $\rho = P_g$, where g is a pure state (see the example considered in the next Chapter, Section 16.2). This happens if both agents feel deep uncertainty about the possible states of the world.

The prior probability for possible states of the world is combined with the information representations used by the agents and given by their question-operators, see (15.1) (or simply the corresponding partitions of unity, see (15.3)). As in the classical framework, information representations are based on questions which agents can ask. In the political poll example which was discussed in Chapter 14 (see also the next Chapter, Section 16.2 for details), these are the questions $A^{(1)} = $ "Is Bill Clinton honest and trustworthy?" (so, for the first agent, the information representation of the world is reduced to answers, "yes"/"no" to this question) and $A^{(2)} = $ "Is Al Gore honest and trustworthy?" (so, for the second agent, the information representation of the world is reduced to answers, "yes"/"no" to this question). As in the classical case, the agents know about the information representations of each other, i.e., in the example with the political poll, the first agent knows that the second agent will ask respondents about the honesty of Al Gore and the second agent knows that the first agent will ask respondents about the honesty of Bill Clinton.

We now compare the informations which classical and quantum agents can gain from the common prior. As was emphasized in Section 14.2, by agreeing on the prior, classically thinking agents agree on the very detailed probabilistic description of the state of affairs given by the collection of conjunctive probabilities $p_{j_1...j_N} \equiv p(P_{j_1}^{(1)} \cap \cdots \cap P_{j_N}^{(N)})$, see (14.2).

In the quantum case, such a detailed probability description is in general impossible, since the agents' information partitions can be incompatible, i.e., it can happen that all projectors $P_{j_1...j_N} \equiv P_{j_1}^{(1)} \wedge \cdots \wedge P_{j_N}^{(N)} = 0$. This is a reflection of the quantum logical structure of reasoning. First of all, the violations of the distributivity law for the quantum generalizations of the operations of conjunction and disjunction can occur, see (13.21). Hence, in general

$$I = I \wedge \cdots \wedge I = \bigvee_{k_1} P_{k_1}^{(1)} \wedge \cdots \wedge \bigvee_{k_1} P_{k_N}^{(N)} \neq \bigvee_{k_1...k_N} P_{k_1}^{(1)} \wedge \cdots \wedge P_{k_N}^{(N)}$$

$$(15.11)$$

Thus, *quantum agents can gain essentially less information from the common prior state than the classical ones.* One may speculate that this is one of the sources of the violation of the classical Aumann theorem for quantum agents. Although they also have a common prior, this prior gives less information which can lead to the agreement about posterior probabilities. One can say that the quantum prior is fuzzy compared with the classical prior. This situation is well illustrated by the political polls example (see the next chapter, Section 16.2). However, this is just *one of the sources* of the violation of the Aumann theorem, since it can be violated even for agents having compatible information representations. In the latter case, the probabilities

$$p_{j_1...j_N} \equiv Tr\rho P_{k_1}^{(1)} \wedge \cdots \wedge P_{k_N}^{(N)} \qquad (15.12)$$

can be used in the same way as the classical conjunctive probabilities given by (14.2).

We remark that the inter-relation of quantum and classical information models is a complex issue. Although for incompatible observables, the conjunctive probabilities (15.12) are unapproachable (they are simply not well defined) and hence, as was emphasized, each agent can gain from the prior state less information, which can be useful to match the posterior probabilities. This does not mean that the quantum state contains less information than the classical state. It is just the opposite. However, the volume of information approachable by each agent is restricted. Consider, e.g., N agents with dichotomous "no"/"yes" question-observables and suppose that their information partitions are based on one dimensional projectors, i.e., each information partition is given just by an orthonormal basis in the state space H, which is two dimensional, $(e_0^{(1)}, e_1^{(1)}), \ldots, (e_0^{(N)}, e_1^{(N)})$. Consider a quantum state given by a density matrix ρ which is a 2×2 matrix. In the case of incompatible observables, the information which an agent can gain from ρ cannot be reduced to information which can be gained from ρ by other agents. Thus ρ contains a huge volume of information. Where does it come from? This a complicated problem from quantum information theory (see, e.g., [23–25] for speculations).

15.5.2. *Disagree from quantum(-like) interference*

Now in the quantum(-like) framework, we repeat the classical Aumann scheme of (dis)agreement on disagree. The only difference from the classical case is that the agents use another (non-Bayesian) rule for the updating of probabilities. In our work, this rule is based on quantum conditional probabilities. In principle, other rules can also be tested to see the effect of the modification of the probability update procedure. In particular, in Hild *et al.* [58]

a measure-theoretical deformation of the classical Bayes rule was considered (applied to (dis)agreeing on disagree reasoning). However, this modification did not imply such a brutal violation of the Aumann theorem as is the case with the quantum one.

Consider some event E. The agents assign to it, probabilities after conditioning ρ on the answers to their questions (on their information representations of the world):

$$\mathbf{q}_{ik} = p_\rho(E|P_k^{(i)}) = \frac{\mathrm{Tr}P_k^{(i)}\rho P_k^{(i)}E}{\mathrm{Tr}P_k^{(i)}\rho P_k^{(i)}}. \tag{15.13}$$

Thus $\mathbf{q}_{ik}$ is the probability which the ith agent would assign to the event E under condition that she gets the answer $a_k^{(i)}$ to her question-observable $A^{(i)}$. We remark that the agents can assign probabilities conditioned on the results of observations only for the answers $a_k^{(i)}$ such that $\mathrm{Tr}P_k^{(i)}\rho P_k^{(i)} > 0$. It is clear that for the ith agent some of these conditional probabilities can coincide. Denote the set of possible values of the posterior probabilities for i by the symbol V_i. Suppose that the jth agent, for $j \neq i$, gets to know that the ith agent assigned the value $q_i \in V_i$ to the probability for the event E. Then the jth agent does not know precisely which answer the ith agent obtained as the result of her measurement. This is just one of the $a_k^{(i)}$ such that the corresponding posterior probability equals to q_i. We shall study the situation when these probabilities ($q_i, i = 1, 2, \ldots, N$) are common knowledge. We perform the corresponding quantum formalization of this situation.

For each i, consider the event

$$C_{q_i} \equiv \{\mathbf{q}_{ik} = q_i\}$$

that after observing her result, the ith agent assigned the value q_i (one of the elements of V_i) to the event E (i.e., i observed one of the values $a_k^{(i)}$ leading to the probability $\mathbf{q}_{ik} = q_i$). In the quantum formalism, this event is represented as a disjunction of the projectors

$P_k^{(i)}$ representing the events of obtaining the answers $a_k^{(i)}$:

$$C_{q_i} = \bigvee_{\{k:\mathbf{q}_{ik}=q_i\}} P_k^{(i)}. \tag{15.14}$$

We also consider the event

$$C_{q_1\ldots q_N} = \{\mathbf{q}_{1k} = q_1, \ldots, \mathbf{q}_{1k} = q_N\}$$

that after observing their results, the agents assigned the values $q_i \in V_i, i = 1, 2, \ldots, N$, to the event E. In the quantum formalism, this event is represented as a conjunction of the projectors C_{q_i}:

$$C_{q_1\ldots q_N} == \bigwedge_i C_{q_i}.$$

Remark 1. Consider the classical Aumann model. Here,

$$\mathbf{q}_i(\omega) = p(E|P^{(i)}(\omega)) = \frac{p(E \cap P^{(i)}(\omega))}{p(P^{(i)}(\omega))} \tag{15.15}$$

and $C_{q_i} \equiv \{\omega: \mathbf{q}_i(\omega) = q_i\}$. We remark that if for some ω_0 the probability $q_i(\omega_0) = q_i$, then, for any $\omega \in P^{(i)}(\omega_0)$, the probability $q_i(\omega) = q_i$. Thus

$$C_{q_i} = \bigcup_{\{k:\mathbf{q}_{ik}=q_i\}} P_k^{(i)}, \tag{15.16}$$

cf. (15.14).

We remark that, in fact, as a consequence of the mutual orthogonality of projectors from the spectral family of any Hermitian operator, the event C_{q_i} can be represented as

$$C_{q_i} == \sum_{\{k:\mathbf{q}_{ik}=q_i\}} P_k^{(i)}.$$

Thus the event $C_{q_1\ldots q_N}$ has representation:

$$C_{q_1\ldots q_N} = \left(\bigvee_{\{k:\mathbf{q}_{1k}=q_1\}} P_k^{(1)} \right) \wedge \cdots \wedge \left(\bigvee_{\{k:\mathbf{q}_{Nk}=q_N\}} P_k^{(N)} \right).$$

$$\tag{15.17}$$

By taking into account the violation of the distributivity law we know that in general:

$$C_{q_1 \ldots q_N} \neq \bigvee_{\{k_1 : q_{1k_1} = q_1\}} \cdots \bigvee_{\{k_N : q_{Nk_N} = q_N\}} P_{k_1}^{(1)} \wedge \cdots \wedge P_{k_N}^{(N)}. \quad (15.18)$$

In principle, $C_{q_1 \ldots q_N}$ can be non-trivial even if all "its conjunction components" are trivial, i.e., $P_{k_1}^{(1)} \wedge \cdots \wedge P_{k_N}^{(N)} = 0$. A similar argument is applicable to the common knowledge about $C_{q_1 \ldots q_N}$ to $\kappa C_{q_1 \ldots q_N}$. This is not the case for classically thinking agents.

Roughly speaking, *the quantum logic leads to "more possibilities to have common knowledge" than the classical logic.*[h] Thus, again heuristically, *quantum agents gain less information from the common prior, but they have more possibilities to get common knowledge.* We remark that in some contexts the use of "fuzzy priors" can be advantageous for information processing. Agents can save a lot of resources that otherwise they should use to obtain detailed common priors.

Suppose that the possibility of $C_{q_1 \ldots q_N}$ becoming common knowledge is not ruled out completely:

$$p_\rho(\kappa C_{q_1 \ldots q_N}) > 0. \quad (15.19)$$

Now we shall try to repeat in the quantum setting the standard proof of the Aumann theorem, which is presented in the set-theoretic framework.

By Lemma 1, the common knowledge projector (for the event $C_{q_1 \ldots q_N}$) can be represented as

$$\kappa C_{q_1 \ldots q_N} = \sum_j P_{k_j}^{(i)}, \quad i = 1, \ldots, N.$$

(Here, for each i, the collection of projectors $(P_{k_j}^{(i)})$ is determined by the iteration procedure for the common knowledge operator, see

---

[h]This is only a heuristic statement. It is not clear how quantum agents can gain more information from the situation than classical ones.

Chapter 17, Section 17.1.) For each such $P_{k_j}^{(1)}, \ldots, P_{k_j}^{(N)}$, we have

$$p_\rho(E|P_{k_j}^{(1)}) = q_1, \ldots, p_\rho(E|P_{k_j}^{(N)}) = q_N. \qquad (15.20)$$

In particular, for any such projector conditional probabilities are well defined, i.e., $\mathrm{Tr} P_{k_j}^{(i)} \rho P_{k_j}^{(i)} > 0$. Consider now the conditional probability:

$$p_\rho(E|\kappa C_{q_1 \ldots q_N}) = \frac{\mathrm{Tr}\kappa C_{q_1 \ldots q_N} \rho \kappa C_{q_1 \ldots q_N} E}{\mathrm{Tr}\kappa C_{q_1 \ldots q_N} \rho \kappa C_{q_1 \ldots q_N}}.$$

First we remark that, for any projector M, $\mathrm{Tr} M\rho M = \mathrm{Tr}\rho M$. Thus:

$$p_\rho(E|\kappa C_{q_1 \ldots q_N}) = \frac{\mathrm{Tr}\kappa C_{q_1 \ldots q_N} \rho \kappa C_{q_1 \ldots q_N} E}{\mathrm{Tr}\rho \kappa C_{q_1 \ldots q_N}}.$$

By using representation given by Lemma 1, we obtain

$$p_\rho(E|\kappa C_{q_1 \ldots q_N})$$

$$= \frac{1}{\mathrm{Tr}\rho \kappa C_{q_1 \ldots q_N}} \left(\sum_j \mathrm{Tr} P_{k_j}^{(i)} \rho P_{k_j}^{(i)} E + \sum_{j \neq m} \mathrm{Tr} P_{k_j}^{(i)} \rho P_{k_m}^{(i)} E \right).$$

$$(15.21)$$

By using (15.20) the first (diagonal) sum can be written as

$$\frac{1}{\mathrm{Tr}\rho \kappa C_{q_1 \ldots q_N}} \sum_j \frac{\mathrm{Tr} P_{k_j}^{(i)} \rho P_{k_j}^{(i)} E}{\mathrm{Tr}\rho P_{k_j}^{(i)}} \mathrm{Tr}\rho P_{k_j}^{(i)}$$

$$= \frac{q_i}{\mathrm{Tr}\rho \kappa C_{q_1 \ldots q_N}} \mathrm{Tr} \sum \rho P_{k_j}^{(i)}$$

$$= \frac{q_i}{\mathrm{Tr}\rho \kappa C_{q_1 \ldots q_N}} \mathrm{Tr}\rho \sum P_{k_j}^{(i)} = q_i.$$

In the absence of the off-diagonal term in (15.21), we get (cf. (14.6)):

$$p_\rho(E|\kappa C_{q_1 \ldots q_N}) = q_i, \qquad (15.22)$$

i.e., $q_1 = \cdots = q_N$. This corresponds to the classical case. However, in general, the off-diagonal term does not vanish — this is *the interference type effect.* Hence, in general, the proof of the Aumann theorem cannot be generalized to quantum logic. Although mathematically this does not imply that in the quantum framework this theorem is not valid, in reality it does, because the standard proof of the Aumann theorem represents the essence of the "impossibility of agreeing on disagree" argument. And later we shall present the corresponding counterexample.

Thus, *agents processing information in the quantum logic framework can agree on disagree,* see the next chapter (Section 16.1) for examples.

Although the probabilities are not equal, it is useful to know the degree of mismatching between them and the quantum formalism provides such information in the form of the interference term.

Theorem 1. *Let condition (15.19), the assumption of common prior, holds. Then:*

$$q_i - q_s = \frac{1}{\mathrm{Tr}\rho\kappa C_{q_1...q_N}} \left(\sum_{j\neq m} \mathrm{Tr}P_{k_j}^{(i)}\rho P_{k_m}^{(i)}E - \sum_{j\neq m} \mathrm{Tr}P_{k_j}^{(s)}\rho P_{k_m}^{(s)}E \right).$$
$$(15.23)$$

If the amplitude of the right-hand side of (15.23) (the interference term [62–67] between updates of the probability of the event E by two different agents), is small, we can say that the agents named i and s practically agree. The interference term can be considered as a measure of "agreement on disagree" between the agents.

Remark 2. From the representation (15.23), we can see that the compatibility of information representations of all agents with either the prior state ρ, i.e.,

$$[\rho, P_k^{(i)}] = 0, \qquad (15.24)$$

or the event E, i.e.,

$$[E, P_k^{(i)}] = 0, \qquad (15.25)$$

are sufficient conditions for the absence of interference, i.e., the impossibility to agree on disagree even for agents using quantum logic. But these conditions are not necessary. Even if both conditions (15.24) and (15.25) are violated, the interference term in (15.23) can be zero as the result of the consistency of the agents "self-interference".

15.6. Agent with information representation based on incompatible question-observables

In the presented model, the quantum extension of Aumann's approach to the possibility of agreement on disagree was directed to the accounting of incompatibility of the information representations (question-observables $A^{(i)}$) of different agents, i.e., in general $[A^{(i)}, A^{(j)}] \neq 0, i \neq j$, and their incompatibility with the prior common state ρ and the event E, i.e., in general $[\rho, A^{(i)}] \neq 0$, or (and) $[E, A^{(i)}] \neq 0$. One can proceed towards a more general framework by taking into account that even information representations of an individual agent can be based on incompatible question-observables; $A_k^{(i)}, k = 1, \ldots, K_i$, for the ith agent, where in general $[A_k^{(i)}, A_n^{(i)}] \neq 0, k \neq n$.

One of the ways to handle this more complex mental context is to consider such an agent as simply a group of individual agents (using the same brain). In such an approach, our previous multi-agent model can be applied to any individual agent unifying incompatible pictures of the state of the world. This model may have interesting consequences for cognition and psychology.

The main consequence of this approach is that in some contexts, even an individual quantum agent may agree on disagree with her/himself.[i] And such a mental phenomenon has many fingerprints in cognition and psychology. For example, cognitive dissonance can

---

[i]It seems that a "classical agent" does not have such a problem. In the classical Aumann framework, the only possibilities to agree on disagree can come from the absence of the common prior probability distribution or (and) the absence of common knowledge. It is natural to assume that, for an individual agent these possibilities are excluded. Of course, we cannot exclude completely multipersonal behavior of an individual. However, in opposition to the quantum(-like) case, such a behavior based on the absence of the integral mental state and the ignorance

be treated (at least in some cases) as living in the agreement on disagree about the posterior probabilities for some events (posterior probabilities corresponding to the mental state updates with the aid of incompatible question-observables). In the simplest case, this is just the impossibility to perform the probability update on the basis of the available information. Decision making based on incompatible question-observables has its advantages and disadvantages. The main advantage is the possibility to gain complementary information. The main disadvantage is the possibility of the internal agreeing on disagree. The latter makes decision making more complex or even impossible. For now, we cannot say more, because we do not have the expertise in this problem (namely, the existence of decision-making contexts in which individuals proceed with internal agreement on disagreement).

It seems that in the standard decision making context, an agent has to try to prevent using incompatible information representations. It is natural to assume that, although such representations can be available at the individual level, by concentrating on the concrete problem, an agent selects just one representation based on the fixed question-operator or equivalently (at least from the mathematical viewpoint) on a family of commuting question-operators. This gives her/him the feeling of self-confidence in the trade with other agents.

In short, we think that the model presented here of "one agent — one spectral decomposition of the state space", matches well with the real situation in cognitive (quantum-like) processing of information. At the same time, the possibility to use incompatible information representations for the solution of different problems, improves the mental power of a decision maker. It is also clear that self-reflecting individuals living in agreement on disagree exist and the modeling of their behavior is important and it may have even consequences for medical treatment.

---

of "common knowledge" (presented in her/his own brain) is rather pathological although possible (Freudian affects can also be included).

Chapter 16

Examples

16.1. Examples illustrating agreement on disagree

Example 1. Consider a two-dimensional complex Hilbert space H and fix some orthonormal basis (e_1, e_2). Set

$$\mathcal{P}_1 = \{P_1^{(1)} = I\}; \quad \mathcal{P}_2 = \{P_1^{(2)} = P_{e_1}, P_2^{(2)} = P_{e_2}\}.$$

The common prior state is chosen as the pure state:

$$\phi = c_1 e_1 + c_2 e_2, \quad |c_1|^2 + |c_2|^2 = 1, \quad \text{and} \quad \rho = P_\phi.$$

We remark that

$$P_1^{(1)} \rho P_1^{(1)} / \text{Tr} P_1^{(1)} \rho P_1^{(1)} = \rho, \quad P_m^{(2)} \rho P_m^{(2)} / \text{Tr} P_m^{(2)} \rho P_m^{(2)} = P_{e_m},$$

$$m = 1, 2. \tag{16.1}$$

Select also an event E corresponding to some pure state, $E = P_\Psi$, where

$$\Psi = d_1 e_1 + d_2 e_2, \quad |d_1|^2 + |d_2|^2 = 1.$$

Then $p_\rho(E|P_1^{(1)}) = |\langle \phi|\Psi \rangle|^2$, since $\rho = P_\phi$ is a pure state. At the same time we have

$$p_\rho(E|P_m^{(2)}) = \text{Tr} P_m^{(2)} \rho P_m^{(2)} E / \text{Tr} P_m^{(2)} \rho P_m^{(2)}$$

$$= |\langle \Psi|e_m \rangle|^2 = |d_m|^2, \quad m = 1, 2.$$

Select $d_1 = d_2 = 1/\sqrt{2}$ and suppose that $|\langle \phi|\Psi \rangle| \neq 1/\sqrt{2}$.

Take $q_1 = |\langle\phi|\Psi\rangle|^2$ and $q_2 = 1/2$. Then $C_{q_1} = I$ and $C_{q_2} = P_{e_1} \vee P_{e_2} = I$. Thus, $C_{q_1 q_2} = C_{q_1} \wedge C_{q_1} = I$. It is evident that $\kappa C_{q_1 q_2} = C_{q_1 q_2} = I$. Moreover, $p_\rho(C_{q_1 q_2}) = p_\rho(I) = 1 > 0$. Nevertheless, $q_1 \neq q_2$. Thus posterior probabilities are different, in spite of complete certainty in common knowledge about these probabilities.

The crucial point of the above construction is the selection of the common prior state and an event which does not commute with one of the information representations, namely, $[\rho, P_m^{(2)}] \neq 0$ and $[E, P_m^{(2)}] \neq 0$. (We remark that, since $E = P_\Psi$, commutativity $[E, P_m^{(2)}] = 0, m = 1, 2$, implies that $\Psi = e_1$ or $\Psi = e_2$. In both cases $|\langle\phi|\Psi\rangle| = 1/\sqrt{2}$.)

Example 2. To illustrate the first part of the aforementioned issue of (non)commutativity, consider now the $\rho = (P_{e_1} + P_{e_2})/2$, i.e., the classical statistical mixture of states P_{e_1} and P_{e_2}. Here again we have (16.1). Select $E = P_\Psi$ such that $d_1 = d_2 = 1/\sqrt{2}$. Then we have again $p_\rho(E|P_m^{(2)}) = 1/2, m = 1, 2$. However, $p_\rho(E|P_1^{(1)}) = \langle\Psi|\Psi\rangle/2 = 1/2$. Here, $q_1 = q_2 = 1/2$. Thus, commutativity of the common prior state with the agents' information representations destroys the quantum anti-Aumann effect (although the event E does not commute with $\mathcal{P}_2$).

Example 3. The same happens in the case of the commutativity of an event with both information representations (even if the common prior state does not commute with at least one of the representations). Let $\rho = P_\phi$ and let $E = P_{e_1}$. Here $p_\rho(E|P_1^{(1)}) = 1/2, p_\rho(E|P_1^{(2)}) = 1, p_\rho(E|P_2^{(2)}) = 0$. Although probabilities are different, there is no contradiction with the Aumann theorem, since the condition (15.19) is not satisfied. Set, e.g., $q_1 = 1/2$ and $q_2 = 1$. Then $C_{q_1} = I, C_{q_2} = P_{e_1}$. Thus, $C_{q_1 q_2} = P_{e_1}$ and $\kappa C_{q_1 q_2} = 0$.

16.1.1. *Exercises*

Exercise 61. For agents with the information representations given by the Pauli matrices, find a prior state ρ and an event E such that the Aumann theorem is violated. Find the coefficients of pairwise interference (of the mismatching of the posterior probabilities) given by (15.23).

Exercise 62. Solve the same exercise for spin-1 matrices.

Exercise 63. Generalize the quantum-like model of common knowledge to agents having the information representation given by positive operator valued measures (POVMs).

16.2. Example: Agreement on disagree from two opinion polls

In this section, we consider a more interesting example illustrating the possibility of agreement on disagree from *two opinion polls* in the situation of very deep uncertainty about the public's opinion. Although, for a moment this example is of a purely theoretical and illustrative nature, it seems that in the future it can serve as the basis for real experimental studies in the domain of cognitive psychology.

This example was motivated by studies on public opinion about the honesty of Bill Clinton and Al Gore. In particular, in the well-known study of Moore [82], a group of participants was asked one question at a time, e.g., $A^{(1)} = $ "Is Bill Clinton honest and trustworthy?" and $A^{(2)} = $ "Is Al Gore honest and trustworthy?" Moore's study was oriented toward demonstrating the statistical significance of the *order effect.* As was shown in Wang and Busemeyer [97], this data can be represented in the quantum(-like) framework. Here the incompatibility of observables played the crucial role. As we have seen, in the common knowledge framework, the incompatibility of questions-observables is not the main issue, although this incompatibility also can contribute to the interference term in (15.23). Now we associate one of the questions observables, e.g., "Is Bill Clinton honest and trustworthy?", with the information representation of one agent, $i = 1$, and another question "Is Al Gore honest and trustworthy?" with another agent, $i = 2$. Thus, we do not plan to model the mutual influence of questions.

In short, we suppose that now that there are two agents, $i = 1, 2$, working in the branch of opinion polling. One of them, $i = 1$, plans to perform opinion polling about the honesty of one top politician TP_1 (cf. with Bill Clinton in Moore [82]) and another, $i = 2$, about the honesty of another top politician TP_2 (cf. with Al Gore in Moore [82])). The common prior mental state of these agents (in fact, its component related to the honesty of top politicians) was formed by the social environment, which is first of all the media. The commonality of this state means that no agent has insider information about this problem which was not available to another. The main quantum specialty is that, although the agents were "prepared" in this state, it is not available for them at the conscious level. Their "measurements" in the form of two opinion polls ($i = 1$, (about honesty of TP_1) and $i = 2$, (about honesty of TP_2)), destroy the initial common prior state. Then they update probabilities of possible events on the basis of the results of questionings. The event E is by itself "nonclassical". This event expresses the maximal possible uncertainty in society about honesty of $TP_i, i = 1, 2$. In practice, the example's context can be expressed as the task given to both agents (or more generally opinion polling agencies) to estimate the probability that society is in the state of such maximal uncertainty.[a]

Now we turn to a quantum(-like) mathematical model. The corresponding classical mathematical model will be presented at the very end of this section. There are two agents, $i = 1, 2$, with dichotomous question-observables $A^{(i)}, i = 1, 2$, taking values $0, 1$. In the simplest model, we can select their state spaces as two dimensional Hilbert spaces, H_1 and H_2. The eigenvectors of the operators corresponding to their eigenvalues $0, 1$ are denoted by the symbols $|0\rangle, |1\rangle$. This is Dirac's notation, which is widely used in quantum information: if operator A has the eigenvalue α then the corresponding eigenvector is denoted as $|\alpha\rangle$ (in the case of a non-degenerate spectrum, i.e., one

---

[a]One might argue that knowing the degree of uncertainty is meaningless. However, this is not the case. In particular, in the example under consideration the event E means that the society is equally uncertain about the honesty of Clinton and Gore.

dimensional eigen-subspace corresponding to α). To be more explicit, we have to put the index i for eigenvectors, $|0\rangle_i, |1\rangle_i, i = 1, 2$, pointing to their operators. However, typically such indices are omitted for simplicity.

Consider the tensor product $H = H_1 \otimes H_2$ of the state spaces of the agents $i = 1, 2$. The canonical basis of this space has the form $(e_{nm} = |nm\rangle \equiv |n\rangle \otimes |m\rangle), n, m = 0, 1$. Consider two orthogonal decompositions of H: $H = H_0^{(1)} \oplus H_1^{(1)}$ and $H = H_0^{(2)} \oplus H_1^{(2)}$, where the subspaces are determined by the bases in them: $(|00\rangle, |01\rangle)$ in $H_0^{(1)}$, $(|10\rangle, |11\rangle)$ in $H_1^{(1)}$, and $(|00\rangle, |10\rangle)$ in $H_0^{(2)}$, $(|01\rangle, |11\rangle)$ in $H_1^{(2)}$. The corresponding projectors are denoted as $P_j^{(i)}, i = 1, 2, j = 0, 1$. We have $P_0^{(i)} + P_1^{(i)} = I$ and, hence, we can define two spectral families $\mathcal{P}^{(i)} = (P_0^{(i)}, P_1^{(i)})$ determining the information representations of the agents $i = 1, 2$.

It is important to point out that the projectors corresponding to different agents commute, so the two spectral families are compatible. Thus, the non-classical information effects leading to a violation of the Aumann theorem are not a consequence of the incompatibility of the information representations of agents.

Now we select the common prior state ρ. We shall consider a special case: ρ is determined by a pure state. Hence, it represents a deep uncertainty about the situation. Set

$$\phi = c_{00}|00\rangle + c_{01}|01\rangle + c_{10}|10\rangle + c_{11}|00\rangle,$$

where $c_{nm} \in \mathbb{R}$ (to demonstrate non-classicality, it is sufficient to proceed with the real coefficients) and

$$c_{00}^2 + c_{01}^2 + c_{10}^2 + c_{11}^2 = 1, \tag{16.2}$$

it is also assumed that $c_{nm} \neq 0$. Suppose that $\rho \equiv \rho_\phi = |\phi\rangle\langle\phi|$.

Finally, we consider the event $E = |\Psi\rangle\langle\Psi|$, where

$$\Psi = (|00\rangle + |01\rangle + |10\rangle + |00\rangle)/2.$$

This is the state of maximal uncertainty.

The prior probabilities for this event are given as

$$q(E) = |\langle\phi|\Psi\rangle|^2 = \frac{1}{4}|c_{00} + c_{01} + c_{10} + c_{11}|^2.$$

Now we consider this state update with the aid of information representations of the agents. We can proceed with the corresponding pure states (since the state update with the aid of the Lüders projection rule always transfers pure states into pure states). For the first agent, we have

$$\phi \to \phi_0^{(1)} = (c_{00}|00\rangle + c_{01}|01\rangle)/\sqrt{|c_{00}|^2 + |c_{01}|^2},$$

$$\phi \to \phi_1^{(1)} = (c_{10}|10\rangle + c_{11}|11\rangle)/\sqrt{|c_{10}|^2 + |c_{11}|^2}.$$

For the second agent, we have

$$\phi \to \phi_0^{(2)} = (c_{00}|00\rangle + c_{10}|10\rangle)/\sqrt{|c_{00}|^2 + |c_{10}|^2},$$

$$\phi \to \phi_1^{(2)} = (c_{01}|01\rangle + c_{11}|11\rangle)/\sqrt{|c_{01}|^2 + |c_{11}|^2}.$$

We now consider posterior probabilities for the event E (we remark that for simplicity we proceed with the real coefficients). For the first agent, we obtain

$$q_{10} = |\langle\phi_0^{(1)}|\Psi\rangle|^2 = \frac{1}{4}|c_{00} + c_{01}|^2/(|c_{00}|^2 + |c_{01}|^2)$$

$$= \frac{1}{4}[1 + 2c_{00}c_{01}/(c_{00}^2 + c_{01}^2)];$$

$$q_{11} = |\langle\phi_1^{(1)}|\Psi\rangle|^2 = \frac{1}{4}|c_{10} + c_{11}|^2/(|c_{10}|^2 + |c_{11}|^2)$$

$$= \frac{1}{4}[1 + 2c_{10}c_{11}/(c_{10}^2 + c_{11}^2)];$$

This is the crucial point: the appearance of terms of the form $|c_{00} + c_{01}|^2$, instead of simply $|c_{00}|^2 + |c_{01}|^2$, implies a non-trivial interference effect, which can lead to a violation of the Aumann theorem. Otherwise, the numerators would be equal to denominators and we would obtain that all probabilities are equal (no disagree).

For the second agent, we obtain

$$\mathbf{q}_{20} = |\langle \phi_0^{(2)} | \Psi \rangle|^2 = \frac{1}{4} |c_{00} + c_{10}|^2 / (|c_{00}|^2 + |c_{10}|^2)$$

$$= \frac{1}{4} [1 + 2 c_{00} c_{10} / (c_{00}^2 + c_{10}^2)];$$

$$\mathbf{q}_{21} = |\langle \phi_1^{(2)} | \Psi \rangle|^2 = \frac{1}{4} |c_{01} + c_{11}|^2 / (|c_{01}|^2 + |c_{11}|^2)$$

$$= \frac{1}{4} [1 + 2 c_{01} c_{11} / (c_{01}^2 + c_{11}^2)].$$

In the case of dichotomous observables (and agents having different information representations), the only way to obtain non-trivial common knowledge is to have it as represented by the unit operator. Therefore, we have to have

$$\mathbf{q}_{i0} = \mathbf{q}_{i1}, \quad i = 1, 2.$$

At the same time to violate to agree on disagree, the probabilities for different agents have to be different.

Thus we obtain the following system of non-linear equations:

$$c_{00} c_{01} / (c_{00}^2 + c_{01}^2) = c_{10} c_{11} / (c_{10}^2 + c_{11}^2);$$

$$c_{00} c_{10} / (c_{00}^2 + c_{10}^2) = c_{01} c_{11} / (c_{01}^2 + c_{11}^2),$$

or

$$\frac{c_{00}}{c_{01}} + \frac{c_{01}}{c_{00}} = \frac{c_{10}}{c_{11}} + \frac{c_{11}}{c_{10}}; \tag{16.3}$$

$$\frac{c_{00}}{c_{10}} + \frac{c_{10}}{c_{00}} = \frac{c_{01}}{c_{11}} + \frac{c_{11}}{c_{01}}. \tag{16.4}$$

For our purpose, it is sufficient to find a particular solution of this system. We shall consider the case:

$$\frac{c_{00}}{c_{01}} = \frac{c_{10}}{c_{11}} = k, \tag{16.5}$$

where k is a real number (we state again that we proceed with the real coefficients). For our purpose, it suffices to choose $k > 0$.

This relation gives a class of solutions of Equation (16.3). However, the relation (16.5) also can be written as

$$\frac{c_{00}}{c_{10}} = \frac{c_{01}}{c_{11}}. \tag{16.6}$$

This relation gives a class of solutions of Equation (16.6). Thus, we obtained a class of solutions of the system (16.3), (16.6) parametrized by two real parameters:

$$c_{01} = t, \quad c_{11} = s, \quad c_{00} = kt, \quad c_{10} = ks. \tag{16.7}$$

The normalization condition (16.2) imposes the following constraint on the parameters:

$$(t^2 + s^2)(1 + k^2) = 1. \tag{16.8}$$

Hence,

$$k = \sqrt{\frac{1 - (t^2 + s^2)}{t^2 + s^2}}, \tag{16.9}$$

in particular, we get the following restriction on the parameters t, s:

$$t^2 + s^2 < 1. \tag{16.10}$$

For this class of solutions, the posterior probabilities have the form:

$$q_1 \equiv \mathbf{q}_{10} = \mathbf{q}_{11} = \frac{1}{4}[1 + 2k/(1 + k^2)]; \tag{16.11}$$

$$q_2 \equiv \mathbf{q}_{20} = \mathbf{q}_{11} = \frac{1}{4}[1 + 2ts/(t^2 + s^2)] \tag{16.12}$$

Now let us consider the following special case:

$$t = s = \lambda \tag{16.13}$$

(the condition (16.10) implies that $|\lambda| < \frac{\sqrt{2}}{2}$). Here

$$q_2 = \frac{1}{2}. \tag{16.14}$$

Hence, by updating the prior knowledge state with the aid of his information partition, the second agent obtains coinciding posterior probabilities of the event E, which are equal to $1/2$.

Now we find the results of the corresponding update for the first agent. In the case under study, the parameter k has the form:

$$k = \sqrt{\frac{1 - 2\lambda^2}{2\lambda^2}}. \tag{16.15}$$

To get to a concrete example, we select the concrete value of λ. We want to have an easily interpretable value of the posterior probability for $i = 1$. Unfortunately, this leads to an "unpleasant expression" for the parameter λ. For example, to assign $q_1 = 1/3$, we have to have $1/3 = [1 + 2k/(1 + k^2)]/4$. This gives us, e.g., the value $k = 3 - 2\sqrt{2}$ which leads to $\lambda = 1/2\sqrt{9 - 2\sqrt{2}}$.

Under this choice of the parameter λ and the corresponding choices of the parameters k and t, s, the first agent assigns coinciding posterior probabilities to the event $E, q_1 = 1/3$, and for the second agent, $q_2 = 1/2$. At the same time, the common knowledge projector is the unit operator, representing maximally available (for this context) common knowledge.

16.2.1. *Still possible to agree on the posterior probabilities*

We remark that in this example, the event E is not compatible with the information representations of agents, i.e., $[E, A^{(i)}] \neq 0, i = 1, 2$. The same is valid for the prior state ρ, i.e., $[\rho, A^{(i)}] \neq 0$. These incompatibilities contribute to the interference term responsible for the violation of the Aumann theorem.

However, as we have seen from our previous analysis of possibilities to agree on disagree for agents using the quantum(-like) representation of information, the inverse is not valid. *The contributions of the agents to the interference term may cancel each other and the Aumann theorem can be valid even for events and prior states which are incompatible with the information representations of agents.* This can be easily shown with the aid of our example.

We now want the coincidence of posterior probabilities of the agents under the condition of non-trivial (in fact, maximally possible) common knowledge. Hence, the following equality $1 = 2k/(1+k^2)$ has to hold, i.e., $k = 1$. This can be approached by selecting the parameter $\lambda = 1/2$. Since here, all parameters k, t, s are still positive, the prior state is incompatible with the agents' questions (incompatibility of questions and the event E does not depend on the parameters of the model). Thus, the agreement on posterior probabilities is possible only for the very special prior state corresponding to the pure state

$$\phi = (|00\rangle + |01\rangle + |10\rangle + |11\rangle)/2. \tag{16.16}$$

The probability given by Equation (16.11) can be considered as a function of the continuous parameter k: $q_1 = q_1(k)$. It is impossible to agree on disagree only for one value of the parameter k, namely, $k = 1$. For all other values of k, the agents agree on disagree. Thus, in this model, the agents come to the agreement on the posterior probabilities only in the very special situation and roughly speaking the chance of such agreement is zero. Of course, this statement is about the class of the common prior states corresponding to the pure states of the form:

$$\phi = k\lambda|00\rangle + \lambda|01\rangle + k\lambda|10\rangle + \lambda|11\rangle, \tag{16.17}$$

with the parameters coupled as (16.15) and the discussed chance is with respect to the uniform distribution of the parameter k. The state (16.16) is very special and there are psychological and information-theoretical reasons to select it (and not another state of the form (16.17) as the common prior state).

16.2.2. *Is entanglement important?*

We remark that neither the state ϕ nor Ψ are entangled.[b] We have $\Psi = \Psi_1 \otimes \Psi_2$, where $\Psi_1 = (|0\rangle + |1\rangle)/\sqrt{2}$ and $\Psi_2 = (|0\rangle + |1\rangle)/\sqrt{2}$ (these vectors belong to different state spaces; and to be precise, we have to label the basis states with the agents indices $i = 1, 2$).

---

[b]In this book we do not discuss cognitive issues related to quantum entanglement. See, e.g., Ref. [4–12].

And we also have $\phi = k\lambda|00\rangle + \lambda|01\rangle + k\lambda|10\rangle + \lambda|11\rangle = \lambda(|0\rangle + |1\rangle) \otimes (k|0\rangle + |1\rangle)$. Thus these are separable states. If $k \neq 1$, the Aumann theorem is violated and if $k = 1$ then it is not violated. It seems that this example can be considered as a sign of the irrelevance of entanglement relative to the (im)possibility to agree on disagree. Of course, this is just an example; a more extended study of this problem is needed.

16.2.3. *Classical model*

The corresponding classical model can be represented as follows. The space of the world's states consists of four points, $\Omega = \{\omega_{00}, \ldots, \omega_{11}\}$. The prior probability distribution is given as $p(\omega_{ij}) = |c_{ij}|^2$, where $c_{nm} \neq 0$. Information representations of the agents, $i = 1, 2$, are given by partitions $\mathcal{P}^{(1)} = (P_0^{(1)}, P_1^{(1)})$ and $\mathcal{P}^{(2)} = (P_0^{(1)}, P_1^{(2)})$, where

$$P_0^{(1)} = \{\omega_{00}, \omega_{01}\}, \quad P_1^{(1)} = \{\omega_{10}, \omega_{11}\};$$

$$P_0^{(2)} = \{\omega_{00}, \omega_{10}\}, \quad P_1^{(2)} = \{\omega_{01}, \omega_{11}\}.$$

The tricky point is to present a classical analog of the event E expressing total uncertainty. The only way to establish a correspondence is to select $E = \Omega$. In this case (independently of the prior probability distribution), all posterior probabilities are equal to one, so any possibility to agree on disagree is excluded.

16.3. A concluding discussion on approaching agreement between quantum agents

The formalism of quantum(-like) decision making was explored to analyze the applicability of Aumann's theorem to, so to say, "quantum-like thinking" agents. In the present framework, the latter (using of quantum logic, instead of the Boolean logic) is practically reduced to using the quantum rule for conditional probabilities generalizing (in a non-trivial way) the classical Bayesian rule. One can consider the present model as an attempt to generalize the Aumann's theorem to a new class of probability updating rules (see [7], cf. [58]).

We demonstrated that quantum updating is too general to keep the Aumann's theorem true. People can, in principle, agree on disagree. The latter happens very often in various situations and our model matches better with the reality of decision making than the classical model based on Boolean logic and the measure-theoretic approach to probability (Kolmogorov, 1933). In our approach, the disagreement is neither a consequence of the absence of the common prior state nor of the common knowledge about assigned probabilities. Thus, "quantum agents" can agree to disagree even while having the common prior state and the common knowledge. The main reason for disagreement is the use of the non-classical rule for the updating of probabilities. We remark that [58] also considered non-classical updating, and they found conditions for the validity of the Aumann theorem. It is possible to find such conditions even for "quantum agents" (see Chapter 15 (Remark 2 after Theorem 1 in Section 15.5)). The validity of the Aumann theorem for "quantum agents" depends on the inter-relations between the common prior state of the world ρ and the information representations of "quantum agents" $(P_j^{(i)})$ as well as $(P_j^{(i)})$ and the event E under the update analysis.

Chapter 17

Appendix

17.1. Operator approach to common knowledge formalization

We now define the *knowledge operator* K_i which applied to any event E, yields the event "ith agent knows that E." Here we repeat the classical scheme by using the quantum representation of states and events, instead of the standard classical representation.

Definition 2. $K_i E = P_{H_{K_i E}}$, where $H_{K_i E} = \{\phi \colon Q^{(i)}_{\phi/\|\phi\|} \leq E\}$.

Proposition 1. *For any event E, the set $H_{K_i E}$ is a linear subspace of H.*

Proof. Take two vectors $\phi_1, \phi_2 \in H_{K_i E}$ and consider their linear combination $\phi = a_1 \phi_1 + a_2 \phi_2$. We consider also the corresponding pure states $\Psi_1 = \phi_1/\|\phi_1\|$, $\Psi_2 = \phi_2/\|\phi_2\|$ and $\Psi = \phi/\|\phi\|$. We have $Q^{(i)}_{\Psi_m} \leq E$. Thus, $\Psi_m = \sum_{j \in O^{(i)}_{\phi_m}} P^{(i)}_j \Psi_m$. It is clear that ϕ can be represented in the form $\phi = \sum_{j \in O^{(i)}_{\phi_1} \cup O^{(i)}_{\phi_1}} P^{(i)}_j \Psi$. Therefore, $O^{(i)}_\Psi \subset O^{(i)}_{\Psi_1} \cup O^{(i)}_{\Psi_2}$ and, hence, $Q^{(i)}_\Psi \leq E$.

Thus, definition 2 is consistent. The operator K_i has the properties similar to the properties of the classical knowledge operator. We present these properties in the form of propositions.

Proposition 2. *For any event E,*

$$\mathcal{K}1: \quad K_i E \leq E. \tag{17.1}$$

Proof. Take non-zero $\phi \in H_{K_i E}$. Then $Q^{(i)}_{\phi/\|\phi\|} \leq E$ and, hence,

$$H_{Q^{(i)}_{\phi/\|\phi\|}} \subset H_E.$$

This implies that $\phi \in H_E$ and that $H_{K_i E} \subset H_E$.

We also remark that trivially

$$\mathcal{K}2: \quad I \leq K_i I, \tag{17.2}$$

in fact,

$$I = K_i I.$$

Proposition 3. *For any pair of events E, F,*

$$E \leq F \text{ implies } K_i E \leq K_i F. \tag{17.3}$$

Proof. Take non-zero $\phi \in H_{K_i E}$. Then $Q^{(i)}_{\phi/\|\phi\|} \leq E \leq F$. Thus $\phi \in K_i F$.

Proposition 4. *For any event pair of events E, F,*

$$\mathcal{K}3: \quad K_i E \wedge K_i F = K_i E \wedge F. \tag{17.4}$$

Proof. (a) Take non-zero $\phi \in H_{K_i E} \cap H_{K_i F}$. Then $Q^{(i)}_{\phi/\|\phi\|} \leq E$ and $Q^{(i)}_{\phi/\|\phi\|} \leq F$. Hence, $Q^{(i)}_{\phi/\|\phi\|} \leq E \wedge F$ and $\phi \in H_{K_i E \wedge F}$. Therefore $K_i E \wedge K_i F \leq K_i E \wedge F$.

(b) Take non-zero $\phi \in H_{K_i E \wedge F}$. Then $Q^{(i)}_{\phi/\|\phi\|} \leq E \wedge F$ and, hence, $Q^{(i)}_{\phi/\|\phi\|} \leq E$ and $Q^{(i)}_{\phi/\|\phi\|} \leq F$. Therefore $\phi \in H_{K_i E} \cap H_{K_i E} = H_{K_i E \wedge K_i F}$ and $K_i E \wedge F \leq K_i E \wedge K_i F$.

Proposition 5. *For any event E,*

$$K_i E = \sum_{P_j^{(i)} \leq E} P_j^{(i)}. \tag{17.5}$$

Proof. (a) First we show that $K_i E \leq \sum_{P_j^{(i)} \leq E} P_j^{(i)}$. Take non-zero $\phi \in H_{K_i E}$. Then $Q^{(i)}_{\phi/\|\phi\|} \leq E$ and $\phi = \sum_{j \in O^{(i)}_{\phi/\|\phi\|}} P_j^{(i)} \phi$. Since

$\sum_{j \in O^{(i)}_{\phi/\|\phi\|}} P^{(i)}_j \le E$, then for any $j \in O^{(i)}_{\phi/\|\phi\|}, P^{(i)}_j \le E$. Therefore $\phi = \sum_{P^{(i)}_j \le E} P^{(i)}_j \phi$.

(b) Now we show that $\sum_{P^{(i)}_j \le E} P^{(i)}_j \le K_i E$. Let $\phi = \sum_{P^{(i)}_j \le E} P^{(i)}_j \phi$. Then $Q^{(i)}_{\phi/\|\phi\|} \le \sum_{P^{(i)}_j \le E} P^{(i)}_j \le E$.

We also remark that

$$E = \sum P^{(i)}_{j_k} \text{ implies } K_i E = E. \tag{17.6}$$

This immediately implies that

$$K_i E = K_i K_i E \tag{17.7}$$

and, in particular, we obtain the following result (important for a comparison with the classical operator approach to the definition of common knowledge):

Proposition 6. *For any event E,*

$$\mathcal{K}4: \quad K_i E \le K_i K_i E. \tag{17.8}$$

Proposition 7. *For any event E,*

$$(I - K_i E) = K_i (I - K_i E). \tag{17.9}$$

Proof. Take for simplicity that $K_i E = \sum_{j=1}^{m} P^{(i)}_j$, see (17.5). Then $I - K_i E = \sum_{j>m} P^{(i)}_j$. By using (17.6) we obtain that $K_i(I - K_i E) = (I - K_i E)$.

In particular, we obtained that

$$\mathcal{K}5: \quad (I - K_i E) \le K_i (I - K_i E). \tag{17.10}$$

We remark that $\mathcal{K}1 - \mathcal{K}5$ are quantum analogs of the classical axioms for the knowledge operator.

Now, as in the classical case, Monderer and Samet [81]; Binmore and Brandenburger [17], we define:

$$M_0 E = E, M_1 E = K_1 E \wedge \cdots \wedge K_N E, \ldots, M_{n+1} E$$
$$= K_1 M_n E \wedge \cdots \wedge K_N M_n E, \ldots$$

As usual, $M_1 E$ is the event "all agents know that E" and so on. We can rewrite this definition by using subspaces, instead of projectors:

$$H_{M_1 E} = H_{K_1 E} \cap \cdots \cap H_{K_N E}, \ldots, H_{M_{n+1} E}$$
$$= H_{K_1 M_n E} \cap \cdots \cap H_{K_N M_n E}, \ldots$$

Now we define the *"common knowledge"* operator, as mutual knowledge of all finite degrees:

$$\kappa E = \bigwedge_{n=0}^{\infty} M_n E.$$

We now repeat the formulation of Lemma 1 and present its proof.

Lemma 1. *If $\kappa E \neq 0$, then $\kappa E \in \tilde{\mathcal{P}}$.*

Proof. Thus, we have to prove that if $\kappa E \neq 0$, then, for each i, it can be represented as

$$\kappa E = \sum_m P_{jm}^{(i)}. \tag{17.11}$$

Take any non-zero vector $\phi \in H_{\kappa E}$. Then it belongs to $H_{K_i M_n E}$ for any n. Thus $Q_{\phi/\|\phi\|}^{(i)} \leq M_n E$ and, hence, $Q_{\phi/\|\phi\|}^{(i)} \leq \wedge_{n=0}^{\infty} M_n E = \kappa E$. Hence, for each $\phi \in H_{\kappa E}$, we have $\phi = Q_{\phi/\|\phi\|}^{(i)} \phi$. Thus (17.11) holds.

This lemma was used in our analysis of the possibility of a quantum generalization of the Aumann theorem. Although the following statement was not used for this purpose, it is better to present it, so as to have the complete picture.

Lemma 2. *If, for each i, an event E can be represented as*

$$E = \sum_m P_{jm}^{(i)}. \tag{17.12}$$

Then $\kappa E = E$.

Proof. It is sufficient to show that, for each i, $E = K_i E$. We know that always $K_i E \leq E$. Thus, it is sufficient to show that $E \leq K_i E$. Let $\phi \in H_E$. Then $\phi = \sum_m P_{jm}^{(i)} \phi$. Hence, $Q_{\phi/\|\phi\|}^{(i)} \leq E$ and by definition $\phi \in H_{K_i E}$.

17.1.1. *What does it mean to know? Quantum probabilistic formulation*

Let Ψ be a state of the world. Suppose that the ith agent is able to repeat measurements, to ask her/his question represented by the quantum observable $A^{(i)}$, many times (ideally infinitely many times) without disturbing the state of the world Ψ (so to say, the world's state is not sensitive to her questions).[a] She/he gets answers $a_j^{(i)}$ with probabilities $p_\Psi(a_j^{(i)}) = \mathrm{Tr} P_\Psi P_j^{(i)}$. We can restrict consideration to the answers for which

$$p_\Psi(a_j^{(i)}) > 0. \tag{17.13}$$

We remark that $\sum_j P_j^{(i)}$ for the set of indices given by condition (17.13) coincides with the projector $Q_\Psi^{(i)}$, i.e., (17.13) is equivalent to the condition

$$P_j^{(i)} \Psi \neq 0. \tag{17.14}$$

---

[a]Consider our example with the opinion polls, Section 16.2. In this case, the state of the world is the "mental state of American society". Each American individual can be considered as a carrier of this state (at least some age group of individuals). Thus, measurements can be repeated.

Under this assumption on the possibility of repeatable measurements, for the ith agent, the state of knowledge about the world based on her/his information representation, is given by the density operator:

$$\rho_\Psi^{(i)} = \sum_j p_\Psi(a_j^{(i)})\rho_{j;\Psi}^{(i)}, \tag{17.15}$$

where

$$p_\Psi(a_j^{(i)}) = \|P_j^{(i)}\Psi\|^2, \quad \rho_{j;\Psi}^{(i)} = \frac{P_j^{(i)} P_\Psi P_j^{(i)}}{\mathrm{Tr} P_j^{(i)} P_\Psi P_j^{(i)}}. \tag{17.16}$$

We also remark that $\rho_{j;\Psi}^{(i)}$ is the projector onto the pure state $\frac{P_j^{(i)}\Psi}{\|P_j^{(i)}\Psi\|}$. Thus, for the ith agent who is able to gather information about the state of the world in a long (infinitely long) run of measurements, the information representation of the world is given by the mixture of pure states corresponding to her partition of the unity (the spectral family of her question-operator).

Theorem 2. *For the Ψ-state of the world and the event E, if the ith agent knows it, then*

$$p_{\rho_\Psi^{(i)}}(E) = \mathrm{Tr}\rho_\Psi^{(i)} E = 1. \tag{17.17}$$

Proof. Select an orthonormal basis in H in the following way. The first block of vectors (e_k) is the orthonormal basis in H_E and the second block of vectors (f_k) is the basis in the orthogonal complement to H_E. Then

$$p_{\rho_\Psi^{(i)}}(E) = \sum_k \langle e_k|\rho_\Psi^{(i)}|e_k\rangle = \sum_k \sum_j |\langle e_k|P_j^{(i)}|\Psi\rangle|^2. \tag{17.18}$$

Since Ψ is a pure state, we have

$$1 = \|\Psi\|^2 = \sum_j \|P_j^{(i)}\Psi\|^2$$

$$= \sum_j \left(\sum_k |\langle e_k | P_j^{(i)} | \Psi \rangle|^2 + \sum_k |\langle f_k | P_j^{(i)} | \Psi \rangle|^2 \right).$$

$$(17.19)$$

Since $Q_\Psi^{(i)} \leq E$, we have

$$\langle f_k | P_j^{(i)} | \Psi \rangle = 0 \qquad (17.20)$$

Therefore $p_{\rho_\Psi^{(i)}}(E) = \sum_j \| P_j^{(i)} \Psi \|^2 = 1$.

References — Part III

[1] de Barros, A.; Suppes, P. (2009). Quantum mechanics, interference, and the brain. *Journal of Mathematical Psychology* 53, 306–313.

[2] Accardi, L.; Boukas, A. (2007). The quantum Black-Scholes equation. Infinite dimensional analysis. arxiv.org/pdf/0706.1300.pdf [Quantum Probability and Related Fields]. Cornell University Library.

[3] Aerts, D.; Sozzo, S.; Tapia, J. (2012). A quantum model for the Ellsberg and Machina paradoxes. Quantum Interaction. *Lecture Notes in Computer Science* 7620, 48–59.

[4] Aerts, D.; Gabora, L.; Sozzo, S. (2013). Concepts and their dynamics: A quantum-theoretic modeling of human thought. *Topics in Cognitive Science* 5(4), 737–772.

[5] Asano, M.; Ohya, M.; Tanaka, Y.; Khrennikov, A.; Basieva, I. (2011). On application of Gorini-Kossakowski-Sudarshan-Lindblad equation in cognitive psychology. *Open Systems and Information Dynamics* 18, 55–69.

[6] Asano, M.; Ohya, M.; Tanaka, Y.; Khrennikov, A.; Basieva, I. (2011). Dynamics of entropy in quantum-like model of decision making. *Journal of Theoretical Biology* 281, 56–64.

[7] Asano, M.; Basieva, I.; Khrennikov, A.; Ohya, M.; Tanaka, Y. (2012). Quantum-like generalization of the Bayesian updating scheme for objective and subjective mental uncertainties. *Journal of Mathematical Psychology* 56(3), 166–175.

[8] Asano, M.; Basieva, I.; Khrennikov, A.; Ohya, M. (2012). Quantum-like dynamics of decision-making. *Physica A* 391(5), 2083–2099.

[9] Asano, M.; Basieva, I.; Khrennikov, A.; Ohya, M., Yamato, I. (2013). Non-Kolmogorovian approach to the context-dependent systems breaking the classical probability law. *Foundations of Physics* 43(7) 2083–2099.

[10] Asano, M.; Basieva, I.; Khrennikov, A.; Ohya, M., Tanaka, Y., Yamato, I. (2012). Quantum-like model for the adaptive dynamics of the genetic regulation of *E. coli*'s metabolism of glucose/lactose. *Systems and Synthetic Biology* 6(1–2), 1–7.

[11] Asano, M.; Basieva, I.; Khrennikov, A.; Ohya, M., Tanaka, Y., Yamato, I. (2012). Quantum-like model of diauxie in Escherichia coli: Operational description of precultivation effect. *Journal of Theoretical Biology* 314, 130–137.

[12] Asano, M.; Basieva, I.; Khrennikov, A.; Ohya, M., Tanaka, Y., Yamato, I. (2013). A model of epigenetic evolution based on theory of open quantum systems. *Systems and Synthetic Biology* 7, 161–173.

[13] Atmanspacher, H.; Filk, T. (2012). Contra classical causality: Violating temporal Bell inequalities in mental systems. *Journal of Consciousness Studies* 19(5/6), 95–116.

[14] Atmanspacher, H.; Römer, H. (2012). Order effects in sequential measurements of non-commuting psychological observables. *Journal of Mathematical Psychology* 56, 274–280.

[15] Aumann, R.J. (1976). Agreeing on disagree. *Annals of Statistics* 4, 1236–1239.

[16] Aumann, R.J. (1995). Backward induction and common knowledge of rationality. *Games and Economic Behavior* 8, 6–19.

[17] Binmore, K.; Brandenburger, A. (1988). Common knowledge and game theory. ST/ICERD Discussion Paper 88/167, London School of Economics.

[18] Basieva, I.; Khrennikov, A.; Ohya, M.; Yamato, I. (2011). Quantum-like interference effect in gene expression: Glucose-lactose destructive interference. *Systems and Synthetic Biology* 5(1), 59–68.

[19] Birkhoff, G.; von Neumann, J. (1936). The logic of quantum mechanics. *Annals of Mathematics* 37(4), 823–843.

[20] Boole, G. (1958). *An Investigation of the Laws of Thought.* Dover Edition, New York.

[21] Brandenburger, A.; Dekel, E. (1987). Common knowledge with probability 1. *Journal of Mathematical Economics* 16, 237–245.

[22] Brandenburger, A. (2010). The relationship between quantum and classical correlation in games. *Games and Economic Behavior* 69, 175–183.

[23] Brukner, C.; Zeilinger, A. (1999). Operationally invariant information in quantum mechanics. *Physical Review Letters* 83, 3354–3357.

[24] Brukner, C.; Zeilinger, A. (2001). Conceptual inadequacy of the Shannon information in quantum measurements. *Physical Review A* 63, 022113, 1–10.

[25] Brukner, C.; Zeilinger, A. (2002). Young's experiment and the finiteness of information. *Philosophical Transactions of the Royal Society A* 360, 1061.

[26] Bruza, P.D.; Cole, R.J. (2005). Quantum logic of semantic space: An exploratory investigation of context effects in practical reasoning. In: S. Artemov, H. Barringer, A. S. d'Avila Garcez, L.C. Lamb, J. Woods (Eds.). *We Will Show Them: Essays in Honour of Dov Gabbay.* College Publications, London.

[27] Busemeyer, J.R.; Townsend, J.T. (1993). Decision field theory: A dynamic cognition approach to decision making. *Psychological Review* 100, 432–459.

[28] Busemeyer, J.R.; Wang, Z.; Townsend, J.T. (2006). Quantum dynamics of human decision making. *Journal of Mathematical Psychology* 50, 220–241.

[29] Busemeyer, J.R.; Santuy, E.; Lambert-Mogiliansky, A. (2008). Comparison of Markov and quantum models of decision making. In: P. Bruza, W. Lawless, K. van Rijsbergen, D.A. Sofge, B. Coecke, S. Clark (Eds.). *Quantum Interaction: Proceedings of the Second Quantum Interaction Symposium*, pp. 68–74 College Publications, London.

[30] Busemeyer, J.R.; Wang, Z.; Lambert-Mogiliansky, A. (2009). Empirical comparison of Markov and quantum models of decision making. *Journal of Mathematical Psychology*, 53(5), 423–433.

[31] Busemeyer, J.R.; Pothos, E.M.; Franco, R.; Trueblood, J. (2011). A quantum theoretical explanation for probability judgment errors. *Psychological Review* 118, 193–218.

[32] Busemeyer, J.R.; Bruza, P.D. (2012). *Quantum Models of Cognition and Decision*. Cambridge University Press, Cambridge.

[33] Busemeyer, J.R.; Wang, Z.; Khrennikov, A.; Basieva, I. (2014). Applying quantum principles to psychology. *Physica Scripta* 2014, T163. 014007

[34] Cheon, T.; Takahashi, T. (2010). Interference and inequality in quantum decision theory. *Physics Letters A* 375, 100–104.

[35] Conte, E.; Todarello, O.; Federici, A.; Vitiello, F.; Lopane, M.; Khrennikov, A.; Zbilut, J.P. (2007). Some remarks on an experiment suggesting quantum-like behavior of cognitive entities and formulation of an abstract quantum mechanical formalism to describe cognitive entity and its dynamics. *Chaos, Solitons and Fractals* 31(5), 1076–1088.

[36] Conte, E., Khrennikov, A.; Todarello, O.; Federici, A.; Mendolicchio, L.; Zbilut, J.P. (2009). Mental state follow quantum mechanics during perception and cognition of ambiguous figures. *Open Systems and Information Dynamics*, 16, 1–17; A preliminary experimental verification on the possibility of bell inequality violation in mental states. *NeuroQuantology* 6(3), 214–221 (2008).

[37] Carlyle, Th. Ed. (1855). *Oliver Cromwell's Letters and Speeches 1*. Harper Publishers, New York.

[38] de Finetti, B. (1990). *Theory of Probability*. J. Wiley, New York.

[39] Dzhafarov, E.N.; Kujala, J.V. (2012). Quantum entanglement and the issue of selective influences in psychology: An overview. *Lecture Notes in Computer Science* 7620, 184–195.

[40] Dzhafarov, E.N.; Kujala, J.V. (2012). Selectivity in probabilistic causality: Where psychology runs into quantum physics. *Journal of Mathematical Psychology* 56, 54–63.

[41] Dzhafarov, E.N.; Kujala, J.V. (2013). All-possible-couplings approach to measuring probabilistic context. *PLoS ONE* 8(5): e61712.

[42] Dzhafarov, E. N.; Kujala, J.V. (2014). On selective influences, marginal selectivity, and Bell/CHSH inequalities. *Topics in Cognitive Science* 6, 121–128.

[43] Geanakoplos, J. (1994). Common knowledge. In: *Handbook of Game Theory*, Vol. 2. R. Aumann and S. Hart (Eds.), Amsterdam, Elsevier Science B.V., pp. 1438–1496.

[44] Feynman, R.; Hibbs, A. (1965). *Quantum Mechanics and Path Integrals*. McGraw-Hill, New York.

[45] Friedell, M. (1969). On the structure of shared awareness. *Systems Research and Behavioral Science* 14, 28–39.

[46] Fuchs, C.A. (2002). Quantum mechanics as quantum information (and only a little more). In: Khrennikov, A. Yu. (Eds.). *Quantum Theory: Reconsideration of Foundations*, pp. 463–543. Ser. Math. Model. 2, Växjö University Press, Växjö.

[47] Fuchs, C. (2007). Delirium quantum (or, where I will take quantum mechanics if it will let me). In: Adenier, G., Fuchs, C. and Khrennikov, A. Yu. (Eds.). *Foundations of Probability and Physics-3*, 889, American Institute of Physics, Ser. Conference Proceedings, Melville, New York, pp. 438–462.

[48] Fuchs, C.A. (2011). Interview with a quantum Bayesian. In: *Elegance and Enigma: The Quantum Interviews*. M. Schlosshauer (Ed.). Springer Frontiers Collection. pp. 1–20.

[49] Fuchs, C.A.; Schack, R. (2013). Quantum-Bayesian coherence. *Review of Modern Physics* 85, 1693–1715.

[50] Fuchs, C.A.; Schack, R. (2015). QBism and the Greeks: Why a quantum state does not represent an element of physical reality. Available at: https://pure.royalholloway.ac.uk/portal/files/23282396/FuchsSchack.pdf.

[51] Harsanyi, J. (1967). Games with incomplete information played by 'Bayesian' players, I: The basic model, *Management Science* 14, 159–82.

[52] Harsanyi, J. (1968). Games with incomplete information played by 'Bayesian' players, II: Bayesian equilibrium points. *Management Science* 14, 320–324.

[53] Harsanyi, J. (1968). Games with incomplete information played by "Bayesian" players, III: The basic probability distribution of the game. *Management Science* 14, 486–502.

[54] Hume, D. (1740) [1888 1976]. *A Treatise of Human Nature*. L. A. Selby-Bigge (Ed.), rev. 2nd. edn. P. H. Nidditch (Ed.), Clarendon Press, Oxford.

[55] Haven, E.; Khrennikov, A. (2009). Quantum mechanics and violation of the sure-thing principle: The use of probability interference and other concepts. *Journal of Mathematical Psychology* 53, 378–388.

[56] Haven, E.; Khrennikov, A. (2013). *Quantum Social Science*. Cambridge University Press, Cambridge.

[57] Haven, E.; Khrennikov, A. (2016). Statistical and subjective interpretations of probability in quantum-like models of cognition and decision making. *Journal of Mathematical Psychology*. Forthcoming. http://dx.doi.org/10.1016/j.jmp.2016.02.005.

[58] Hild, M.; Jeffrey, R.; Risse, M. (1987). Aumann's "no-agreement theorem" generalized. In: C. Bicchieri, R. Jeffrey, and B. Skyms (Eds.). *The Logic of Strategy*. Oxford University Press, Oxford.

[59] Khrennikov, A. (1999). Classical and quantum mechanics on information spaces with applications to cognitive, psychological, social and anomalous phenomena. *Foundations of Physics* 29(7), 1065–1098.

[60] Khrennikov, A. (1999). *Superanalysis*, Nauka, Fizmatlit, Moscow, 1997 (in Russian). English translation: Kluwer, Dordrecht.

[61] Khrennikov, A. (2003). Quantum-like formalism for cognitive measurements. *Biosystems* 70, 211–233.

[62] Khrennikov, A. (2004). On quantum-like probabilistic structure of mental information. *Open Systems and Information Dynamics* 11(3), 267–275.

[63] Khrennikov, A. (2006). Quantum-like brain: Interference of minds. *BioSystems* 84, 225–241.

[64] Khrennikov, A. (2004). *Information Dynamics in Cognitive, Psychological, Social, and Anomalous Phenomena. Fundamental Theories of Physics*, Kluwer, Dordrecht.

[65] Khrennikov, A. (2009). *Interpretations of Probability.* 2nd edn. de Gruyter, Berlin.

[66] Khrennikov, A. (2009). Quantum-like model of cognitive decision making and information processing. *Biosystems* 95, 179–187.

[67] Khrennikov, A. (2010). *Ubiquitous Quantum Structure: From Psychology to Finance.* Springer, Berlin.

[68] Khrennikov, A. (2011). Quantum-like model of processing of information in the brain based on classical electromagnetic field. *Biosystems* 105(3), 250–262.

[69] Khrennikov, A.; Basieva, I. (2014). Possibility to agree on disagree from quantum information and decision making. *Journal of Mathematical Psychology* 62–63, 1–15.

[70] Khrennikov, A. (2015). Quantum-like model of unconscious–conscious dynamics. *Frontiers in Psychology* 6, art. 997.

[71] Khrennikov, A. (2015). Quantum-like modeling of cognition. *Frontiers in Physics* 3, art. 77.

[72] Khrennikova, P. (2012). *Evolution of quantum-like modeling in decision making processes.* 1508, AIP Conference Proceedings, 108.

[73] Khrennikova, P. (2013). A Quantum Framework for 'Sour grapes' in Cognitive dissonance. In: Quantum Interaction (7th International Conference). Atmanspacher, H.; Haven, E.; Kitto, K.; Raine, D. (Eds.). *Lecture Notes in Computer Science* (LNCS) 8369; 270–328. Springer, Berlin.

[74] Kolmogorov, A.N. (1933). *Grundbegriffe der Wahrscheinlichkeitsrechnung.* Springer-Verlag, Berlin. English translation: Kolmogorov, A.N. (1956). *Foundations of the Theory of Probability.* Chelsea Publishing Company, New York.

[75] Kolmogorov, A.N.; Fomin, S.V. (1975). *Introductory Real Analysis.* Dover Publications, New York.

[76] Lambert-Mogiliansky, A.; Zamir, S.; Zwirn, H. (2009). Type indeterminacy: A model of the KT (Kahneman-Tversky)-man. *Journal of Mathematical Psychology* 53(5), 349–361.

[77] Lewis, D. (1969). *Conventions: A Philosophical Study.* Harvard University Press, Cambridge.

[78] Lewis, D. (1998). *Making Decisions* (2nd edn.). J. Wiley Publishing, New York.

[79] Littlewood, J.E. (1953). *A Mathematical Miscellany*. Methuen, London, reprinted as *Littlewood's Miscellany*, B. Bollobas (Ed.), Cambridge University Press, Cambridge.

[80] McKelvey, R.; Page, T. (1986). Common knowledge, consensus and aggregate information. *Econometrica* 54, 109–127.

[81] Monderer, D.; Samet, D. (1989). Approximating common knowledge with common beliefs. *Games and Economic Behavior* 1, 170–190.

[82] Moore, D.W. (2002). Measuring new types of question-order effects. *Public Opinion Quarterly* 66, 80–91.

[83] Nielsen, L. (1984). Common knowledge, communication and convergence of beliefs. *Mathematical Social Sciences* 8, 1–14.

[84] Nozick, R. (1963). *The Normative Theory of Individual Choice*. Ph.D. dissertation, Princeton University, Princeton.

[85] Ozawa, M. (1997). An operational approach to quantum state reduction. *Annals of Physics (New York)* 259, 121–137.

[86] Pitowsky, I. (1982). Resolution of the Einstein-Podolsky-Rosen and Bell paradoxes.*Physical Review Letters* 48, 1299; Erratum, *Physical Review Letters* 48, 1768.

[87] Plotnitsky, A.; Khrennikov, A. (2015). Reality without realism: On the ontological and epistemological architecture of quantum mechanics. *Foundations of Physics* 45(10), 269–1300.

[88] Pothos, E.M.; Busemeyer, J.R. (2009). A quantum probability explanation for violation of rational decision theory. *Proceedings of the Royal Society B* 276, 2171–2178.

[89] Pothos, E.M.; Busemeyer, J.R. (2013). Can quantum probability provide a new direction for cognitive modelling? *Behavioral and Brain Sciences* 36(3), 255–274.

[90] Pothos, E.M.; Busemeyer, J.R.; Trueblood J.S. (2013). A quantum geometric model of similarity. *Psychological Review* 120(3), 679–696.

[91] Schelling, T. (1960). *The Strategy of Conflict*. Harvard University Press, Cambridge.

[92] Trueblood, J.S.; Busemeyer, J.R. (2011). A quantum probability account of order effects in inference. *Cognitive Science* 35, 1518–1552.

[93] Shafer, G. (2006). *Why did Cournot's principle dissapear?* Slides which can be found at: www.glennshafer.com/assets/downloads/disappear.pdf.

[94] Vanderschraaf, P.; Sillari, G. (2013). *Common knowledge*. The Stanford Encyclopedia of Philosophy, E.N. Zalta (Ed.). Available at: http://plato. stanford.edu/ archives/fall2013/entries/common-knowledge.

[95] von Mises, R. (1957). *Probability Statistics and Truth*. Macmillan, London.

[96] von Neumann, J. (1955). *Mathematical Foundations of Quantum Mechanics*. Princeton University Press, Princeton.

[97] Wang, Z.; Busemeyer, J.R. (2013). A quantum question order model supported by empirical tests of an a priori and precise prediction. *Topics in Cognitive Science* 5, 689–710.

[98] Wikipedia contributors. Common Knowledge (logic). *Wikipedia. The Free Encyclopedia.* See sections: 'Example': '*Puzzle*'; '*Solution*'. Available at: https://en.wikipedia.org/wiki/Common_knowledge_(logic).

Index

Printed in the United States
By Bookmasters